MEMORY AND MISCARRIAGES OF JUSTICE

Memory is often the primary evidence in the courtroom, yet unfortunately this evidence may not be fit for purpose. This is because memory is both fallible and malleable; it is possible to forget and also to falsely remember things which never happened.

The legal system has been slow to adapt to scientific findings about memory even though such findings have implications for the use of memory as evidence, not only in the case of eyewitness testimony, but also for how jurors, barristers, and judges weigh evidence. *Memory and Miscarriages of Justice* provides an authoritative look at the role of memory in law and highlights common misunderstandings while bringing the modern scientific understanding of memory to the forefront.

Drawing on the latest research, this book examines cases where memory has played a role in miscarriages of justice and makes recommendations from the science of memory to support the future of memory evidence in the legal system. Appealing to undergraduate and postgraduate students of psychology and law, memory experts, and legal professionals, this book provides an insightful and global view of the use of memory within the legal system.

Prof. Mark L. Howe holds a Chair in Cognitive Science at City, University of London, UK. His research on memory has addressed questions concerning memory development, memory illusions, the emergence and adaptive functions of memory, links between reasoning and memory, memory in traumatized and maltreated children, as well as memory and the law. He has published numerous peer reviewed articles and book chapters on memory, as well as authored and edited a number of books.

Dr. Lauren M. Knott is a Senior Lecturer in the Department of Psychology at City, University of London, UK. She specializes in the investigation of false memory development in children and the role of retrieval processes in false recognition.

Prof. Martin A. Conway is a Professor of Psychology at City, University of London, UK. Having researched human memory for over 32 years he has published numerous papers, books, and articles as well as making contributions to television, radio, and newspapers.

MEMORY AND MISCARRIAGES OF JUSTICE

Mark L. Howe, Lauren M. Knott, and Martin A. Conway

Routledge
Taylor & Francis Group

LONDON AND NEW YORK

First published 2018
by Routledge
2 Park Square, Milton Park, Abingdon, Oxon OX14 4RN

and by Routledge
711 Third Avenue, New York, NY 10017

Routledge is an imprint of the Taylor & Francis Group, an informa business

© 2018 Mark L. Howe, Lauren M. Knott, and Martin A. Conway

British Library Cataloguing in Publication Data
A catalogue record for this book is available from the British Library

Library of Congress Cataloging in Publication Data
Names: Howe, Mark L., author. | Knott, Lauren M., author. |
Conway, Martin A., 1952–, author.
Title: Memory and miscarriages of justice / Mark L. Howe, Lauren M.
Knott, and Martin A. Conway.
Description: New York, NY : Routledge, 2017.
Identifiers: LCCN 2017007986| ISBN 9781138805583 (hardback : alk.
paper) | ISBN 9781138805606 (pbk. : alk. paper)
Subjects: LCSH: Evidence, Circumstantial. | Admissible evidence. |
Memory. | Judicial error.
Classification: LCC K5490 .H69 2017 | DDC 347/.066—dc23
LC record available at https://lccn.loc.gov/2017007986

ISBN: 978-1-138-80558-3 (hbk)
ISBN: 978-1-138-80560-6 (pbk)
ISBN: 978-1-315-75218-1 (ebk)

Typeset in Bembo
by Florence Production Ltd, Stoodleigh, Devon, UK

Printed and bound by CPI Group (UK) Ltd, Croydon, CR0 4YY

CONTENTS

PART 1

Memory and the law

Miscarriages, misuse, and naïve beliefs

1

MEMORY AND MISCARRIAGES OF JUSTICE

Memory is fallible. Fallible not just because we forget information (errors of omission) but fallible because we also "remember" things that did not happen (errors of commission). This can be a simple case of misremembering, for example, that we had eggs for breakfast when in fact we had cereal, or sometimes, more seriously, we mistakenly remember entire events (e.g., going for a hot air balloon ride when you were a child) that never happened. We do this not because memory is fundamentally flawed but because it is reconstructive. That is, memory of events is not a verbatim playback of what happened. Rather, it is a reconstruction based on the retrieval of some stored remnants of the original experience that may have persisted in memory, along with schema-driven information that serves to make the memory coherent and that fills in any blanks. Of course, there are times when we simply reconstruct an entire event, sometimes based on the remnants of previous experiences that are pieced together to make a new experience or may simply be based on imagination.

Memory is also malleable. That is to say, once created, a memory is not necessarily a fixed stable entity. When we reactivate that memory, whether it be to discuss an event with friends and family, or to provide an account of an event when questioned by the police, the mere act of reactivating changes that memory, as we recount a narrative with new details, details suggested by others, and details that fill in the gaps of the narrative we are telling.

This type of reconstructive memory system is, however, very adaptive (e.g., see various chapters in Schwartz, Howe, Toglia, & Otgaar, 2014). It is likely that memory evolved not as a system that retains verbatim information about past experience but rather one that helps us understand experience and interpret the world around us, and, based on this understanding, make predictions about the future (e.g., Howe, 2011). This ability to extract meaning from experience rather than remember copies of those experiences is important to survival. For example, a flexible memory system allows us to plan for and imagine a future, a function of memory that is integral to survival.

Despite the inherent reconstructive nature of memory, memory often serves as the centerpiece in the legal arena. Witnesses attempt to identify perpetrators from memory, remember criminal events they witnessed, and convey what they remember in police interviews and courtroom testimony. But if memory is reconstructive how can we know which parts (if any) are correct and which ones are reconstructed? This is the conundrum that faces legal professionals and jurors alike and this book attempts to shed some scientific light on exactly how reliable memory evidence can (and cannot) be. This is critical when memory is evidence in the courtroom and often, as we shall see, is the *only* evidence.

To take a recent example of this memory conundrum that made headlines in the English press, consider the case of Sir Cliff Richard. He is a British pop star who was very successful in the late 1950s and 1960s selling over 250 million records worldwide and is the third top-selling artist in UK single chart history, being eclipsed only by the Beatles and Elvis Presley. In August 2014, in response to a complaint to the Metropolitan Police's Operation Yewtree (set up in the wake of the Jimmy Savile scandal), Richard's apartment in Berkshire was searched, but there were no arrests. The complainant said that he had been abused by Richard as a teenager at a religious rally in the 1980s. Richard, now 75, strongly denied the allegations of historic sexual abuse. He voluntarily met with and was interviewed by members of the police but again, he was never arrested or criminally charged. Subsequently, David Crompton, chief constable of South Yorkshire Police, was criticized for his interactions with the press and publicly apologized to Richard.

In February 2015, South Yorkshire Police announced that the inquiry into the alleged offences had increased and that it would be continuing. Richard subsequently released a statement maintaining that the allegations were "absurd and untrue" (Gander, 2015). The development came a day after an independent report had concluded that South Yorkshire Police had "interfered with the star's privacy" (BBC News, 2015) by telling the BBC about the impending August 2014 raid on Richard's apartment. The BBC's tip-off regarding the search reportedly came from within Operation Yewtree, although Crompton said he could not be certain that the leak originated from there.

In May 2016, South Yorkshire Police sent a file of evidence to the Crown Prosecution Service (CPS). The following month, the CPS announced that after reviewing evidence relating to claims of historic sexual offences dating between 1958 and 1983 made by four men that there was "insufficient evidence" to charge Richard with an offence, and that no further action against him would be taken. Richard said his naming by the media, despite not being charged, meant he had been "hung out like live bait" (BBC News, 2016). South Yorkshire Police later apologized to Richard after its investigation into the singer was dropped on 16 June 2016.

It was subsequently reported that during the 22-month police investigation a man was arrested over a plot to blackmail Richard. The unnamed man in his forties contacted Richard's aides and threatened to spread "false stories" unless he received a sum of money. On 21 June 2016 the BBC apologized publicly to Richard for causing distress after the controversial broadcast of the police raid on his property in 2014.

The police undoubtedly have a duty to follow-up and investigate these cases, we only need look to the Jimmy Savile case to understand the potential seriousness of ignoring such allegations. However, the legal system and the media have an obligation to protect those involved in the allegations before proven guilty. Unfortunately for Richard, his life was turned upside down for approximately two years, causing considerable distress. As we shall see in upcoming chapters, there are a number of infamous cases where people have come to believe that they were not only sexually abused when they were younger (e.g., see Maran, 2010), but that they participated in satanic ritual abuse (e.g., see Felstead & Felstead, 2014) and acts of cannibalism (Loftus, 1998). Although in some cases these memories are retracted (e.g., the Burgus case discussed by Loftus, 1998; also see Maran, 2010), others have led to criminal convictions and worse, to the death of the person who came to believe these memories (Felstead & Felstead, 2014).

It is important to make the clear statement here that we are well aware that not all cases of historic sexual abuse are based on faulty or retracted memories. Indeed, many people do accurately remember their abuse. For example, a number of years ago one of us (Howe) became involved as a memory expert for the prosecution in a series of trials when now-grown men recounted their sexually abusive experiences during their stay at a Christian Brothers orphanage (Archdiocesan Commission, 1990). For the majority of these men, their experiences were accurately recounted in their memory narratives and their statements vindicated by additional corroborative evidence. Alexander et al. (2005) discuss numerous cases where documented child abuse can be accurately remembered, for the most part, over a 12- to 21-year interval. But this is the crux of the matter – how can we know when memory evidence is based on mostly correctly reconstructed remembering and when is it based on mostly incorrectly reconstructed remembering?

So, what is at issue here? Unfortunately, it is often the case that many of these allegations typically involve only two witnesses: the victim and the perpetrator. In court, it is up to the triers of fact to determine which memory is most reliable, something that is no easy task. We have learned from science, however, about the types of factors that could easily distort our fragile memories. It is here that the memory expert can offer valuable advice to the courts. Over the years, both Howe and Conway have evaluated hundreds of complainants' (both male and female) statements concerning historic childhood abuse and have written numerous case reports concerning the reliability of memory for witnessed events that have occurred decades earlier.

Such cases were discussed in a special issue of the journal *Memory* in 2013 where in one article Howe reflected on his years as an expert memory witness (Howe, 2013c). Many of these cases followed a classic pattern where memories lie "dormant" for 10–40 years and are suddenly "recovered" through some type of memory work. For example, Howe refers to the case of WM (fictitious initials are used to hide the identities of those involved):

> WM had no memory for her traumatic experiences until she received religious counseling and "prayer" therapy: ". . . it's all coming back now, for a long time I didn't remember it until last year." In addition, when specifically queried as to how her memories suddenly came back, WM reveals the following:
>
> PO: So, what was it that triggered it, what . . . how did it come back into your memory?
>
> WM: We were praying . . . It was, it was two years ago, prayer week, so it must've been about May/June two years ago.
>
> PO: Right.
>
> WM: . . .that's when it all started coming back bit by bit. I mean, it's coming back now, it's come back, some of the bits have come back as I've been talking to you.
>
> (Howe, 2013c, p. 581)

Howe goes on to explain that these alleged memories emerged as a consequence of intense memory work through prayer therapy and also from nightmares the complainant said she had experienced. We know from the scientific literature that such "memory work" can result in the production of memory errors when events experienced during these times of altered consciousness come to be believed as real (see Chapter 2).

Memories of long ago childhood events are not the only form of memory evidence that is under examination in the courts. For example, in cases of murder, assault, or burglary the statements and identifications made by the eyewitnesses or victims can be the key evidence leading to a guilty verdict. As we will see in Chapter 7, before the inclusion of DNA evidence, eyewitness misidentification was one of the greatest causes of wrongful convictions worldwide. Today the Innocence Project (non-profit legal clinics set up across the USA and the UK) works to support appeal cases of those wrongfully convicted, using post-conviction DNA testing. Appeal cases much like Kirk Bloodsworth's:

> An honorably discharged former Marine, Kirk Bloodsworth was the first person in the United States to be exonerated from death row by DNA testing. In 1984 he was arrested for the rape and murder of nine-year-old Dawn Hamilton. He was sentenced to death in Baltimore County, Maryland, in 1985.
>
> Dawn Hamilton died on July 25, 1984. Two young boys witnessed Dawn walking into the woods with a man they described as skinny, six foot-five, with a bushy moustache and blond hair. Bloodsworth was six feet tall, had red hair, and was well over 200 pounds. The police produced a composite drawing of the man based on the eyewitness testimony of the two young boys. The slim resemblance to the composite drawing and the eyewitness

identification of three others who placed him near the scene of the crime, two of whom were not able to identify him during a lineup but had recognized him when the composite picture was shown on the news, ultimately led to the conviction and death sentence.

In 1986 Kirk was retried after an appeal but convicted again, this time sentenced to two lifetime sentences. Finally, in 1992, after eight years in prison, DNA fingerprinting taken from evidence collected at the scene of the crime proved that Kirk was innocent, and in fact, a known suspect at the time, Kimberly Shay Ruffner, already serving a sentence for rape, was the rapist and murderer of Dawn Hamilton, the nine-year-old girl, found dead in the woods, having been sexually assaulted, strangled, and beaten to death with a rock.

(Kirk Bloodsworth, Innocence Project, 2016)

In these opening accounts, we have seen that memory is not quite what the legal system assumes or indeed, wants it to be. In the following chapters of this book, we will examine the various reasons why this is the case. In addition, we will provide theoretically sound and empirically tested suggestions to guide the interpretation of memory evidence. We will first consider the phenomena of repressed memories for long ago childhood events and highlight the cautionary tale with regard to recovered memories from highly suggestive therapeutic techniques (Chapter 2). We will then consider in Chapter 3 what we refer to as naïve beliefs of memory and the problems this causes for the legal system. In Chapters 4 and 5 we will discuss the science behind autobiographical memory and what we know with regard to early childhood memories. Chapter 6 summarizes the latest research examining the sensitivity of memory to stress and highly emotional experiences, something that is commonplace when we are dealing with memories that make up the majority of evidence in legal settings. Chapter 7 reviews the specific research regarding eyewitness identification, an area that in itself warrants an entire book. Here we will consider some of the pertinent research that has examined errors in the procedural aspects of eyewitness identification. Chapter 8 follows on from this with a discussion of the methods used in witness and victim interviewing, focusing on both adult, but mainly, child interviewing. More specifically, what factors can lead to admissions and omissions in detail, and knowing these, what methods can we use to elicit the most accurate recall of an event. We finish this scientific section about the nature of memory with two chapters (Chapters 9 and 10), ones that examine the more collaborative nature of remembering in both jurors and eyewitnesses as well as the pitfalls that ensue when we consider the fallible nature of memory for evidence in jurors.

Caution is always prudent in these matters, but the science of memory has provided us with a set of tools that can guide us when memory serves as (the only) evidence. In anticipation of our review of that evidence, and the more in-depth recommendations and conclusions detailed in the final chapter (Chapter 11), we close this opening chapter with four simple guidelines that we recommend should inform decision-making about memory as evidence:

1. Memories are *psychological mental representations* and should not be compared to, or considered as being like, videos, photographs, or any other forms of recording.
2. Because they are psychological representations they have properties that other non-psychological mediums do not have. For example, they are selective in what they retain, all memories are time-compressed relative to the events they represent, and the fragments they retain are of internal *experience* (not reality!).
3. Any memory, but most especially ones recalled from early childhood, reported fluently with considerable highly specific details should be treated with some caution. With particular attention needed as to how these reports were uncovered (e.g., forced through extensive questioning, multiple discussions with friends, family members, practitioners).
4. All memories contain inferences and details that have been added, often non-consciously.

2

THE ORIGINS OF FALSE AND REPRESSED MEMORIES

> Approaches to memory-recovery work range across a wide continuum, from practices that likely pose little risk if any of iatrogenic illusory memories or false beliefs regarding CSA to those that likely pose substantial risk . . . existing science is insufficient to enable precise specification of which approaches do and do not pose substantial risk . . .
>
> (Lindsay, 1998, p. 483)

Although still present (e.g., see Wypijewski, 2009; Zezima & Carey, 2009), few cases based on *repressed* memories make it to court today. The story was a little different in the late 1980s with a surge of claims that were specifically related to historic childhood sexual abuse (CSA) based on repressed memories. The alleged abuse was often highly traumatic and intrusive, but the victims reported no memory of the abuse until after entering therapy or after reading self-therapy books (e.g., Bass & Davis, 2008; Dolan, 1991).

More recent approaches to psychotherapy that adopted a variety of memory therapy techniques use the term "repression" when a patient was believed to have a history of CSA but has no memory of it. The extreme interpretation of repression is that highly traumatic events can be involuntarily lost from consciousness but later be accurately retrieved in adulthood when it is psychologically "safe" to do so. A special memory mechanism, qualitatively different from normal forgetting mechanisms, is thought to be responsible for this. The special memory mechanism is instantly able to encapsulate the entire record of the event and maintain it outside of conscious awareness, in a pristine and unmodifiable condition, until it is ready to be recovered in a safe psychological environment.

The existence of a special mechanism is at the heart of a controversial debate and polarization in the professional community. According to one extreme view,

l mechanism can help the mind defend itself by repressing memories of
ᴜᴀᴜᴄ experiences from our conscious awareness, preventing them from being
remembered until many years later when it is safer to do so (Brown, Scheflin, &
Hammond, 1998). At the other end of this debate are those that question the
scientific evidence for the existence of these special memory mechanisms. Here,
when forgetting of CSA occurs, it is likely due to ordinary forgetting processes.
For example, the abuse victim may actively avoid thinking about the event, falsely
deny that the event occurred, or avoid environmental cues that would trigger
memories of the event, and eventually "forget" the event altogether (also see Chapter
4). Thus, memories of CSA do not require special and separate memory systems
that differ in qualitative ways from ordinary memory and recovered memories, if
they exist, need not rely on a special mechanism of repression. As Lindsay (1998)
states, at least some kinds of CSA histories can be forgotten and later remembered
via ordinary mechanisms of memory. Indeed, there are a substantial number of
surveys which show that people who report CSA also report prior periods of not
remembering CSA, and there are cases where CSA victims fail to remember well-
documented abuse events (see below).

However, theorists who espouse this latter side of the debate also suggest
that it is unlikely that people who experience extreme events or repeated CSA
after the age of 3-4 are unlikely to forget the abuse (although see Chapter 6 and
memory for repeated versus single traumatic events). Thus, if such memories are
"recovered" using suggestive therapeutic techniques to "unlock" the repressed
memory, then caution is needed when interpreting the reliability of such memories. Such caution is based on a long history of research and scientific data
supporting the premise that human memory is highly suggestible and malleable
(see Ceci & Loftus, 1994). Based on this evidence it is plausible that false memories may be inadvertently created by risky therapeutic methods that have been
used in many recovered memory claims (e.g., hypnosis, guided imagery; Ceci &
Loftus, 1994). It is important to note here that prominent critics of memory-recovery
work, such as Loftus (1993), and Lindsay (1998) do not assert that all recovered
memory reports are false as there are some cases where memories of CSA emerge
after long periods of forgetting. Such critics claim that there is no scientific
evidence for a special repression mechanism and that memory-recovery work can
lead to iatrogenic false memories. However, this does not imply that all accounts
of recovered CSA are false, or that all memory-recovery techniques will inevitably
lead to the formation of false memories, but that the creation of false memories
does occur, and that false beliefs in these events can be held confidently (e.g.,
Lindsay, 1998; Loftus, 1993). Thus, when CSA memories emerge following the
reading of self-help books (e.g., *Courage to Heal*; Bass & Davis, 2008) or therapy
where memory-recovery techniques have been used, suggestion and influence
must be given serious consideration when assessing the reliability of the alleged
memories.

Recovered-memory therapy

A number of memory-recovery techniques such as hypnosis, survivor groups, guided imagery, dream interpretation, sodium amytal, and ideomotor questioning, as well as self-help books such as *Courage to Heal,* run the risk of creating false memories for events that never happened. There are advocates of recovered memories that claim that adults who were abused as children, but have complete amnesia for the abuse, will demonstrate a variety of symptoms as a result of the abuse (Bass & Davis, 2008; Dolan 1991; Fredrickson, 1992). Bass and Davis (2008) list 74 *characteristics* associated with sexual abuse. The list includes attributes such as relationship difficulties, feeling dissatisfied with family relationships, sexual dysfunction, trouble expressing feeling, and feeling different.

When a client is exhibiting *symptoms* indicative of abuse, it is the role of the therapist to assist the client in recalling the repressed memory of that abuse (Dolan, 1991). These symptoms are said to include dreams of being pursued, sleep disturbances, eating disorders, substance abuse, compulsive sexuality, sexual dysfunction, chronic anxiety attacks, depression, difficulties with relationships, distrust of others, guilt, impaired self-esteem, self-destructive behaviors, and personality disorders (see Bass & Davis, 2008). Unfortunately, these very general attributes are not particularly diagnostic of abuse and could apply to any number of behavioral and psychological problems, or indeed, to some extent, be applied to everyone (Kihlstrom, 1998). Kihlstrom (1998) suggests that although it may be true that abuse victims display many of these signs and symptoms, it does not follow that everyone who displays these attributes is a victim of abuse. However, when patients come to therapists, they are looking for answers to explain any behavioral or psychological problems they are experiencing. If the therapist concludes that the patient is a victim of abuse, then with the help of recovered-memory techniques, it is not surprising when reports of abuse arise throughout the course of therapy. When a criminal or civil claim is made on the basis of this newly remembered abuse, the problem the court faces is knowing whether the report reflects a real experience or an iatrogenic false memory. Indeed, contrary to popular belief (see Chapter 3), a memory is not triggered, it is reconstructed (Bartlett, 1932; Kihlstrom & Barnhardt, 1993). Whether the recollection is reconstructed from the kernel of an historically accurate event is the critical question, one that science is not yet able to answer definitely. However, as seen throughout this book, there are some telltale signs that signal when memories are more likely to be false than true.

A further confounding factor in relation to memory-recovery techniques is the fact that we remember very little from early childhood (see Chapter 4). The absence of a mature autobiographical memory system and its subsequent emergence and development in later childhood (after the age of 5–7 years) has been well documented in both behavioral and neurobiological studies (Howe, 2011, 2013b, 2015). Before this age, we are typically in a period of amnesia commonly referred to as infantile and childhood amnesia where memories are poorly formed and typically forgotten very rapidly (see Chapter 4). In fact, Howe (2013b) states that more stable, adult-like autobiographical memories are rarely seen before the age of 9–10 years, and even then, recalling events from this period during adulthood will only be possible if they are particularly distinctive and memorable.

A reason we refer to this as a confounding variable is because of the perverse logic some self-help guides (e.g., Bass & Davis, 2008) and therapists have taken concerning the recollection of childhood events by adults. A good illustration of this can seen when therapists take the view that because someone cannot remember their abuse, this absence of memory constitutes "evidence" that they must have been abused. For example, Bass and Davis make no reference to infantile or childhood amnesia or to the maturation of brain structures that allow for the long-term recollection of autobiographical memories. Instead, they make such claims as:

> If you don't remember your abuse, you are not alone. Many women don't have memories, and some never get any memories. This doesn't mean they weren't abused.
>
> (p. 81)

> If you are unable to remember specific instances . . . but still have a feeling that something abusive happened to you, it probably did.
>
> (p. 21)

And also:

> Many survivors suppress all memories of what happened to them as children. . . . Survivors often doubt their own perceptions. Coming to believe that the abuse really happened, and that it really hurt you, is a vital part of the healing process.
>
> (p. 58)

Bartlett (1932) refers to remembering as being a reconstructive activity. Bass and Davis (2008) refer to a reconstructive memory technique in their self-help guide:

> If you don't remember what happened to you, write about what you *do* remember. Recreate the context in which the abuse happened even if you don't remember the specifics of the abuse yet. Describe where you lived as a child. What was going on in your family, in your neighbourhood, in your life? Often when women think they don't remember, they actually remember quite a lot.
>
> (p. 83)

Although there is research that supports the use of context reinstatement to improve memory for an event, as Kihlstrom (1998) notes, when doing this based on speculation, what *might* have happened can often be confused with what *did* happen. In fact, there is research that shows this in controlled laboratory-based conditions. For example, Ceci, Loftus, Leichtman, and Bruck (1994) interviewed 48 children aged 3–6 years old about real and fictional events. Children were invited to play a "picture in the head" game. They had to picture in their head what the event would look like. Following this imagining task, children's false assent rates for fictional events (saying that they really happened) increased across multiple sessions and continued to be high even when the children were informed that the interviewer asked them to imagine events that did not really happen. Although in this instance participants were children, highly suggestive, repetitive situations that patients often find themselves in during therapeutic sessions could also lead to difficulties in distinguishing between what they have imagined happening from what actually happened. In fact, research with both children and adults, using a related technique where people are asked to perform or only imagine performing an action, produces similar results (e.g., Castelli & Ghetti, 2014). That is, even adults confuse whether something actually occurred or they only imagined it occurring. Interestingly, there is research suggesting that people who report having recovered/repressed memories are extremely poor at discriminating between real and imagined events (McNally, Clancy, Barrett, & Parker, 2005). Thus, inviting speculation can have a profound effect on later recall because it is a form of self-generated misinformation (Bruck & Ceci, 1995).

Therapists will use a variety of different treatment plans to help patients recover memories of sexual abuse. These include direct questioning, hypnosis, reading books, attending survivors' groups, age regression, and dream analysis. More unconventional techniques include: prayer, meditation, age regression, reflexology, channelling, psychodrama, casting out demons, yoga, trance writing, and primal scream therapy (Underwager & Wakefield, 1998). Fredrickson (1992) maintains that because few survivors experience spontaneous recall, various memory retrieval techniques are necessary in order to elicit trauma memories. Indeed, Fredrickson explicitly recommends the use of dream interpretation, free association writing, massage therapy, body manipulation, hypnosis, feelings work, art therapy, and expanding on imagistic memories.

The dreams, images, and thoughts that come as a result of these recovered memory techniques are seen as an implicit expression of memory for abuse. However, there are other plausible explanations. A patient may enter into therapy because they are anxious or depressed and looking for an explanation for their problems. If the therapist suggests they are likely a victim of child abuse and explains the theory of repressed memories, it is not unlikely that with repeated therapy sessions the patient will start thinking and dreaming about child abuse. As Brenneis (1994) states, the problem comes when these dreams become attributed to actual past experiences without independent corroboration. Of course, all such memories should be taken seriously and investigated. Child abuse and trauma occur with unacceptable frequency and survivors must be supported. However, that does not mean that uncorroborated memories "unlocked" under these conditions should be accepted uncritically as evidence of abuse by either the therapist or the patient.

In these vulnerable situations, it is the responsibility of the therapist to provide an unbiased view of possible recovered memories and question the historical truth. It does not help the patient to persuade them of something that is not true, and the consequences to their quality of life and that of those around them can be devastating (Kihlstrom, 1998; Maran, 2010).

The family of Carol Felstead are all too aware of this problem, as are many families who have faced allegations of child abuse, and have maintained their innocence (also see the False Memory Syndrome Foundation [FMSF] and the British False Memory Society [BFMS]). The story of Carol Felstead's life and death can be found in full in the recently published book *Justice for Carol* (Felstead & Felstead, 2014). Carol Felstead (although her name was changed by deed poll to Myers) died in June 2005 at the age of 41 under mysterious circumstances. Her family were only informed two weeks after her death. Her case has alarming parallels with the satanic abuse cases of the late 1980s and early 1990s (see Jenkins & Maier-Katkin, 1991). Carol was registered as mentally ill for the last 13 years of her life, and she first expressed her claims of ritual abuse only after she entered therapy. In a document handed to the coroner's office by one of Carol's early therapists Dr. Fleur Fisher, Carol claimed that her family had satanically abused her in inconceivable ways. They supposedly killed her sister and placed a dead baby on top of Carol and then set the family house on fire. It was claimed that her family also murdered Carol's own children by ritual sacrifice. There is no evidence for any of these acts but it is possible that Carol's account drew, in part, on a series of real life family tragedies that took place before she was born – her fifth brother was stillborn, her baby sister died a natural death from a hole in the heart, and there was also a fire at the family home.

In the late 1980s Carol was seeing a succession of psychiatric professionals, many of whom believed in the existence of ritual abuse. By the late 1990s, medical records indicated further allegations of extreme abuse. She believed her parents were high priests of a satanic cult and claimed that a friend she had confided in as a teenager was murdered by the cult in front of her and that she had been regularly fed urine and faeces.

Carol's medical records indicated that she underwent recovered memory therapy and only then began to make the claims of satanic abuse. Although the claims were so bizarre and extreme, her therapists, who were prominent believers in satanic abuse, accepted them without question and without attempting to corroborate or challenge the events. This story is a tragic one, full of lies and deceit. At the time of this writing, the Felstead family are still fighting the battle to find out the whole truth behind the events that led to Carol's death and there has been a successful application for a new inquest. The events can be followed through the BFMS.

Today, we have a clearer understanding of the uncertainty of recovered memory techniques and their use to "unlock" recovered memories of abuse. Official statements from the American Psychiatric Association (Board of Trustees, 1993) and the American Medical Association (AMA; Council of Scientific Affairs, 1993) have been made regarding uncorroborated recovered memories of CSA. They clarify the need to be aware of the issues of false accusations while at the same time not discrediting the reports of patients who have indeed been traumatized by actual previous abuse. Basic clinical and ethical principles should guide the psychiatrist's work in this difficult area. Such statements emphasize that care must be taken to avoid prejudging the cause of the patient's difficulties, or the veracity of the patient's reports. A strong prior belief by the psychiatrist that sexual abuse, or other factors, are or are not the cause of the patient's problems is likely to interfere with appropriate assessment and treatment. Clinicians should not exert pressure on patients to believe in events that may not have occurred and they need specialized training to treat patients who report the emergence of memories during specialized interview techniques (e.g., hypnosis, guided imagery).

As Rogers (1992, 1994) notes, valid claims may arise in therapy, but typically in these cases the therapist did not use intrusive and suggestive techniques and the patient will not have been placed into influential group treatment until the abuse had been fully documented. Thus, it is important to carefully examine such medical records in any court case. The overwhelming issue is that there is no litmus test to distinguish between true and false memories (also see Bernstein & Loftus, 2009). Therefore, when a memory is "uncovered" in therapy, it is the role of the therapist to assess the veracity of that event before such reports are used to launch legal action. Although the scientific community has failed to produce evidence of repressed/recovered memories, there are those who would argue that this absence of evidence is not proof that they do not exist, just proof that they do not exist using the methods tried to date. Because of this, as well as the inability to determine truthfulness of a specific repressed memory allegation without corroborative evidence, repressed memory claims present special equitable and evidentiary problems for the courts (Amicus curiae: *Minnesota Supreme Court, Doe 76C v. Archdiocese of St. Paul and Minneapolis and Diocese of Winona*, 2011). We turn to a discussion of this matter next.

An historical account of recovered memory in the courtroom

In cases involving claims of recovered memories, one party aims to prove the existence of repressed memories, while the other party provides a counterclaim, denying the abuse occurred and argues that memories recovered in therapy should be inadmissible in court (Underwager & Wakefield, 1998). There was a surge of such cases involving claims of recovered memories when courts and legislatures in many US states created legal mechanisms for both criminal and civil actions based on recovered memories (Loftus & Rosenwald, 1993). The statute of limitations restricts the period during which lawsuits may be filed after the date of injury. However, several states passed legislation extending the statutory period in civil cases so that the statute of limitations does not begin until two to three years after the alleged abuse is *remembered* or after the *claimant understands that the abuse caused injury* (Loftus 1993; Loftus & Rosenwald, 1993). This was termed the "delayed discovery rule" and courts have usually held that the statute of limitations begins to run when the plaintiff recovers their first memory. Amendments to existing statutes, enacted after 1994 and 1995, are more complex and give greater weight to avoiding fraudulent claims and include the need for independent corroboration of the recovered memory before the delayed discovery rule can be applied (Underwager & Wakefield, 1998). It is also common for courts to hold pretrial hearings to determine the admissibility of testimony from expert witnesses on the phenomenon of repression. Taub (1999) refers to an example of ten trial courts that have considered this question, where all but three concluded that the repressed memory testimony in question had not been demonstrated to be reliable and was therefore inadmissible. The three rulings where recovered memory testimony was admitted were overturned due to a later demonstration that there were errors in applying the scientific standard of admissibility (*Isely v. Capuchin Province, 877 F. Supp. 1055* (E.D. Mich. 1995)), or because the scope of expertise was restricted such that it only included therapists who specialized in trauma, ignoring memory researchers and professional organizations that have contributed to the scientific debate over the validity of recovered memories (*Shahzade v. Gregory, 923 F.Supp. 286* (D. Mass 1996)).

During this period, The False Memory Syndrome Foundation was formed (founded in 1992 in the USA and the British False Memory Society founded in 1993) by professionals working with victims of trauma, scientists studying memory, and families affected by accusations of CSA. Although abhorring actual cases of childhood sexual abuse, these societies raised awareness of the dangers of iatrogenic false memories created using memory-recovery techniques to "unlock" repressed memories. Between 1992 and 1998 the False Memory Syndrome Foundation conducted a Legal Survey to compile reports of litigation related to repressed memory claims. At its conclusion, the survey contained 633 civil cases and 103 criminal actions where specific repressed memory claims led to litigation.

The picture is very different today, with fewer new repressed memory claims being filed without corroborative evidence. A large percentage of repressed memory claims do not make it to trial and repressed memory testimony is considered by many courts to be unreliable and therefore, inadmissible if there is no corroborative evidence due to the suggestive circumstances under which "repressed memories" are often "recovered." A subsequent set of legal actions are related to malpractice and have been brought against mental health care providers by former patients and third parties who claim therapeutic negligence led to the development of false memories, which resulted in injury to the patient, a third party, or both (e.g., *Ramona v. Isabella*, 1994). Taub (1999) provides a full review of the FMSF Legal Survey, but here we highlight some of the prominent historical cases based on claims of recovered memory.

Criminal cases

The Survey contains records of 103 criminal cases that were filed in 25 US states. The majority of cases on record were resolved during 1992–1994. Prior to 1994, the majority of cases went to trial; very few cases were dismissed. This tendency changed abruptly in mid-1994, after which such criminal charges were either withdrawn by the state or dismissed by the court.

Paul Ingram

In 1989, defendant Paul Ingram (*State of Washington v. Ingram*) received a 20-year prison sentence after he pled guilty to the sexual and ritual abuse of his two daughters. The sisters asserted that years earlier they had been repeatedly raped and that at least 25 human babies, some born to them, had been sacrificed in rituals in the Ingram's back yard. Police failed to locate the burial grounds for the alleged ritual sacrifices. Furthermore, medical examination of the daughters failed to yield any evidence of sexual activity or of childbearing. Yet Paul Ingram, a deputy sheriff and a member of a Christian church, believed that his children would not lie. Although Ingram insisted he could not remember ever doing anything he was accused of, he worked with the detectives, a pastor, and a therapist to visualize the attacks and eventually reported having flashbacks and images of abusing his two daughters. Dr. Ofshe, a social psychologist, interviewed Mr. Ingram at length and was able to show how he had been persuaded to produce a false confession through the use of long interrogations involving visualization exercises and suggestions to accept that claims about things he allegedly did but that he could not remember doing. However, Ofshe's report was not made available to Ingram to use in the trial and, after pleading guilty, Ingram was charged with six counts of rape in the third degree. Ingram tried without success to withdraw his guilty plea and remained in prison until released in 2003 after serving his sentence.

George Franklin

In what was considered to be a landmark case in 1990, George Franklin was the first American citizen to stand trial and be convicted of murder based on a repressed memory. In 1989, the defendant's daughter, Eileen Franklin-Lipsker (Franklin-Lipsker), informed the police that she had been an eyewitness to the 1969 sexual molestation and murder of her eight-year-old best friend, Susan Nason. She implicated her father, George Franklin (Franklin), and a San Mateo County, California jury convicted him of first-degree murder. Franklin served five years of a life sentence before a federal district court granted him a writ of habeas corpus due to unconstitutional errors in his state court trial.

Franklin-Lipsker claimed that the repressed memory first came back to her in a flashback when she was playing with her two young children. When the case went to trial, Franklin-Lipsker had a rich and detailed memory of the event filled with very specific details, emotions, and word-for-word conversations. She remembered explicit details of her father sexually assaulting Susie (Susan) in the back of a van. She also claimed that she could remember vivid details of the location, the weather, the ring that Susie was wearing on her finger, and seeing her father holding a rock above his head with both hands. Susan raised her hands to her head as Franklin "crashed the rock down against her head where her hands were." He struck Susan a second time with the rock. The blow crushed a silver ring worn by Susan that had had a stone in it. As her father raised the rock above his head, she remembered screaming and seeing Susie lying on the ground, covered in blood, the ring on her finger smashed. The memory was recalled with such confidence and detail, and confirmed many facts of the murder, that when the jury began its deliberations on 29 November 1990, they returned a guilty verdict the next day.

Loftus and colleagues (Loftus, Polonsky, & Fullilove, 1994; Loftus & Rosenwald, 1993) questioned the authenticity of the recovered memory in this case. Although Franklin-Lipsker confided in her brother that she visualized her father killing Nason while being hypnotized, she later denied this had occurred, claiming the memory had only recently returned to her from a "flashback" and that the memory had been repressed but returned spontaneously. Horngrad, the defense attorney for Franklin, believed Franklin-Lipsker learned her memory would not be admissible in court if it had been elicited while she was under hypnosis, which is why she later denied that the memory returned during hypnotherapy. As Loftus and Ketcham (1994) highlighted, there were alternative sources for details that made Franklin-Lipsker's memory so rich and confident. Media reports from when the body was found were filled with some of these same details. It was reported in the newspapers that the murdered girl's skull was fractured and that a crushed ring found on the body showed evidence that she held her hands up to protect her face. Loftus claimed it was at least plausible that under suggestible conditions Franklin-Lipsker incorporated these facts into her memory, picking up details from conservations, rumours, her fantasies and fears, and arrived at the mistaken conclusion that she had witnessed her father raping and murdering her best friend.

The lack of any physical evidence implicating Franklin in the murder were among the grounds for the subsequent reversal of Franklin's conviction. A year after Franklin's conviction was overturned, as prosecutors planned to retry him, it was disclosed that Franklin-Lipsker had in fact been hypnotized by a therapist before the first trial. Post-hypnotic testimony is barred in California because it is seen as unreliable. In July 1996, the prosecutors announced they would not retry Franklin.

Taub (1999) notes that sentences in criminal repressed memory cases have ranged from two life terms plus 25 years, to one year of house arrest. In a significant number of cases the state proceeded against the defendant only to discover later that there was evidence that clearly contradicted the claim or that the allegations were developed under hypnosis or other suggestive circumstances (e.g., *State of Nevada v. Dorsey*, 1995). Some criminal charges were withdrawn when the complainant retracted her claims (e.g., *Commonwealth of Pennsylvania v. Althaus*, 1992). Criminal charges in a New Hampshire case were withdrawn after the state's Supreme Court ruled that repressed memory testimony is insufficiently reliable to be admitted at trial (e.g., *State v. Hungerford*, 1997).

Civil cases

According to the FMSF Legal Survey, civil lawsuits represent 86% of all repressed memory cases in the USA. Of the civil suits that have been resolved, approximately 13% have gone to trial. Between 1995 and 1998 only 8% of civil cases have been resolved at trial (ten in favor of the plaintiffs and four in favor of the defendants). During that same period, 70% of the repressed memory lawsuits were either dropped by the complainant or dismissed by the courts due to the inadmissibility of repressed memory testimony. Three cases highlighted in the legal survey are presented below.

Borawick

In 1992, Borawick (*Borawick v. Shay*), a 38-year-old Connecticut woman sued relatives who, she claimed, had sexually abused her when she was a child. Claims included rituals where she was drugged at the age of three, and then sexually abused and forced to take part in a ritual involving drinking the blood of a dead pig. The appellant initially claimed that the memories returned to her spontaneously, but other court records showed that the alleged abuse was reported during a hypnotic session with her unlicensed therapist. In 1996, the case was dismissed by the USA Second Circuit Court on the grounds that suggestible hypnotic techniques were used to recover the memories, the far-fetched uncorroborated nature of the allegations, and the lack of qualifications and the inaccurate record keeping of the therapist. Following this case, the court proposed that certain factors be considered at a pretrial evidentiary hearing before choosing to admit post-hypnotic testimony and that it is the responsibility of the party seeking to admit the testimony to persuade the court that the evidence is admissible (see Taub, 1999). These factors include: to be aware of the aim or subject of the hypnotic sessions; to be aware of any possible suggestions from the hypnotherapist; seek a record of the hypnotic session if available; and show corroborating evidence.

Ramona

Hypnosis is not the only suggestive memory recovery technique. In 1992 Holly Ramona, at the age of 21, sued her father for childhood sexual abuse based on her recovered memories. The California court of appeals heard the case. Ramona first entered therapy for help with bulimia and depression. Although she had no memories of being abused, her therapist told her that 60–80 percent of her patients had experienced abuse of some kind. After four months in therapy, Ramona began to have "flashbacks" of abuse occurring when she was 5–8 years old. To better understand these flashbacks and discover if they were true memories her therapist asked her to undergo a sodium amytal interview with the belief that a person cannot lie under the drug's influence. During the interview, Ramona described the sexual abuse and her therapist assured her she was not lying. Two years after the interview she experienced new flashbacks of additional abuse and went on to sue her father (*Ramona v. Isabella*).

In 1997, a California appellate court dismissed the claims against her father, holding that Ramona had not demonstrated the reliability of her post-sodium amytal memories and thus barred her from testifying because her memory was tainted by therapeutic administration of the drug. California courts held that sodium amytal interviews were unreliable because despite being called a "truth serum," the drug, while reducing inhibitions and making individuals more willing to talk, does not guarantee the truthfulness of what is being said. In response, Ramona's father sued the therapist for mistakenly causing his daughter to believe she was abused as a child (*Ramona v. Ramona, Super. Ct. Napa County, Cal, 1994*) and the jury awarded Mr. Ramona a $500,000 judgment. Holly Ramona did not appeal the jury verdict.

Franklin

In 1992, Franklin began treatments with a psychologist, Dr. Laurie Hoover after experiencing panic attacks. Using a variety of recovered memory techniques including guided imagery, writing with the non-dominant hand, trance-work, relaxation, communicating with metaphorical "inner children," and journal writing, Franklin began to "recall" previously repressed memories of abuse. At first Franklin believed the abuser had been her father but later became convinced that Stevenson, a cousin seven years her senior, committed the abuse. She filed this action against him (*Franklin v. Stevenson*). Despite Stevenson originally requesting that the trial court exclude any evidence and testimony from either the expert witnesses or Franklin herself, the judge denied this motion, and the jury returned a guilty verdict against Stevenson. In 1999, a Utah District Court judge reversed the jury verdict in favor of the plaintiff and dismissed the claim, drawing a parallel between hypnotic suggestion and communicating with an "inner child." This, along with the other techniques used, was seen to be similar to hypnosis and judged inherently unreliable for recovering memories. Indeed, on cross-examination in this case, Stevenson elicited concessions from Franklin's expert witness, Dr. Bessel van der Kolk, regarding the lack of scientific support for the memory techniques used with Franklin. Dr. van der Kolk testified as follows:

> Q. Is there any scientific literature, any studies that you are aware of that have been done that show that asking a question with one hand and answering the question with the non-dominant hand is a mechanism by which you can recover an accurate memory of the past? Are there studies?
>
> A. It's interesting that you ask the question, actually, because this great Frenchman who knew more about trauma than anybody else, Pierre Janet . . . in 1889 in his book . . . actually wrote about that very phenomenon.

Q. Did his study deal with the issue of validating the accuracy of the recovered memory, Doctor?

A. No, he didn't.

Q. Thank you. And are you aware of a single study as of 1996 that has validated this as a reliable technique for recovering memory, Doctor?

A. Not to my knowledge.

Q. Thank you.

Q. Do you believe that there is any scientific evidence to suggest that I could ask myself [a question] and I could answer that question with my non-dominant hand and expect that I'm really getting the truth?

A. Is there any scientific evidence? I'm not aware of any studies specifically done on non-dominant handwriting to support or disprove that. It is a common clinical technique.

(Taken from: www.law.justia.com/cases/utah/
supreme-court/1999/franklin.html)

Despite the large number of cases filed, a significant number (both civil and criminal) were dismissed or withdrawn due to hypnosis or other suggestible memory techniques used to recover the memory testimony. However, it is important to note that despite the extensive literature in the field, we are not implying that these techniques are conclusively unreliable as a matter of law. Instead, it is, and has been in previous cases, the responsibility of the trial judge to explore this issue in individual cases and determine the reliability of such techniques when counsel has made a proper objection to such evidence.

Malpractice lawsuits

We have already referred to a couple of cases where malpractice claims against therapists have been raised (*Ramona v. Isabella* and the ongoing Carol Felstead case). Even when such an accusation based on therapeutic malpractice is proven to be false, it is unlikely that the social stigma, damage to personal relationships, and emotional turmoil can be ameliorated. Third-party false-memory legal cases are those in which a person who was not a patient sues the therapist of the person who makes the accusations. The questions typically asked in these court cases are about whether, given the potential damage a falsely accused individual may face, the therapist has a duty to that person. Is it the responsibility of the therapist to try to avoid the creation of false memories using suggestive techniques, and should any recovered memories be treated with caution until the events can be corroborated? If the therapist fails to do these things, should they be held liable if a patient decides to act on the basis of their false memories and file a civil or criminal charge? These lawsuits are complicated. What patients discuss in therapy is confidential so it is difficult to prove the role of the therapist in developing false memories. Furthermore, the law does not generally acknowledge that a mental health professional has a duty to those with whom there is no formal client–therapist relationship.

Despite these complicated legal matters, malpractice lawsuits are still ongoing today. Several jurisdictions have struggled with determining whether, and under what circumstances, therapists owe a duty to third parties, and have reached differing conclusions based on competing public policy considerations. As of 2014, Wisconsin is a state that has established case law that provides a possible path for these cases. Two such cases, summarized by the FMSF, are highlighted below.

Susan Jones

Susan L. Jones was a social worker trained to treat repressed memory patients. In August 1992, she began treating Laura B. who before entering therapy had no knowledge or memory of being sexually abused by her father. Jones led Laura to believe that her nightmares and anxiety attacks were actually "flashbacks" and "recovered memories" of episodes of sexual assault and abuse by her father. She also convinced Laura that the physical sensations she was experiencing were "body memories." Here, there may be no conscious memory of abuse but the body is said to remember through supposed physical symptoms that correspond to the childhood abuse. It should be noted that there is no empirical support for the body memory concept (Smith, 1993). Jones used a variety of memory recovery techniques, including visualization, to lead Laura into a self-induced trance to uncover allegedly lost memories of sexual abuse. The social worker directed Laura to stop communicating with her father. Laura filed a police report and her father, Joel Hungerford, was arrested. A trial followed and in May 1995 the Superior Court (Groff, J.) ruled that because Laura's "memories" of assault were recovered during therapy, they were not scientifically reliable and thus inadmissible at trial (*State v. Hungerford, 142 N.H. 110, 134, 697 A.2d 916, 930, 1997*).

Following the initial trial, the father filed a lawsuit against the social worker, claiming that the treatment of his daughter was negligent. As is common in these cases, Jones moved to dismiss claims that she owed the father a duty of care as the relationship was between the client and the therapist. The New Hampshire Supreme Court ruled that a mental health care provider owes a legal duty to the father when the diagnosis is that the father sexually abused or assaulted the patient. It should act with reasonable care to avoid foreseeable harm to the father of an adult patient resulting from treatment arising from the diagnosis of past sexual abuse or assault by said father (*Hungerford v. Jones, U.S. District Court, No. 97–657, 1998*).

Celia Lausted

In 1983, Celia Lausted began treating Nancy Anneatra even though she was unlicensed at the time. In 1985, after two years of therapy, Anneatra accused her parents of sexual abuse based on the repressed memories she had "unlocked" in therapy and filed a lawsuit in Minnesota that was later dismissed. After the confrontation, Anneatra cut off all contact with her parents and in 1995 died of cancer. After Anneatra's death her mother, Mrs. Sawyer, was able to obtain records of Anneatra's therapy that provided evidence of the role the therapist played in her daughter's alleged recovery of false memories. Shortly after, the Sawyers sued their daughter's psychiatrist, H. Berit Midelfort, and therapist, Celia Lausted, for negligence that led to the development of false memories of sexual abuse by her father and various family members. The therapists were accused of using highly suggestive techniques, such as hypnosis, without consideration of the potential risks of using these techniques. The FMSF filed an amicus brief to provide expert opinion on repressed memories in this case. In 2001, a Wisconsin jury awarded $5.08 million to the Sawyers for the pain and suffering they sustained as a result of the false memories of sexual abuse that developed when their daughter was in therapy (*Sawyer v. Midelfort No. 97–1969*, 1998). The court noted:

> We are quite confident that negligent treatment which encourages false accusations of sexual abuse is highly culpable for the resulting injury.

More and more courts are taking the view that "the therapist owes an accused parent a duty of care in the diagnosis and treatment of an adult patient for sexual abuse where the patient, acting on the encouragement, recommendation, or instruction of the therapist, takes public action concerning the accusation" (see *Hungerford v. Jones, U.S. District Court, No. 97–657*, 1998).

Of course, it is not just the families who suffer from these false allegations, but so too does the patient. In an extensive review of repressed memory cases, Taub (1999) notes that it is not just the families that are entitled to sue for malpractice but former patients are similarly entitled, and indeed some have also begun to file malpractice suits against therapists. Here, the charges surround the creation of iatrogenic false memories of abuse through the misuse of intrusive suggestive therapeutic techniques.

The origins of false memories

We know by now that the nature of memory is central to substantiating the recovered memory possibility. A popular view of memory in the public, clinical, and legal arenas is that it is akin to a video playback, where memories are a sort of detailed mental copy of "reality" (Simons & Chabris, 2011). Indeed, it is popularly believed by laypersons and professionals alike that such recordings can be stored in memory and retrieved unadulterated when we "press the replay button." These ideas also form the basic belief behind recovered memories (Loftus & Ketcham, 1994).

However, over 80 years ago Bartlett stated that remembering is an "imaginative reconstruction, or construction," and "it is thus hardly ever exact" (Bartlett, 1932, p. 213). Such a view fits nicely with more contemporary research as well as the current view of memory. Indeed, there has been at least 40 years of research that has shown that memory is not like a video-recorder, is biased during encoding processes, and that people use imaginative (re)construction in both laboratory-based and real-life situations during memory retrieval (see Loftus, 2005, for a review).

Early research by Loftus and colleagues demonstrated that it is relatively easy to distort originally encoded memories by exposing people to misleading information. In one of the original studies by Loftus and Palmer (1974), subtle variations in the wording of a question resulted in changes in the way participants reported an event. Here, participants viewed footage of a car accident and were later asked the question "how fast were the cars going when they _____ into each other?" Participants reported over 20% greater travelling speeds when the adjective "smashed" was used compared with "contacted." The question with the word "smashed" was also more likely to elicit a false memory of broken glass at the site of the crash.

However, it is one thing to be able alter small details of an event, such as the perceived speed of a car, and quite another to be able to implant an entire event. In the mid 1990s, Loftus and colleagues attempted just this. In what has now become known as a landmark study, Loftus and Pickrell (1995) successfully implanted a completely false memory of being lost in a shopping mall. Family members of adult participants provided Loftus and Pickrell with stories about childhood experiences. Four stories were presented to the participants, three of them were actual events from their childhood and the fourth was the "lost in the mall" story. The false event was constructed using plausible information about a shopping trip, including the name of a mall near where they grew up. The lost-in-the-mall scenario included the following elements: lost for an extended period; crying; aid and comfort from an elderly woman; and finally, reunion with the family. Following two successive interviews where they were questioned about each event and asked to remember as much as possible about the event that happened to them as a child, over 25% of the participants falsely remembered the lost-in-the-mall event. In a similar study using doctored photographs as suggestive evidence, Wade, Garry, Read, and Lindsay (2002) successfully implanted memories for false events from the adult's childhood. Through guided imagery exercises (not unlike those used in recovered memory therapy), participants were asked to think about the photograph depicting them on a hot air balloon ride (which they had never taken). They found that 50% of participants created complete or partial false memories for this event.

Such studies have been criticized for implanting memories for mundane events that do not replicate the emotionally traumatic events of child abuse. Although ethically we could not implant false memories of child sexual abuse, memory distortions have been demonstrated for more negative and traumatic experiences from childhood. For example, Porter, Yuille, and Lehman (1999) interviewed participants about highly emotional and stressful events from their childhood (serious animal attack, a serious indoor or outdoor accident), some of which were true and some false. Using guided imagery and repeated retrieval attempts, 26% of participants reported a complete false memory and another 30% recalled aspects of the false experience. Other studies used similar methods to elicit false memories of nearly drowning as a child and being rescued by a lifeguard (Heaps & Nash, 2001), or having to go to hospital at the age of four after being diagnosed with low blood sugar levels (Ost, Foster, Costall, & Bull, 2005). Often, initial interviews elicit little detail, but with repeated questioning across successive weeks, participants are able to provide a detailed recollection, including thoughts at the time into the narration:

> I was living in [place name] at the time. It must have been on a Sunday because my dad was there. He was always around on a Sunday . . . I don't remember much about the hospital except I know it was a massive, huge place. I was 5 years old at the time and I was like 'oh my God I don't really want to go into this place, you know it's awful' . . . but I had no choice. They did a blood test on me and found out that I had a low blood sugar . . .
>
> (Ost et al., 2005, p. 710)

Taken together these (as well as many other) studies show the power of this strong form of suggestion. It has led a significant number of participants to believe in or even remember detailed events that did not happen (Scoboria et al., 2017). Akin to the iatrogenic false memories recovered in therapy, in these laboratory-based studies, false memories are often a fusion of imagined, real, and suggested information. However, as we have mentioned before, there is no reliable test to distinguish between a relatively accurate reconstruction and ones that contain many incorrect aspects or are entirely false. The major concern for the more suggestive memory recovery techniques is the ease with which memories can be distorted.

Critics of recovered memory work do not claim that all memories recovered in therapy must be false. However, it is likely that false recovered memories of CSA arise as a result of a number of factors including the nature of the suggestive influence (Lindsay, 1998). This includes not only the type and strength of the suggestive technique, but also the perceived authority and trustworthiness of the source of the suggestion, repetition of the suggestion, the plausibility of the suggestion, and how well the suggestion fits with the beliefs of the person's past (Lindsay, 1998). These factors may also be augmented by a high level of vulnerability of the patient who is receiving the therapy. Although not entirely impossible, it is less likely that people will develop false CSA memories purely spontaneously or after only a few suggestive questions (Lindsay, 1998).

Although a repression or dissociation interpretation does not withstand empirical scrutiny (McNally, 2003; Piper, Pope, & Borowiecki, 2000), it is clear that while people can develop false recovered memories of CSA, there are also others that do indeed recall memories of CSA that are genuine. This latter group report having been sexually abused during childhood, having not thought about the abuse in years, and then recalled the event either spontaneously or during therapy. There does appear to be some evidence for this. Clinicians have reported cases of recovered memories with documented evidence of CSA (Briere & Conte, 1993, although see Loftus, 1993 for a critique of this study) or where no memory of the documented abuse exists (Williams, 1994; although see Loftus, Garry, & Feldman, 1994 for a critique of this research). Repression theorists believe that such findings support the claim that trauma victims can repress horrific experiences (Brown et al., 1998). However, an alternative explanation, as we have mentioned earlier, is that memories may have been subject to the normal process of forgetting. Indeed, simply not thinking about child abuse for a period of time is not the same as having repressed memories of that abuse.

McNally and Geraerts (2009) refer to several elements that could account for not thinking about abuse for a period of time and then remembering it later. We know from past research that the more traumatic an event, the more likely we are to remember it (Pope, Oliva, & Hudson, 1999). However, experiences of abuse may not always be perceived as traumatic. Clancy and McNally (2005, 2006) interviewed 27 adults who reported CSA. The majority of the participants reported the event as confusing and uncomfortable, but only two of 27 participants remembered the event as terrifying and traumatic. Furthermore, only two participants understood the event to be sexual at the time of its occurrence. As Clancy and McNally (2005, 2006) state, at least some "recovered memory" participants forgot the abuse not because it was so traumatic, but because it was not traumatic.

If not cued or if actively avoided, long periods of time can pass with no memory of the abuse. In the interviews conducted by Clancy and McNally (2005, 2006) participants reported not remembering the abuse due to an absence of reminders, or because they actively avoided thinking about the experience. However, as McNally and Geraerts (2009) state, merely pushing something out of mind does not mean it is inaccessible. They refer to the memory being "suppressed" not "repressed." People will also recall their abuse experiences and then forget they have done so. Such "illusion amnesia" has been termed the "forgot it all along" effect. Schooler, Bendiksen, and Ambadar (1997) found in their case studies participants could believe that the memories had been repressed for many years when they had in fact previously discussed their experiences with others.

Such errors in metamemory have been documented in the laboratory. For example, Merckelbach et al. (2006) examined the ability to estimate prior remembering in participants with continuous or recovered CSA memories. Participants were asked whether they had vivid memories about various childhood events and after a one-hour interval, they completed a second questionnaire containing new but also previously presented childhood questions. They were asked to indicate how recently they had thought about new but also previously presented childhood events. Participants with "recovered memories" underestimated their prior remembering (see also Arnold & Lindsay, 2002, 2005). Thus, as Schooler et al. (1997) documented, people may have a "recovered memory" experience simply because they forget having previously remembered it.

Finally, laboratory-based research has suggested there may exist some cognitive differences between two types of recovered memory experiences, those recovered spontaneously and those recovered during suggestive therapy sessions. For example, research suggests that compared with those who allegedly recover their memory spontaneously, those who gradually recover their memories in therapy are more prone to the production of false memories in laboratory-based experiments using the Deese/Roediger-McDermott (DRM; Deese, 1959; Roediger & McDermott, 1995) paradigm (Geraerts, Lindsay et al., 2009). In comparison, when using a "forgot it all along" task, people who allegedly recovered their memories spontaneously showed heightened forgetting of prior remembering compared with those people who recovered memories in therapy and those who had continuous memories of CSA. Thus, people who recovered memories of abuse through suggestive therapy were susceptible to the construction of false memories, but did not underestimate their prior remembering, whereas, people who reported spontaneous recovered memories, were less susceptible to false memories but showed a heightened proneness to forget prior instances of remembering. Geraerts, Lindsay et al. (2009) argued that such individual differences in memory function suggests differing mechanisms underlying recovered-memory experiences, with some reflecting forgotten recollections of what could be authentic events, whereas others reflect the product of suggestive therapeutic techniques and are ultimately false. They concluded that understanding these different underlying mechanisms of recovered memories might be a first step in resolving the controversial issues concerning the origins of people's experiences leading to their belief that a particular memory has been "recovered."

Conclusion

As we can see, the more modern view of recovered memories is not as extreme as the repressed memory versus false memory debates of the late 1980s and early 1990s. We have no scientific evidence to support the existence of a repressed memory mechanism. Indeed, the evidence from memory research does not suggest that the construct of repressed and recovered memory is invalid, but that these terms have been misused. Instead, the reason for the apparent periods of forgetting is likely a result of normal memory mechanisms, including normal forgetting, failure to understand the traumatic nature of the event, failures of metamemory, intentional avoidance (or forgetting), and infantile and childhood amnesia, all of which have been adequately documented by ample scientific research (Ceci & Loftus 1994).

We have seen that memories for entire events that did not happen can be created. Although we cannot create false memories for sexual abuse in controlled laboratory conditions, there is an abundance of evidence demonstrating the relative ease with which researchers can implant false memories of both mundane and more negative events through suggestion. (Also see Chapters 4 and 6 for how it is easier to implant negative than neutral memories.) The problem in the courtroom, as Spiegel and Scheflin (1994) opine, is that there is no foolproof way in which we can reliably determine with 100 percent accuracy the difference between the retrieval of a real memory and the convincing false belief in a created memory. It is likely that many cases of "recovered memories" can contain both a kernel of accuracy as well as aspects that are illusory (Lindsay, 1998). We have seen that the many techniques used over the years to aid memory recovery in therapeutic contexts are at risk of creating false memories for events that never happened. In many of these cases, without independent corroboration, it can be difficult to trust memory. It is also likely that different approaches to recovered memory work vary in their likely risk to produce iatrogenic false memories. Yet again, science has not yet given us a definitive answer to which approaches pose substantial risk and those that do not (Lindsay, 1998). Certainly, the research to date encourages a "case-specific focus" (Alison, Kebbell, & Lewis, 2006, p. 416) regarding each circumstance that leads to the recovery of a memory for child abuse.

Although it is impossible to postdict the accuracy of recovered memory claims, Lindsay (1998) does consider some important factors to help assess the plausibility of these claims. These include how the recovered memory experience came about (with greater confidence in a memory that was not recovered using suggestive memory work), the likelihood the event could be forgotten (happened early in life, happened a small number of times, represents a common form of abuse that may have appeared in the popular media), and at least some corroborating evidence in support of the claim.

Recovered memories that appear relatively implausible should be treated with caution. A more implausible claim would include reports of abuse that is bizarre and extreme (e.g., satanic ritual abuse), said to have happened numerous times over the period of many years, said to have happened during infancy, emerged via extensive memory-recovery work, and has no supporting evidence. In cases where recovered memories do appear in court, the expert memory witness should be called upon. Although no memory expert will be able to discern the truth or falsity of an allegation, they will be able to inform the courts regarding the effects of any suggestive techniques used to recover the memory, how memory may have been influenced, and how the alleged memory stands up to what science tells us about how memory works. Each case should be evaluated on its own merits but implausible claims such as those listed above and abuse that is only recalled after extensive intrusive memory techniques should be treated with skepticism.

Despite this leap forward in the scientific understanding of false and recovered memories, therapists' experiences of, and beliefs about, cases of recovered memory, satanic abuse, dissociation, and false memory still shows a gap in the scientific and professional fields (see Chapter 3). In an online survey published in 2013 (Ost et al., 2013), Chartered Clinical Psychologists and Hypnotherapists agreed overwhelmingly with the existence of false memories (over 80%), however both reported cases of satanic abuse and repressed memories, with approximately one third reporting that such cases could "usually" or "always" be taken as essentially accurate (also see Ost et al., 2017). This survey shows that a number of therapists hold beliefs that scientists would view as controversial, especially given the last twenty or more years of research and scientific discoveries about memory. Ost et al. (2013) suggest that the reason for this may be because the controversy surrounding this literature in the 1990s no longer exists today and the research is not as prominent as it once was. This is one reason why chapters and books such as this one exist, and why we must continue to publicize the science that has taught us what we know about the risks and realities of false and recovered memories.

3

MYTHS AND NAÏVE BELIEFS ABOUT MEMORY

As we have seen in Chapter 2, eyewitness evidence in criminal cases is one of the most important and most frequently encountered pieces of evidence we see in the courtroom. In a study conducted in 1987 it was estimated that in 77, 000 criminal trials each year in the United States, the primary or sole evidence was testimony provided by eyewitnesses (Wells, Small, Penrod, Malpass, Fulero, & Brimacombe, 1998). Yet we know from the research in this area, and the hard work of the Innocence Project, that eyewitness error is the leading cause of wrongful convictions.

Police officers, lawyers, judges, and jurors regularly face the complex and difficult task of knowing when to accept an eyewitness' testimony as reliable or unreliable depending on the exposure to memory-distorting factors. Similarly, clinicians must consider when a client reveals a memory or personal story within a therapy session, whether this reflects a genuine experience, whether their memories have been distorted by factors associated with time, or whether this memory is one that reflects a fictitious event (Qin, Goodman, Bottoms, & Shaver, 1998). Sorting memories based on fact and memories based on fiction is no easy task, but having knowledge about the fallibility of autobiographical memory and the factors that may lead to the distortion of memory would appear crucial to success (Magnussen & Melinder, 2012). In an ideal world, all those that encounter memory evidence, be it in a legal or clinical setting, should possess sufficient knowledge in order to determine the authenticity of autobiographical recollections. Of course, as it stands now, it appears that many of us (i.e., laypeople, clinicians, police officers, lawyers, jurors, and judges) hold naïve beliefs about how memory operates as well as how we come to decide the reliability of memory when it serves as evidence (Magnussen & Melinder, 2012).

The evidence to support the notion that naïve beliefs about memory are more common than one might anticipate comes from several recent surveys that have probed both the general public (Conway, Justice, & Morrison, 2014; Magnussen et al., 2006) and professional groups including those involved in the judicial system as well as those in clinical settings (e.g., Magnussen & Melinder, 2012; Magnussen et al., 2008; Wise & Safer, 2004; Wise, Safer, & Maro, 2011). The surveys have asked questions about beliefs concerning memory in general as well as about issues relating to the reliability of eyewitness testimony specifically. For example, between 45% (Magnussen et al., 2006) and 81% (Patihis et al., 2014) of jury-eligible lay people believe that frightening and traumatic memories can be blocked or repressed. However, scientific evidence runs strongly against that belief (see Chapter 2; Loftus & Ketcham, 1994). Moreover, 70% of people believe that these repressed memories can be subsequently retrieved accurately in therapy (Patihis et al., 2014), whereas scientific evidence stresses the distortive nature of therapeutic memory recovery techniques (see Chapter 2). Finally, approximately 55% of people believe that memory accuracy can be enhanced by hypnosis (Patihis et al., 2014; Simons & Chabris, 2011), whereas the scientific literature is replete with demonstrations of the highly suggestive qualities of hypnosis (see Chapter 2; Ran, Shapiro, Fan, & Posner, 2002).

Similar findings have been reported by clinical investigators. For example, Dammeyer, Nightingale, and McCoy (1997) found that 71% of clinicians expressed a strong belief that repressed memories exist and that prosecutors (48%) and defense attorneys (78%) were significantly less knowledgeable when it came to factors that would affect the accuracy of an eyewitness' testimony (Wise, Pawlenko, Safer, & Meyer, 2009). As noted, these (and other, see below) naïve beliefs stand in stark contrast to what the science of memory has shown about the manner in which memory operates (Arndt, 2012; Conway, Howe, & Knott, 2017; Howe, 2013a, · 2013b, 2013c).

Despite this, many courts firmly assert the jury's ability to evaluate witness evidence (e.g., see New Jersey Courts [Eyewitness Instruction], 2012). In fact, research has shown that when evaluating the accuracy of witnesses' testimony, jury-eligible individuals rely on factors that are poor predictors of accuracy, ignoring factors that are good predictors (Pawlenko, Safer, Wise, & Holfeld, 2013). As memory-based testimony and identification of suspects are cornerstones of legal evidence, certain USA jurisdictions (e.g., in Arizona, New Jersey, Pennsylvania) have developed enhanced procedures (e.g., in the eyewitness identification of suspects) to help jurors weigh memory evidence. This is an important first step for the judicial system, considering that a single type of memory error, misidentification of suspects, is the largest single source of wrongful convictions in the USA. For instance, according to the Innocence Project, 2015,

> Eyewitness misidentification is the greatest contributing factor to wrongful convictions proven by DNA testing, playing a role in more than 70% of convictions overturned through DNA testing nationwide.
>
> (retrieved from: www.innocenceproject.org/causes-wrongful-conviction/eyewitness-misidentification)

In this chapter we examine the types of naïve beliefs that affect the judicial system and provide the scientific counterpoint to these beliefs. We begin with beliefs about memory in general, including a discussion concerning naïve beliefs about how memories are formed and subsequently retrieved (i.e., reproductive rather than reconstructive). We then turn to naïve beliefs about the effects of stress and trauma on encoding, storage, and retrieval, including views about repressed memories and their subsequent recovery. Finally, we discuss naïve beliefs about children's memories, how these memories are preserved into adulthood, and their subsequent reliability as evidence in the courtroom. Although we devote specific chapters to many of these topics later in this book, our focus here is on long-standing naïve beliefs about memory in these contexts.

Naïve beliefs about eyewitness memory

In a recent survey, Simons and Chabris (2011) asked 1500 members of the general public a series of questions about memory. Respondents were presented with statements such as, "Permanent Memory: *Once you have experienced an event and formed a memory of it, that memory does not change,*" and they had to indicate whether they agreed ("strongly" or "mostly") or disagreed ("strongly" or "mostly") with the statement, or indicate that they did not know the answer. These answers were compared with what the scientific consensus is concerning the correctness of each statement. Interestingly, for the majority of the statements (all but one) education level was negatively correlated with agreement. Table 3.1 shows the percentage agreement – "strongly" and "mostly" combined – for each statement by the general public and by the scientific experts. As can be seen in this Table, whereas the public mainly agreed with each of the statements, the experts mainly disagreed.

What these data clearly document is that people's beliefs about memory run counter to the scientific consensus about how memory actually operates. Because the general public serve on juries, these data make it clear that "common sense" notions about memory will not suffice when jurors must decide guilt or innocence based on memory evidence (for an early discussion of this general problem, see Deffenbacher & Loftus, 1982). However, such common-sense notions are frequently viewed as sufficient in courts of law. Indeed, as one judge (incorrectly) opined:

> Eyewitness testimony has no scientific or technical underpinnings which would be outside the common understanding of the jury; therefore, expert testimony is not necessary to help jurors "understand" the eyewitness' testimony.
>
> (*State v. Coley*; 32 S.W.3d 831; Tenn. 2000)

Consistent with this quote, studies have found that judges routinely overestimate a juror's ability to distinguish reliable from unreliable eyewitnesses as well as their common sense understanding of memory (e.g., Houston, Hope, Memon, & Read,

TABLE 3.1 Percentage agreement to statements about memory by the general public (N = 1500) and memory experts (N = 89)

Statement	General public (%)	Scientific experts (%)
Amnesia. People suffering from amnesia typically cannot recall their own name or identity	82.7	0.0
Confident testimony. In my opinion, the testimony of one confident eyewitness should be enough evidence to convict a defendant of a crime	37.1	0.0
Video memory. Human memory works like a video camera, accurately recording the events we see and hear so that we can review and inspect them later	63.0	0.0
Hypnosis. Hypnosis is useful in helping witnesses accurately recall details of crimes.	55.4	0.0
Unexpected events. People generally notice when something unexpected enters their field of view, even when they're paying attention to something else	77.5	18.8
Permanent memory. Once you have experienced an event and formed a memory of it, that memory does not change	47.6	0.0

Data taken from Simons and Chabris (2011).

2013; Magnussen, Melinder, Stridbeck, & Raja, 2010). Unfortunately, such overestimation is not uncommon even today. Indeed, the use of expert reports to guide the courts is still being shunned because it is believed that the scientific findings are "the same as, or very similar to, commonly held beliefs, common experience, and common sense" (Keane, 2010, p. 24).

Related research has examined judges', jurors', and law enforcement personnel's understanding of issues related to eyewitness memory. Because there has been considerable research on eyewitness memory over the last 25 years, survey-based studies have been designed to assess the impact of this research on those involved in the legal system. Specifically, these studies have focused on ascertaining what prosecutors, judges, jurors, and the law enforcement officers know and believe about eyewitness memory (Wise et al., 2009). For example, Benton, Ross, Bradshaw, Thomas, and Bradshaw (2006) used a questionnaire originally designed by Kassin, Tubb, Hosch, and Memon (2001) to test eyewitness experts' knowledge of eyewitness memory. Benton et al. administered the same questionnaire to 42 criminal and civil state judges, 75 law enforcement officers attending training conferences, and 111 jurors drawn from individuals who had responded to a jury summons in Hamilton County, USA The survey included 30 statements concerning eyewitness issues and three response options were provided for each statement ("Generally true," "Generally false," and "I don't know").

When comparing the responses with those of the eyewitness experts they found that for jurors, 87% differed in their responses. Jurors were the least knowledgeable on items relating to system variables (these are factors having to do with procedures used by the justice system, such as interviewing techniques or line-up procedures; see Chapter 7). They found that the officers' responses differed significantly from the experts' responses on 60% of the 30 eyewitness statements. These included wording of questions, effects of lineup instructions, presentation format (simultaneous or sequential), lineup fairness, and confidence malleability. Law enforcement officers and judges performed better but still not at the level of the eyewitness expert. Both disagreed with the experts on 60% of their responses. Disagreements were mainly focused on items related to the wording of questions, effects of lineup instructions, presentation format, description matching as opposed to suspect matching, and confidence malleability (Benton et al., 2006). Worryingly, law enforcement officers also differed significantly from the experts in relation to the effects of post-event information, child suggestibility, hypnotic suggestibility, child witness accuracy, false childhood memories, identification speed, and long-term repression. Benton et al. reported that the largest differences in law enforcement and experts' responses were found for child witness accuracy. The largest discrepancy between the responses of judges and experts was for hypnotic suggestibility, which was also found for juror responses.

It is important to note that such memory beliefs in these groups are not simply an aberration of sampling in a single study. In a comparison to Wise and Safer's (2004) survey of judges' knowledge of eyewitness testimony, on seven out of eight items that were similar in content, judges in both studies responded comparably. Items included confidence malleability (88% vs. 89%, respectively), weapon focus (67% vs. 69%), post-event information (81% vs. 84%), attitudes and expectations (86% vs. 94%), presentation format (29% vs. 19%), and the forgetting curve (41% vs. 31%) (Benton et al., 2006). These beliefs continue still. Even when law enforcement officers were from departments that have instituted eyewitness reforms (National Institute of Justice's Eyewitness Evidence: A Guide for Law Enforcement (hereafter "Guide"); Technical Working Group for Eyewitness Evidence, 1999), Wise et al. (2011) found that the reform and non-reform officers did not differ in either their knowledge of eyewitness factors or their use of proper interviewing procedures.

These findings show that there is still a large discrepancy between lay understanding of factors that will affect eyewitness accuracy and what we know from years of scientific research. This discrepancy is large and exists not only in jurors but also in judges, lawyers, and law enforcement professionals. Therefore, even those involved more directly with eyewitness evidence exhibit important limitations in their knowledge of eyewitness issues.

What is the solution? We have seen evidence that even with the existence of reforms and guides for law enforcement, these inaccurate beliefs still exist. However, more work is being done on the development and dissemination of standard protocols for collecting evidence and also on instructions for jurors (Lampinen,

Judges, Odegard, & Hamilton, 2005). However, as highlighted by Benton et al. (2006), the rest of the solution would appear to be the use of testimony from eyewitness experts where eyewitness evidence plays a pivotal role. It is clear that such knowledge needed to understand the risks associated with eyewitness memory accuracy is not common sense to everyone. As Benton et al. highlighted some 10 years ago:

> The legal system needs to become aware that the scientific and technical underpinnings of eyewitness memory research are not only outside the purview of common sense but also sufficient to warrant the admission of expert testimony as scientific knowledge. Consequently, eyewitness experts may be best able to serve and assist the court by providing information about the impact of system variables as delineated in the Guide, which is not common sense to jurors, judges or law enforcement personnel.
>
> (Benton et al., 2006, pp. 126–127)

However, who provides the expert testimony? In cases where the reliability of memory reports is an issue, psychologists are occasionally called as expert witnesses. Of course, it is not just the judiciary and laypeople that have naïve beliefs about memory, so too do some of those who provide clinical psychological advice in forensic cases. For example, Melinder and Magnussen (2015) surveyed 177 psychiatrists and psychologists using a similar questionnaire to that used by Wise and Safer (2004). Respondents had all served as expert witnesses in court. Their knowledge of eyewitness memory was compared with that of 819 psychiatrists and psychologists who had never served as expert witnesses. The questions included beliefs about the link between eyewitness confidence and accuracy, the effects of post-event (mis)information, and whether memory for minor or peripheral details was an indicator of eyewitness accuracy. The results showed that many of the beliefs held by psychiatrists and psychologists were inaccurate, and those beliefs contradicted the consensus view of memory experts. Moreover, and contrary to their expectations, those who had testified about eyewitness memory in court did not perform any better on the memory questions than those who had not served as an expert witness. Worse, additional studies have shown that licensed clinical psychologists are no better than legal professionals and laypeople when it comes to understanding issues related to eyewitness memory (Magnussen & Melinder, 2012).

Further surveys conducted in the UK (e.g., Ost et al., 2013) and the USA (Patihis et al., 2014) have all shown similar patterns of naïve beliefs in licensed and unlicensed clinical psychologists. This survey research highlights significant false beliefs about memory that laypeople, clinical psychologists and psychiatrists, and those in the legal system (police officers, lawyers, and judge) labor under when eliciting memory evidence and when evaluating that evidence. Thus, the take home message of this research is that (clinical, counseling) psychologists are not memory experts just because they are psychologists. Professional psychologists in these samples, all of whom will have studied cognitive psychology to some extent at university, do not typically score higher than people in the legal field or those lay-people acting as jury members. Indeed, Magnussen and Melinder (2012) suggested that such results support the recommendations of the British Psychological Society Research Board's report *Guidelines on Memory and the Law* (2008), that memory expertise must be proved in each individual case and that courts are advised not to accept expert witnesses testifying on issues involving the reliability of memory reports unless expertise in memory research has been demonstrated.

Naïve beliefs about the effects of stress and trauma on memory

So far we have considered memory issues that relate to eyewitness accuracy. How-ever, there are other memory issues surrounding the relationship between emotion and memory and the fate of traumatic memories where naïve beliefs can have serious consequences. One very prominent naïve belief is that when events are traumatic, memories for those events are particularly vivid, include considerable peripheral detail, and, depending on the extent of the trauma, are frequently repressed. Indeed, 81% of undergraduate students agreed with the statement that "traumatic memories are often repressed" (Patihis et al., 2014, p. 521). An additional 70% of these same students agreed that "repressed memories can be retrieved in therapy accurately" (Patihis et al., 2014, p. 521). Rubin and Bernstein (2007) also examined the beliefs of lay people for the plausibility that forgotten childhood sexual abuse among people could account for longstanding emotional problems and a need for psychotherapy. In a survey questionnaire, they asked respondents how likely they thought it was that a person with longstanding emotional problems and a need for psychotherapy could have been a victim of childhood sexual abuse. They found that only 17.8% said that this was implausible. Based on this finding, Rubin and Bernstein concluded that, "our results are important in their own right because they document a widespread belief in the general population of a Western Society that an event as memorable as childhood sexual abuse can be forgotten and still have marked effects on current behavior" (p. 777).

Magnussen and Melinder (2012) asked clinical psychologists to respond to the question, "Sometimes adults in psychotherapy remember traumatic events from early childhood, about which they previously had absolutely no recollection. Do you think such memories are real or false?" The results showed that 63% thought these memories were mostly real. Of course, it should be noted that this question does not require the respondent to agree or disagree as to whether the stories that abuse patients tell are generally true or false, but rather simply asks about beliefs regarding the truth of a recovered memory in therapy. Magnussen and Melinder argued that by agreeing with this statement it would seem to suggest a belief in the existence of a special repression or dissociation mechanism of forgetting.

Despite two decades of research on the veracity of recovered memories, it appears that beliefs today are similar to what they were some 20 years ago. Poole, Lindsay,

Memon, and Bull (1995) surveyed clinical psychologists in the UK and the USA and found that 70% of the respondents have utilized various memory-recovery techniques with their clients to help uncover memories of early abuse. The evidence presented above seems to suggest that in many cases, lay people, and to some extent (clinical, counseling) psychologists, still believe in a special memory mechanism that leads to the repression of traumatic childhood memories.

Of course, such a belief runs contrary to the scientific consensus that has emerged in this area. Repression is not among the mechanisms of forgetting acknowledged by current memory science (McNally, 2003). In fact, well-controlled, large-sample studies have routinely showed that the victims of childhood sexual abuse remember these experiences into adulthood (Goodman et al., 2003) and that abuse severity is positively linked to memory longevity (Alexander et al., 2005). Thus, even very severe abuse tends to be remembered continuously throughout childhood and into adulthood. Although there may be some exceptions to this, the evidence suggests that such forgetting is likely due to normal mechanisms of failing to remember early childhood events (e.g., infantile and childhood amnesia) and, in cases of milder abuse (Alexander et al., 2005; Goodman et al., 2003), normal mechanisms of forgetting. As we showed in Chapter 2, there is no substantial or reliable evidence to support the existence of a special repressed memory mechanism (also see McNally, 2003).

Even more extreme beliefs about the effects of trauma on memory can be seen when we consider the notion of satanic ritual abuse (Bottoms, Shaver, & Goodman, 1996; Qin et al., 1998). The late 1980s and early 1990s saw a dramatic rise in the number of claims that people (particularly children) were subjected to satanic ritual abuse (see Chapter 2). Investigations into the reality of such claims in both the UK (La Fontaine, 1998) and the USA (Lanning, 1992) found no basis for the belief in such satanic ritual abuse. In spite of this, accounts of such abuse continued to appear (Scott, 2001). In fact, 32.4% of clinicians who were asked whether they had seen a case of satanic/ritualistic abuse said that they had (Ost et al., 2013). Unfortunately, it is the case that memories of satanic ritual abuse have almost always been reported as having been repressed and thus, many therapists have engaged in suggestive recovered memory techniques to "uncover" such claims. Despite the absence of empirical evidence to substantiate the existence of repressed memories of satanic ritual abuse or childhood sexual abuse, belief in their existence is remarkably widespread (see Lynn, Evans, Laurence, & Lilienfeld, 2015). For example, Poole et al. (1995) found that 71% of clinical and counseling psychologists claimed to have encountered at least one case of repressed memory in their practice. Worse, what these beliefs can inevitably lead to is a very diverse group of therapeutic interventions designed to help the patient "accurately recover" these memories. Common to the various techniques (e.g., brainspotting, somatic transformation therapy, traumatic incident reduction; see Lynn et al., 2015) is that they tend to foster the development of false memories, not the recovery of true memories (see Chapter 2).

Naïve beliefs about children's memory

Survey research has also shown that when it comes to understanding children's ability to remember events, laypeople, clinical psychologists and psychiatrists, and those involved in legal services (e.g., judges, jurors, lawyers, police) share a number of false beliefs. For example, when asked "When a child's description of sexual abuse is disclosed over time, with more details being reported each time the child is interviewed, this indicates that the child's description is true," 52% of jury-eligible respondents agreed (Quas, Thompson, & Clarke-Stewart, 2005, p. 439). Disclosing more details across interviews is not indicative of children's accuracy when reporting abuse (see Chapter 8). Indeed, increasing detail with additional interviews is more an indication that suggestion is at work than that memory has "improved" (also see, Quas et al., 2005).

Curiously, 56% of respondents agreed that "a child cannot describe sexual abuse unless he/she actually experienced it" (Quas et al., 2005, p. 437). Of course, studies of children's knowledge of sexual matters shows that by age four, they have an understanding of some sexually relevant information (including the ability to name sexual body parts) and that sexually abused and nonabused children's rudimentary sexual knowledge does not differ (e.g., Gordon, Schroeder, & Abrams, 1990a, 1990b). Interestingly, only a minority of jury-eligible participants, 38%, agreed that children sometimes make up stories of having been sexually abused when they have not and 46% agreed that children can sometimes come to believe that they were abused when they were not actually abused (Quas et al., 2005).

It is clear that naïve beliefs about children's memory still exist for the majority of jury-eligible (and other) people. However, some progress has been made. For example, 71% of jury-eligible individuals agreed that "children are sometimes led by an adult into reporting that they have been sexually abused when they have not" and 70% agreed that "most children can be manipulated into making a false claim about sexual abuse" (Quas et al., 2005, p. 437). Fifty-eight percent of these same people also agreed that "repeatedly asking children specific questions, such as, 'Did he touch your private parts?' often leads them into making false claims of sexual abuse" (Quas et al., 2005, p. 437). Of course, whether it is a majority or a minority of individuals who hold naïve beliefs about children's memory, it is important to educate those jurors (judges, legal personnel) through expert testimony about the science of children's memory in order to ensure a just verdict (also see, Ceci & Friedman, 2000; Lyon, 2002).

Naïve beliefs about the reliability of adults' recollections of childhood events

Consider the following opinion rendered in a case of accusations concerning historic child sexual abuse:

> It is difficult to see how . . . expert evidence can properly be tendered to establish a justifiable criticism of an adult witness who says that she suffered

abuse throughout her childhood, which must have begun at too early an age for her to remember the first occasion [and who provided] highly specific details of abuse at such an early age . . . the jury should consider their own experiences, searching their recollections for their earliest memories, and analyzing what they could actually remember, and how far back their memories went. They did not require, and would not have been assisted by the evidence of an expert.

(R v. S; R v. W; 2006 EWCA Crim. 1404,
Royal Courts of Justice, London, p. 9)

Naïve beliefs about the ability of adults to remember early childhood events are rife. For example, consider one of the findings from Conway et al.'s (2014) survey of beliefs about memory in the general population. Respondents were asked to judge what was the age from which their own earliest memory dated and what was the age of other people's earliest memory. Figure 3.1 shows the distribution of first memories for one's own first memory (the open bars) and that of the estimated age of first memory of other people (the filled bars). What is interesting here is that the age of one's own first memory largely dates to the period of three to five years of age, in good agreement with many other studies of the age of first memories (e.g., Rubin, 2000). In contrast, however, the estimated age of the first memory of other people dates to the period from two to four years of age. In other words, people believe that other people generally have earlier memories than their own. This is a potentially serious overestimation. For instance, when a person is asked to judge the veracity of another person's earliest memories, as often happens in cases of historic childhood sexual abuse, then following (no doubt implicitly) the belief that other people have earlier memories than they do, they may have a bias to accept as possible, or even true, an account of a memory purportedly from a very early age.

Nonetheless, although many respondents accurately state that remembering events from the first year of life is quite difficult, a significant minority of people, 15.1%, also believe that "with effort, we can remember events back to birth" (see Figure 3.1 and Patihis et al., 2014, p. 521). In a recent UK survey that compared memory beliefs of Chartered Clinical Psychologists, unchartered therapists, and first year undergraduate students in psychology it was found that there is still a strong belief that adults' reports of memories from a very young age are likely to be reliable and may have been unconsciously repressed (Ost et al., 2017).

We have already discussed naïve beliefs concerning trauma and repression, but a related question arises as to the reliability of early childhood memories that arise for the first time in therapy. A large majority of laypeople and professionals in Europe and the USA agree that such memories are likely to be true (see Melinder & Magnussen, 2015; Patihis et al., 2014). Of course, this belief too flies in the face of scientific evidence. Indeed, it is well known that traumatic events are often better remembered than more mundane events (e.g., McNally, 2003). Moreover, with the exception of events occurring during very early childhood (e.g., infantile

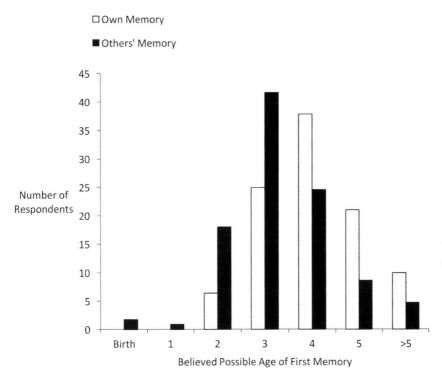

FIGURE 3.1 Believed age of own and others' first memory.

amnesia) or events that are subject to alcohol- or drug-induced blackouts and documented brain anomalies (e.g., epilepsy), complete amnesia for traumatic events has been documented to be faked (see chapters in Christianson, 2007).

Naïve beliefs about quality and quantity of evidence

One prominent naïve belief about memory accuracy is that accounts of events that are rich in detail are more accurate than accounts that are less detailed (Conway, Loveday, & Cole, 2016). When surveyed, laypersons (Magnussen et al., 2008), professionals from the legal field (Wise & Safer, 2004), and clinicians (Magnussen & Melinder, 2012; Melinder & Magnussen, 2015) appear to agree with this assumption. Here, participants were provided with the following statement; "A witness's ability to recall minor details about a crime is a good indicator of the accuracy of the witness's identification of the perpetrator of the crime" (Melinder & Magnussen, 2015, p. 56). The appropriate response, according to the most current science, would be, disagree. Here, it is well established in the scientific literature that false, not true, memories that can be frequently accompanied by such rich details (for a review, see Arndt, 2012). Results from the survey showed that only

33% of clinicians, 16% of laypersons, and 31% of judges (Melinder & Magnussen, 2015) made the correct choice to "disagree."

These findings provide further support for the need to educate both jury eligible laypeople as well as professionals involved in the legal system regarding the fragility of autobiographical memory and the well-documented factors that may undermine the reliability of human memory reports. It provides further evidence in support of the role of the expert witness who has a PhD and relevant expertise on issues involving the reliability of memory. This is an important point, because implausible memory performances are often misunderstood in the courts. Magnussen et al. (2010) review one recent example where the use of a memory expert may have prevented the wrongful convictions of Scottish citizens Thomas Campbell and Joseph Steele, who spent twenty years in prison for murder before finally being exonerated. The ultimate cause of the conviction was the impressive (but ultimately false) testimonies of four police officers who claimed to have overheard an allegedly self-incriminating remark by Campbell. The jurors and judge were so impressed with the confidence and detail of these testimonies, that they convicted Campbell and Steele of the murder.

To explain, in 1984, Thomas Campbell and Joseph Steele were sentenced to life imprisonment for armed assault and for murdering six people. In what is known as the Ice Cream Wars in Glasgow in the 1980s, there was a fierce competition for the most lucrative runs of ice cream vans with intimidation and violence employed by rival vendors. Campbell and Steele were convicted of shooting in the windows of the van owned by Andrew "Fat Boy" Doyle and for later setting his house on fire, resulting in the death of Fat Boy and five of his family members, including a baby. There was no evidence that the men had been at the site of the crime and the case rested on the testimonies of the four police officers who attended Campbell's home when executing a petition warrant that concerned the shooting, and who claimed to have overheard a remark by Campbell, "I only wanted the van windows shot up. The fire at Fat Boy's was only meant as a frightener which went too far." Campbell denied having made such a statement but the confident testimonies by the police officers obviously impressed the court.

However, it was precisely this point that worried the Scottish Criminal Case Review Commission. The commission noted that the police officers' accounts of the remark were identical, despite claims that they had not compared notes, and asked, what is the probability that four witnesses remember, in identical wording, a remark consisting of 23 words dropped under such conditions? The commission engaged a cognitive psychologist who conducted two experiments in which he tested the ability of witnesses to remember Campbell's alleged statement after being presented with a recording made with a Glasgow accent. None of the participants, including fourteen Scottish police officers, were able to remember the statement verbatim, and the majority of the participants remembered less than half the statement. The commission referred the case to the Scottish Appeal Court, the High Court of Judiciary, which decided that the evidence had been fabricated. In 2004, the court quashed the convictions of Campbell and Steele (cited in

Magnussen et al., 2010, p. 1; taken originally from www.scotcourts.gov.uk/ opinions/XC956.html). Magnussen and Melinder (2015) raise the question, would a memory expert have detected the unlikely memory performance of the police officers? They, like us, believe they would. Having such knowledge should help judges and jurors assess, with more skeptical eyes, the truly extraordinary memory feats that are sometimes presented in court.

Limitations of survey research

Much of the evidence discussed in this chapter concerning beliefs about memory has been extracted from studies using large-scale self-report surveys. There are, of course, several limitations to such surveys that should be highlighted before we conclude. First, as noted, these surveys reflect self-reports. Self-reports are not always a true reflection of actual belief or explicit behaviors. For example, results from Benton et al. (2006) may overestimate the extent to which police officers follow appropriate procedures for eyewitness interviews and eyewitness identifications.

Second, some of the statements could have been interpreted differently from how they were originally intended. If true, conclusions reached from responses may not accurately reflect what respondents actually believe. For example, take the statement used by Magnussen and colleagues (Melinder & Magnussen, 2015; Magnussen et al., 2012) regarding recovered memories in therapy; "Sometimes adults in psychotherapy remember traumatic events from early childhood, about which they previously had absolutely no recollection. Do you think such memories are real or false?" Responding "mostly real" leads us to conclude that psychologists believe in a special repressed or dissociative memory mechanism. Although this is a reasonable assumption to make (how else do respondents believe these memories can be true?), this proposition has not been explicitly put in this version of the question. Furthermore, such a question may also be too vague. Psychologists may be aware that recovered memory techniques can be suggestive and are susceptible to memory errors, but this question does not allow them to say this. Nevertheless, these survey results provide some very intriguing insights into people's (naïve) beliefs about memory.

Conclusion

What lessons can we learn from this chapter? Evidence would suggest that, in general, knowledge about the functioning of human memory and its consequences in legal settings is quite poor. Laypeople, police officers, professionals from the legal field, and psychologists hold varying beliefs about critical issues of memory that are not supported by current memory science. When the reliability of memory is in question in the courts, this does have serious consequences (see earlier reference to the Innocence Project).

In the psychiatric and psychological field, mistaken beliefs regarding the complex workings of the human memory system are unlikely to lead to any serious consequences in everyday practice. However, when such false beliefs are brought into the courtroom, they may have catastrophic consequences (Melinder & Magnussen, 2015). As we have seen in Chapter 2, there have been a number of well-documented cases in both the USA and Europe where recovered memories of CSA have led to false convictions of innocent persons and, more so now, we are seeing cases of malpractice claims against therapists. We have also seen misguidance of the court from psychiatric and psychological expert statements relating to the reliability of witness memories when those reports are from individuals who are not memory experts (Goodman et al., 2007; Loftus & Ketcham, 1994). Thus, it is recommended that in order to prevent such wrongful convictions and reduce the number of false allegations caused by highly suggestive recovered memory (and related) techniques, it is important that psychiatric and psychological expert witnesses are updated on current memory science. They should also be aware of what constitutes as normal, memory performance for both children and adult witnesses, and also be able to show an understanding of the malleable nature of memory and the errors that can occur in memory performance. The famous Daubert ruling of the USA Supreme Court (*Daubert vs. Merrell Dow Pharmaceuticals, Inc.*) set the standards for governing expert testimony in court. It is recommended that "the opinions formulated by the expert witness are based on theories and methods that are testable, have been subject to peer review, have an acceptable error rate, and are generally accepted within the expert's community" (Melinder & Magnussen, 2015, p. 59). When it comes to remembering events, ones that play a critical role in convictions in the courtroom, there needs to be a clear set of guidelines concerning what constitutes a memory expert, ones that specify who should provide expert testimony in the courtroom. This, perhaps of all the lessons that can be learned from this chapter, is the most important one.

PART 2

The science of memory and the law

4

WHEN ADULTS' MEMORIES OF CHILDHOOD SERVE AS EVIDENCE

> Memories serve two distinct roles in the legal system. First, they play an indispensable role in fact-finding. We gather memories in depositions, trial testimony, police investigations, lineups, and more to help establish the underlying facts that set the entitlements of disputing parties. We value these memories principally for the information they can provide. Second, memories and their associated affective states can themselves form part of a claim for damages. If you injure me and cause me to have upsetting memories, I can sometimes seek redress for the intentional or negligent infliction of the emotional distress associated with those memories.
>
> (Kolber, 2006, p. 1578)

Nowhere are these two roles of memory in the courtroom better exemplified than in cases where adults claim to have remembered traumatic experiences from their childhoods. Here, typically the *only* evidence is memory and those memories are frequently said to be quite *traumatic*. However, the fact that such memories were formed in childhood, and are frequently only recounted for the first time later in adulthood, can only add to the number and complexity of the issues surrounding their utility as evidence in court.

The notorious unreliability of memory as evidence is documented throughout this book, but nowhere is memory's fallibility greater than when it comes to adults attempting to recall childhood experiences. These early memories not only suffer from the usual reconstructive errors of remembering that all memory evidence does, but there are two additional concerns. First, these early childhood memories were formed when our memory structures and processes were relatively immature. Such memory traces are quite labile and many do not persist even into later childhood let alone into adulthood (see later discussion of infantile and childhood amnesia). Second, not only are these events encoded and stored in an immature memory system, but these memories are often claimed to have survived intact in that dynamically developing system over a number of decades. Thus, not only are these experiences encoded and stored in an immature memory system, they must endure rapid changes in that system over many decades before they are later remembered as evidence.

In this chapter we explore these two frailties of early memories. We begin by examining how information is encoded and stored in an immature memory system and then turn to a consideration of whether such memories can exist intact over the ensuing decades into adulthood. Before we do this, however, consider the following anonymized excerpt from a typical trial where an adult claimed to have remembered a traumatic early childhood event. Here the complainant, a woman in her 40s, tells the police interviewer about an alleged event that happened to her when she was 3-5 years old:

> I remember it was upstairs in my Nan's cottage by the lake. It was early in the morning and the sun was shining in through the dormer window. I was playing in the attic, trying on old clothes. I was wearing an old green dress with lace on the front, one that tied up at the back with a ribbon. I remember him coming up the attic stairs and staring at me . . . he tells me how much he likes the dress as it reminds him of the old days. Then he just picks me up and he just sat me on his lap and gave me a really big hug. He was wearing gray dress pants and a shirt with a collar. He just sat there with his legs out in front of him. When he picked me up he sat me facing the same way, away from his face. He pulled me really close in to him . . . he had his arms around my waist and his legs started to move. Then he put his hands under my dress and started to touch me with the fingers on his right hand. I remember feeling uncomfortable and disgusted, that this was very wrong.

These alleged memories, ones that had ostensibly lain dormant for over 30 years, are very specific and include considerable detail. Indeed, her narrative account of this event includes details that someone so young would have difficulty encoding in the first place (handedness, knowing that something is disgusting). Moreover, her account contains explicit information about what she and the accused were wearing, the precise time of day when the alleged events occurred, and that it was a sunny morning. Of course, as we discuss later in this chapter, detailed memories such as the one given in the narrative of this complainant are extremely unlikely to be formed at such a young age. What the research on early memories has clearly demonstrated is that only sparse fragments of early events are remembered years later, fragments that are decontextualized segments of an experience, such as "I remember sitting in my parents' bedroom, observing my mother as she did some cleaning. There is nothing else to the memory, but I remember having a very different perspective of the room at the time" (Bruce et al., 2005, p. 572).

So why is there such a disconnect between what the scientific research on adult recollections of early memories tells us and the police interviews of alleged victims of childhood maltreatment? Perhaps one such reason has to do with the naïve belief (held by all concerned including the rememberer, the police, the jury, lawyers, and the judge – see Chapter 3) that memories of "real" events should be rich in detail. Indeed, many transcripts of police interviews contain multiple questions concerning these details, including things such as whether the complainant remembers what they were wearing; what the perpetrator was wearing; what was said before, during, and after the event; who else was in the house at the time of the event; what they ate for breakfast that day; what the weather was like that day; and so forth. These questions are asked not just once during interviews, but can appear numerous times within the same interview as well as across different interviews. Of course, most of the time, such peripheral details of events are of low importance and are, therefore, often not well recalled. However, both in police interviews as well as in the courtroom, witnesses are often called to testify on precisely such very specific details. In fact, complainants may feel particularly compelled to answer these questions even in the absence of memory for these details due to their own naïve beliefs about memory and because such answers appear to have particular importance because these questions are asked repeatedly within and across interviews. As we suggested in Chapter 3, because memories do not contain such peripheral information, especially for events occurring during childhood some 20-40 years earlier, perhaps interviewing techniques should eliminate questions of this sort in order to avoid potential contamination of memories by inviting inference and speculation.

It is also important to remember that real cases of childhood sexual abuse exist, ones where victims do remember their abuse even after twenty or more years have elapsed (e.g., see Alexander et al., 2005). In the majority of these latter cases, victims have continuous memory for the abuse, often forget peripheral details (e.g., it was sunny) of the event(s), but frequently remember the personally salient, central details of what happened. For example, consider the following transcript from an anonymized case of documented child sexual abuse (details were corroborated by the victim's grandmother who found the defendant in bed with the child and a medical exam confirmed sexual abuse):

> Interviewer: How old were you when the sexual abuse/assault first happened?
> Child: Four. That I can remember. He'd (grandfather) would punish me with sex. He'd hold me down and make me give him oral sex.
> Interviewer: How severe was the sexual abuse/assault that led to the legal case?
> 1 = mild (exhibitionism)
> 2 = moderate (nongenital touching)
> 3 = severe (oral sex, genital touching w/out penetration)
> 4 = very severe (rape, penetration, anal/genital sex)

Child: Um, 3; the one case that we prosecuted him on was just um oral. My grandmother walked in and caught him.

Interviewer: So you had a witness?

Child: Uh huh. She almost killed him.

Interviewer: How old were you (when the abuse started)?

Child: I was little. I was four or five. And then he would wake up and I remember – you know, and he would punish us by not giving us food for the whole day. He would take whatever we got and not give us anything else. I always got special punishment (referring to sexual abuse).

Interviewer: Do you know why that was?

Child: Cause I was the oldest and I was supposed to set a good example for my sisters and when I'm given rules, I am to obey them.

Interviewer: How old were you at the time of the *last* incident?

Child: 11 years old.

Interviewer: How did you cope with the abuse, that is, how did you deal with it as it was occurring?

Child: In the beginning I didn't have to because I didn't know. It hurt but pain eventually went away. I didn't know any better. There wasn't – I mean I didn't know that it was wrong.

Interviewer: Later?

Child: I didn't cope well at all. I tried to separate myself from it. Leave my body. No emotions. It was like watching it instead of it happening to me.

By contrast, in some cases where complainants have very detailed recollections, there has been little if any continuity of memory, the alleged victims remember large amounts of peripheral detail, and often include emotions, timelines, and observations that are not typically encoded by children about their experiences (e.g., see Chapter 1 and Conway, 2013; Howe, 2013a, 2013b, 2013c). Frequently, these latter cases involve missing or absent memories of the abuse, with "recollections" of abuse suddenly appearing following some kind of cue (e.g., reading or hearing about abuse in the media) or therapeutic intervention for lifestyle problems (e.g., marital issues).

To illustrate, consider AD, a woman who was 30 years old at the time of her complaint, who recounts what she believes to be sexual abuse from her childhood. She states that starting around three years of age the abuse consisted of sexual touching and that when she turned five years old she was raped by the perpetrator on at least ten different occasions. She also stated that she never remembered any of these events until, following counseling at the age of 27 or 28 years, she began to remember each of the alleged incidents, one at a time in a retrograde manner:

AD:. . . I did not remember these events until I entered counseling when it suddenly came back to me. I remembered the last time he raped me first and then the others also came back, one at a time.

Curiously, when these "memories" did come back, they included considerable verbatim details about what the alleged perpetrator said even during an alleged rape incident when she was five years old:

> AD: . . . he told me "not to say anything cos no one would believe me." After he was done, he told me to "just act normal and keep watching the TV".

AD also provided remarkable amounts of detail to the police concerning the various rape events. To illustrate, when she described an alleged rape incident from the age of five years, she is asked:

> Police Officer (PO): So, would he lie on your right or left side?
> AD: He'd lie down on my right side.
> PO: Okay, can you remember what the bed was like?
> AD: Erm, I think it was only a small, single bed, if I can remember rightly . . . I think it was, no, sorry, it was a double bed, with a green textile head board.
> PO: Okay. What time of day it was?
> AD: Erm, it was in the afternoon before teatime when everyone would be home.
> PO: Okay. So there was nobody else in the house.
> AD: No.
> PO: So he took your pants off. What did he do then?
> AD: He put them on the floor. He laid me down, cos I was sat up.
> PO: Were you wearing underwear?
> AD: Yeah, so he took off my pants and my underwear and put them on the floor and lay me, he laid me down on the bed.

AD also claims to remember that the defendant's penis was not very big, that he ejaculated inside her, and that he did not wear a condom. Of course, these descriptions are about things that most 5-year-olds would probably know very little about and stand in stark contrast to her inability to remember personally salient events during that same time period (e.g., what school she attended, who her teachers and friends were).

Of course, there are other cautionary signs in AD's case including the counseling she received before having sudden "flashbacks" of these alleged rape incidents, how the number of events and details within events grew over time with the counseling sessions, as well as conversations she had with close friends concerning their sexual abuse experiences (for more details on the role of therapy in the creation of possible false memories, see Chapter 2). For example, before AD "remembered" any of these alleged experiences, she reports that she was:

> . . . told that it's [sexual abuse] happened to a couple of girls that I used to know when we were children . . . and they're the ones that told me about

it happening to them . . . and they believed it happened to me too . . . so I said, "Yeah."

To understand what can be remembered some decades after a traumatic experience one needs to know something about (1) what the experiencer's memory capacities were at the time of the experience (in this case, memory in children), (2) how experiences are retained over time, and (3) the conditions under which the memory of this experience(s) came to serve as the basis of a legal proceeding (e.g., cued by something in the media, a conversation with a friend about their similar experience). We turn to each of these topics in turn next.

Memory throughout childhood

Early childhood memories are fragile at best and tend to be forgotten quite rapidly (for recent in-depth reviews of early memory development, see Bauer, 2015; Howe, 2011, 2014, 2015). In fact, although memories can be formed very early in life, our ability to remember them in later childhood and adulthood can be quite limited. This paucity of memories from early development (especially the first two years of life) is referred to as infantile amnesia whereas the term childhood amnesia refers to a similar paucity of memories from the ages of three to eight years of age. To put a finer point on this, Figure 4.1 shows that people have little or no memory for experiences that occurred before the age of two, few memories for events that occurred between two and three years of age, and that the number of memories of events one is able to remember later increases with the person's age at the time the event occurred. Thus, infantile amnesia is considered to be a relatively dense amnesia inasmuch as few if any memories can be retrieved from that period of life, regardless of whether such memories are traumatic or not. Childhood amnesia is not quite so dense as some memories from this period can be reconstructed in later childhood and adulthood. Importantly for forensic purposes, it is not until around the age of seven or eight years that we begin to see more mature, adult-like levels of autobiographical remembering (e.g., see Bauer & Larkina, 2014). These data are consistent with the growing consensus that experiences occurring at or after the age of seven or eight can be reliably remembered in adulthood (see Howe, 2011, for a review).

So why does this amnesia occur? One position is that memories that are formed during the infantile and childhood amnesia periods are still available in memory (are still in storage) but they are no longer accessible (cannot be retrieved). This *retrieval failure* hypothesis is based on *encoding specificity theory*, which states that in order to retrieve memories (any memories, not just ones from childhood), you have to reinstate the conditions (both internal and external) that pertained during the original encoding episode in order to access the information that was stored at that time. Because it is impossible to reinstate the conditions of encoding from early childhood (especially the mental state of an infant or toddler at the time

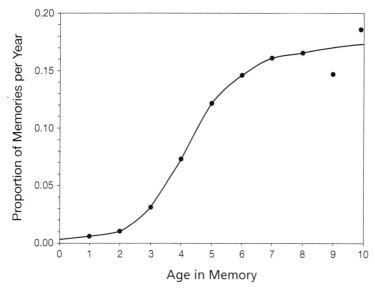

FIGURE 4.1 The distribution of adult recall of 11,000 childhood memories (adapted from Rubin, 2000; reproduced with permission from Taylor & Francis). Points along the distribution (Y-axis) represent the proportion of memories retrieved by adults, memories that were stored at different ages across their childhoods (X-axis). These data represent a summary across many studies of autobiographical recall of childhood events by adults using different recall techniques.

of encoding), such memories are said to remain irretrievable in later childhood and adulthood. Although certainly a plausible theory, there are many reasons why a pure retrieval account of infantile and childhood amnesia is not tenable (see Howe, 2011).

Another, more plausible *storage* account states that infantile and childhood amnesia occurs because the memory traces laid down early in life are extremely labile, being neither durable nor stable over long-term retention intervals. There is considerable evidence to support this view. For example, memory during early infancy fades much more rapidly than it does in toddlerhood, subsequent childhood, or adulthood. In fact, the ability to consolidate information in storage (i.e., to create stable and durable encodings of events in memory) develops considerably during the period of infantile and childhood amnesia (Bauer, 2009). If early memory traces are labile, then they will be subject to more rapid deterioration so that regardless of which retrieval mechanisms are brought to bear to recover these early memories, they may simply not exist, after even a short period of time (Hayne, 2004). Indeed, major developments in memory across childhood consists of both qualitative and quantitative changes in what gets stored, something which in turn increases the binding of various aspects of a memory trace, enhancing the durability of that trace (Howe, 2013b).

Of course, infantile and childhood amnesia both wane over time. This is due in part to the development of an organizational structure, the cognitive self (e.g., for an in-depth review, see Howe, 2014). That is, the infant begins (at around 18 to 24 months of age) to understand that events that are occurring are happening to a "me," a self that not only experiences events, but also thinks, feels, and reacts to these events. Thus, events are no longer just memories of experiences but become autobiographical; that is, they are memories of things that happened to me. Because organization is key to creating stable, durable memories, binding current experiences to this self who experiences, thinks, and feels, provides a strong "glue" that helps consolidate memories in storage, imbuing them with greater longevity (also see Sui & Humphreys, 2015). In addition, it is around this time when language is quickly developing, and children can translate their experiences into words and share them with others. This redescription of experience can also enhance memory through verbal rehearsal of experiences and elaborating them through sharing them with others (e.g., Nelson & Fivush, 2004).[1]

In fact, language can be an important gauge as to what can and cannot be remembered by adults about their childhoods. That is, if words are not available for labeling experiences at the time they occur, such experiences rarely cross the infantile/childhood amnesia barrier. For example, Simcock and Hayne (2002) used a "magic shrinking machine" to examine children's early event memory. Preschoolers (27-, 33-, and 39-month-olds) were shown how to operate the magic shrinking machine by pulling on a lever that activated a set of lights that ostensibly indicated that the machine was now on and ready to work. The experimenter then took a toy and placed it inside the machine where it disappeared from view. The experimenter then turned a handle on the side of the machine which produced a series of unique sounds. When the sounds stopped, the child retrieved a smaller yet identical toy from the machine. This sequence was repeated a number of times with a different toy being "shrunk" each time. Children's language skills were also assessed at this time and six months and a year later when children were also retested for their memory of the magic shrinking machine. After a 6- to 12-month delay interval they found that, despite improvement in children's language skills, preschoolers could not translate preverbal aspects of this experience into verbal recall. That is, children did not use words to describe the magic shrinking machine event that had not been part of their earlier vocabulary at the time of the event despite the subsequent acquisition of those words during the retention interval.

In another experiment, Morris and Baker-Ward (2007) looked at children's memory for a unique event using a "bubble machine." Here, bubbles were produced only when the correctly colored liquid was poured into the machine. Thus, in this experiment, color was causally linked to the desired outcome – the production of bubbles. Morris and Baker-Ward measured children's color vocabulary before the experiment and then trained the children in color naming during the two-month retention interval. Using physical prompting during this later test, a few of the children (29%) were able to correctly remember and name the color of the liquid needed to produce the desired bubbles. What these findings show is that through the use of very rigorous training procedures, supplemented by a highly supportive retrieval environment during testing, a minority of children can provide verbal labels for what was originally a non-verbal experience.

Bauer and her associates (Bauer et al., 2004; Cheatham & Bauer, 2005) have obtained similar findings using imitation tasks. Their research has shown that only older children are able to provide verbal recall of earlier studied behaviors. In fact, it turns out that the best predictor of later verbal recall is the child's verbal recall ability at the time of the original event. Together, the studies by Bauer and her colleagues suggest that only older children, those who already express their memories using language, provide verbal recollection of earlier events following a long retention interval.

Finally, studies have also examined memory for early events using a variety of cuing techniques (e.g., Bauer, Burch, Scholin, & Güler, 2007). In a recent study of this sort, Tustin and Hayne (2010) used a "timeline template" to cue children's, adolescents', and adults' earliest memories. Here, participants were shown a physical timeline (i.e., a large piece of cardboard with a horizontal line drawn along the midline to indicate time), with the year a person was born being depicted on the far left with progression rightward representing each ensuing year up to the present time. Photographs of the participant at different ages were placed along the timeline and participants were asked to remember their earliest memories using the timeline. Their recollections were then authenticated by comparing them with those of their parents.

The findings showed that although all of the participants reported an earliest memory before the age of three years, their memories were very fragmented (i.e., contained little contextual meaning or detail). Indeed, Jack and Hayne (2010), using the same timeline procedure but only with adult participants, found that the earliest autobiographical memories, even those up to the age of about six years, were very sparse. This very fragmented recall is consistent with other reports (e.g., Bruce et al., 2005). More importantly, at least from a forensic perspective, early memories (whether recalled by children or adults) are devoid of concepts such as time, emotion, or verbatim information (Strange & Hayne, 2013). Thus, regardless of whether verbal or pictorial props are used to assist recall of early memories, such recollections are inherently impoverished, being fragmentary, containing very little specific detail, and are devoid of context and meaning (also see Wells, Morrison, & Conway, 2014).

Although these lines of research demonstrate the importance of language in the retention of early memories, it is important to point out that children (and perhaps adults) only express a small fraction of the content of their memories using language, leaving a considerable part of what is actually remembered left unspoken (see Bauer, 2015; Howe, 1998; Simcock & Hayne, 2003). However, the forensic importance of this research cannot be denied. That is, these studies clearly demonstrate that the vestiges of early experiences do not easily cross over the infantile/childhood amnesia barrier, certainly not in terms of consciously available autobiographical memories (also see Richardson & Hayne, 2007).

This line of research portends another important area of development that is key to memory longevity, namely, changes in semantic or conceptual knowledge. As children develop, so too does their knowledge of the world and how it works. New concepts emerge and old concepts are reorganized in light of new knowledge (e.g., see Bjorklund, 1987; Ceci, Fitneva, & Williams, 2010; Ceci, Papierno, & Kulkofsky, 2007). The advent of language to describe conceptual knowledge is also critical because it turns out that later memory for events is constrained by the language available at the time the event occurred. For example, Morrison and Conway (2010) discovered that there is a systematic relationship between the age of a person's earliest memory and the age at which the words describing that memory were acquired. More complex concepts (including emotional terms) do not appear until sometime later in childhood and, thus, adult recollections of early childhood experiences should be devoid of these terms. However, as we have seen earlier in this chapter (and in Chapters 1 and 3), and as will be discussed later (see Chapter 6), oftentimes memory evidence, particularly in cases of historic child sex abuse, routinely contain such terms.

Of course, as development proceeds across the early school years, children's conceptual knowledge changes and memory for autobiographical experiences improves. Children become better at using conventional indices of time (e.g., using calendar dates; see Friedman, 2014; Friedman, Reese, & Dai, 2011), include emotional terms reflecting their feelings about the experience (e.g., concepts such as *disgust* emerge around 5 years of age; see Widen & Russell, 2013), and become contextually grounded (i.e., they contain a context in which to understand the nature of the event; see Howe, 2011, 2014, 2015; Wells et al., 2014). That is, across development in childhood, autobiographical memories contain more and more relevant features that become encoded and stored in thematically coherent memory traces (see Bauer & Larkina, 2016; Peterson, Morris, Baker-Ward, & Flynn, 2014). In addition, as children's knowledge base continues to expand and leads to a more efficient restructuring of information already in memory, the individual features themselves that get encoded are better elaborated and bound more tightly within the memory trace (Ceci et al., 2007, 2010). What this does is increase the longevity of such memories, something that is maximized when the self also serves as the "glue" that binds the features together (Howe, 2011; Sui & Humphreys, 2015).

What happens during retention?

The next problem is what happens to stored information during its long-term retention into adulthood. Memories, even those from childhood (whether traumatic or not, see Chapter 6), once consolidated (i.e., where the neural activity corresponding to the trace becomes stabilized in storage – see Chapter 5) do not remain immune to forgetting or alteration due in large measure to subsequent re-experiencing. Forgetting, primarily of peripheral and verbatim details of an experience, is relatively common and occurs even in the face of attempts to rehearse and preserve the memory for that experience through re-experiencing. In fact, rehearsal itself can interfere with the original memory. This is because autobiographical recollections when told to others (either through conversation or questioning), sometimes repeatedly, result in the reactivation and reconstruction of memories of that event. This reactivation causes the trace to become labile again and in need of reconsolidation, something that can result in modifications to the original memory trace (for a review, see Sandrini, Cohen, & Censor, 2015). In this section we briefly review the variables that affect the integrity of childhood memories, including forgetting and interference, as well as what happens during repeated remembering and subsequent reconsolidation (also see Chapter 2).

Forgetting and interference

Perhaps the most pernicious effect on memory for childhood (or any) events is forgetting. With the passage of time and the constant barrage of new and potentially interfering experiences throughout childhood and adolescence, early memories are likely to fall into that abyss of weakened and forgotten memories for experiences that fade into the background of other, unused traces (see Brainerd, Reyna, Howe, & Kingma, 1990; Howe, 2000). That is, during and even after the infantile/childhood amnesia periods are over, what memories remain in storage are subject to forgetting through disuse, decay, or interference with new memories for more recent experiences. Indeed, when remembered, earlier experiences are not simply dragged from their repository in storage unadulterated, rather but, they are *reconstructed* based on what fragments remain for the original encoding along with filling-in-the-gaps using our rich knowledge base (semantic memory). Indeed, as research over the past century or two has shown, when we encounter new experiences, new synaptic connections are made, ones that may involve existing memories. What this means is that when memories for prior experiences that are stored in memory interact with new experiences, they become blended, rewritten, and altered irrevocably. Thus, what we are remembering today about events that happened many years ago is an amalgam of those fragments of early experience along with the changes that have ensued in light of subsequent experiences. The problem here, at least from a forensic perspective, is that the reconstruction of long-held memories from childhood is not necessarily a reliable representation of those original events.

Reconsolidation

How can memories that have been stored change with subsequent experiences? One idea is that when new experiences are similar in some way to stored ones, the earlier memories become reactivated and this reactivation can lead to modification of the original trace (e.g., Sandrini et al., 2015). This is also true when we relate these memories through conversation with others or are questioned (e.g., by the police) – that is, the original memories become labile and must go through a process of reconsolidation, one that is very similar to the original consolidation process used to encode and store these memories in the first place. The problem here is that when these memories get reconsolidated, they can contain updated information encountered in the reconsolidation environment. That is, reconsolidation allows the modification of existing memory traces by altering their strength or by updating their content through the integration of new information being automatically added to the memory trace (Sandrini et al., 2015). These amendments mean that the memory trace is not a reliable representation of the original experience – at best, it is a reconstructed amalgam of like experiences and at worst it is a memory so distorted that it can be considered false (see Chapter 2).

These effects are particularly detrimental when they occur in a therapeutic or forensic setting when the therapist or forensic questioner is looking to confirm a particular hypothesis (e.g., that the person has been sexually abused in childhood). Here, the person being questioned faces a series of questions that tacitly seek to confirm the questioner's hypothesis, and experiences that are retrieved in the process of answering these questions can be reinterpreted in terms of the questions themselves. That is, if one is being queried about whether they had experienced sexual abuse as a child, memories of childhood experiences that are retrieved during this questioning process can be reinterpreted as possibly having something to do with an as yet uncovered memory of abuse. Later, after these memories are reconsolidated, they can serve as the basis for a newly constructed childhood abuse experience (see Chapter 2). Thus, although memory reconsolidation can be quite useful in some therapeutic circumstances (e.g., reducing fear responses to traumatic memories – e.g., see Schwabe, Nader, & Pruessner, 2014), it can also have a more sinister side in which memories can be irrevocably altered, entirely erased, or a new but entirely false memory created (see Chan & LaPaglia, 2013; Kroes et al., 2014; Schwabe & Wolf, 2009; Spiers & Bendor, 2014).

Together, these considerations cast serious doubt on whether memories from childhood are successfully retained, at least untainted, into adulthood. Although not all experiences may be subject to the extreme levels of modification that occur through forgetting, reinstatement, and reconsolidation, it can be reasonably argued that most (if not all) childhood memories undergo some degree of alteration. Importantly, these alterations take place outside of the rememberer's conscious awareness. Indeed, reconsolidation processes occur outside of consciousness and the changes that ensue in one's memory of childhood (or any other) events is not something that one can guard against.

The question of forensic interest is where the memories that are being retrieved and used as evidence in court fall on this continuum of revision: are they the ones that are least tainted by these processes that occur during the retention period, or are they the ones that have undergone considerable revision? As we saw earlier (Chapter 3), one of the naïve beliefs that is often used as a criterion to determine the extent of memory distortion is whether the event being remembered is negative or traumatic. This belief goes something like this: although memory revision might occur with relatively innocuous or mundane memories, personally consequential memories for negative or traumatic experiences are immune to the effects of forgetting, reinstatement, and reconsolidation. However, as we will see in Chapter 6, negative and traumatic memories are equally affected by (if not more affected by in some circumstances) memory revision processes than are non-traumatic memories. In addition, there are some reports indicating that, once created, negative memories that are entirely false are easier to implant than memories that are neutral or positive (e.g., Otgaar, Candel, & Merckelbach, 2008). As well, negative false memories, rather than declining over time like true memories, tend to increase and do so more quickly than other types (e.g., neutral) of false memories (e.g., Howe, Candel, Otgaar, Malone, & Wimmer, 2010). Finally, processes that are used to "suppress" or "avoid" memories for traumatic events (including falsely denying the experience) tend to lead to distortions of what is later remembered about those experiences (e.g., Otgaar, Howe, Memon, & Wang, 2014; Otgaar, Howe, Smeets, & Wang, 2016). Thus, when the reliability of childhood memories is being assessed when they are being presented as evidence, we need to consider at least two things. First, what was the age of the person at the time the event was encoded and stored in memory – something that determines not just the endurance of such a memory, but also its content. Second, we also need to consider what processes transpired between the time the memory for that event was formed and the time it is being presented as evidence in a court of law. Although it might be easier to establish documentation concerning the first than the second issue, there is still no litmus test that can effectively and reliably provide an index that reflects the degree to which a childhood (or any other) memory has been modified over time.

Memories of childhood in the courtroom: conditions for litigation

How does it happen, then, that memories for (alleged) childhood abuse come to mind during adulthood and form the basis of legal proceedings? There are obvious cases in which people who have continuously remembered their abuse feel intimidated (are scared or feel ashamed or embarrassed) and do not come forward right away. In fact, there is considerable evidence that delayed disclosure is more common than first thought (for a review, see McElvaney, 2015). As it happens, full disclosure may only occur later in childhood or adulthood when the person is psychologically prepared to come forward with public allegations of their abuse.

There are two important issues that need to be confronted when children delay disclosure, both having to do with the memorial consequences of strategies (e.g., false denials, intentional forgetting) children use when they withhold information. False denial strategies are ones where the person simply denies to themselves that the events actually happened. Of course, whether such denials represent actual denials of true events is often unclear because of the lack of evidence verifying the abusive incidents. However, false denials can alter what is in memory (Otgaar et al., 2014,

2016) and can, therefore, have devastating consequences for remembering in forensic settings (see also McWilliams, Goodman, Lyons, Newton, & Avila-Mora, 2014; Vieira & Lane, 2013).

In addition to using false denial strategies, victims of abuse attempt to forget (intentional forgetting) their experiences and the question arises as to how successful such attempts are and what the impact of these attempts are on memory for the event. Recent research with maltreated children has demonstrated that they are as good as non-maltreated children at intentionally forgetting emotionally negative information at least over short delays (Howe, Toth, & Cicchetti, 2011). More generally, studies that have focused on the effects of intentional forgetting on memory show that for both children and adults, deliberate attempts to forget impoverish the recollections of events (e.g., Aslan, Staudigl, Samenieh, & Bäuml, 2010; Howe, 2005; Kimball & Bjork, 2002). In fact, some research has shown that strategies to intentionally forget can increase the production of false memories (Kimball & Bjork, 2002).

Although some theorists have argued that attempts to forget, to falsely deny, or to keep secret events that have actually occurred makes memories for these events more readily accessible (e.g., Lane & Wegner, 1995), we argue that what the evidence shows is actually quite the opposite. In fact, there are many reasons to suspect that using strategies such as false denial and intentional forgetting might impair memory and increase false memory levels. For example, both of these strategies prevent victims from rehearsing memories for these events, something that will inevitably lead victims to remember less of the event. Often in these circumstances, a victim might begin to "fill in the memory gaps" with what they infer or imagine must have happened, in an attempt to make the memory sensible. Indeed, even at the best of times when memories are many years old, a victim's ability to distinguish what actually happened from what they infer or imagine could have occurred is exceedingly difficult. Worse still, as we saw in Chapter 2, information that is internally generated by using imagination can lead to the formation of false memories (also see Ackil & Zaragoza, 1998; Mazzoni & Memon, 2003). Indeed, it is well known that simply imagining that an event has occurred when in fact it has not increases the belief that the event has occurred. This, in turn, frequently leads to the production of false memories for that event (i.e., what is known as the imagination inflation effect). Moreover, research has shown that children are more prone to false memories fueled by imagination than adults (Castelli & Ghetti, 2014).

An important issue that has not been studied in depth is whether strategies to withhold information might have similar adverse effects on the retrieval of imagined events as they do on the retrieval of experienced events. That people who have reported being sexually abused might have used strategies to forget even *imagined* events is evident from legal cases in which people recovered false memories of child sexual abuse triggered by imaginative and suggestive techniques used in therapeutic sessions (see Chapter 2; also see Raymaekers, 2013; Raymaekers, Smeets, Peters, Otgaar, & Merckelbach, 2012). These people tend to be highly confident that their (false) memories were accurate and often try to cope with these false memories using strategies such as intentional forgetting (Maran, 2010). Indeed, there exists some experimental work which shows that intentional forgetting exacerbates the distorting effects of imagination on memory (Delaney, Sahakyan, Kelley, & Zimmerman, 2010).

Although the majority of memories of actual abuse may preserve only the core details of that abuse (see Chapter 6), some complainants reconstruct other, more peripheral details in order to satisfy (1) the misconception held by many that for a memory to be "real" there should be lots of "details" they can recall, or (2) the interviewer who persistently requests such information in their questioning of the complainant. Again, memories such as these are still subject to the same issues that all memories face when being retained for considerable periods of time, and it is still difficult to tell which parts of the complainant's narrative have been reconstructed (preferably only the peripheral details), which parts serve as the kernel of memory from which the narrative has been reconstructed (preferably the core of the experience), and which, if any, parts are entirely false (see Chapter 2). It is of more than passing interest to note that even in cases where the events being litigated did indeed happen, delayed recollection of these events always contain some reconstructed components. Of course, this is the issue we face in court – how can we tell which part is the reconstruction and which part is the kernel of memory upon which the reconstruction is woven.

In other circumstances, the complainant has not had a continuous memory for abuse during childhood and these "new" memories have arisen in adulthood as a result of self-questioning, talking to others who have been abused, reading newspaper or magazine articles about historic child sex abuse, or they have undergone therapy for perceived dysfunctional aspects of their current adult life. These spontaneous "recollections" should be treated with some degree of caution especially when there is no additional verification that such events took place (see Chapter 2). Unfortunately, even in the absence of corroboration, the complainant often comes to believe that these memories for events are true. Whether true or not, these alleged memories of early childhood experiences often contain adult-like emotions (e.g., disgust), temporal aspects of events that children do not encode, and other peripheral details that are not found in children's memories (Conway, 2013; Howe, 2013a, 2013c; Howe & Knott, 2015). Moreover, these details are often reconstructed unconsciously and are not explicitly created in an attempt to deceive. However, once created and (re)consolidated, the person comes to believe that these memories are true.

So the problem remains – regardless of how memory evidence has arisen, the problem confronting the court is whether these memories provide a reliable account of events that happened in the person's past. Although all memories are reconstructed, the question is whether they are reconstructed from kernels of truth, have been distorted through the use of strategies to prevent the person from thinking about their childhood, or perhaps influenced by interventions designed to tease long-forgotten memories from the recesses of the person's mind. The problem here is that when disclosure is delayed, there is good reason (and science) to suggest that the memories that serve as courtroom evidence may not resemble the facts as they were at the time of the alleged incidents. Even in circumstances where memory for childhood events is continuous, there are still processes at play that can modify these memories. Perhaps the prudent course is a conservative one where jurors and judges are advised as to the potential for memory distortion in such cases and to view any memory evidence with a comprehensive understanding of both the strengths and failures that are a part of our reconstructive memory system.

Conclusion

In this chapter we have seen that children encode event information differently from how adults do, that early memories are extremely labile and often do not survive into later childhood and adulthood (i.e., infantile and childhood amnesia), and that even if they do, they are fragmented, devoid of contextualized meaning, and lack emotional content and temporal markers. Understanding how memory develops is critical to understanding how children's encoding, storage, and retrieval of information changes with age and how these changes affect what adults will be able to remember about their childhoods. As we saw, many of these changes are moderated by parallel developments in children's cognitive abilities and growth of their knowledge base. These changes, in turn, are correlated with underlying neuro-biological developments in memory-related structures in the medial temporal lobe (e.g., the hippocampus and the dentate gyrus) and the prefrontal cortex, as well as the connectivity among these structures (for reviews, see e.g., Howe, 2011, 2013b, 2015; Mullally & Maguire, 2014; Riggins, Blankenship, Mulligan, Rice, & Redcay, 2015) (for more specific details, see Chapter 5).

Moreover, childhood memories are subject to reactivation and subsequent reconsolidation, processes that can lead to systematic distortion and modification of the original memory trace. These processes occur automatically, outside of conscious awareness, and as such represent critical changes to memories for originally experienced events that transpire without the rememberer even knowing they have happened. Thus, when adults present evidence that consists of recon-structed memories of childhood events, extreme caution needs to be exercised when adjudicating such evidence (see Howe, 2013b).

This problem is exacerbated because it is not clear that "true" components of memory can ever be distinguished from "false" components of memory. Even at a neurobiological level, neuroimaging research concerned with detecting differences between true, false, and imagined memories is only in a nascent stage and no consistent, reliable, or courtroom-ready techniques are available as yet to help triers-of-fact decide the veracity of memory evidence (Schacter, Chamberlain, Gaesser, & Gerlach, 2012; van de Ven, Otgaar, & Howe, in press). As Lacy and Stark (2013) point out, there is no neurobiological measure or marker that we can use to say that a particular recollection is based on an event that did or did not happen to that person as a child. They (and we) conclude that,

Given what we know about the neurobiology of memory and the cognitive psychological research on memory, "perfect" memories that are accompanied by a high level of confidence and detail should be taken with a grain of salt, and "imperfect" memories that are vague and missing details should not be immediately discredited. However "good" a witness's memory of an event may be, their memory may not actually be accurate, and currently there is no clear way to measure the accuracy. This does not mean that memory-based evidence should be disregarded but rather that police, judges, and jurors should be educated on these nuances so that they may give memory-based evidence its proper weight.

(Lacy & Stark, 2013, p. 655)

Note

1. Although talking about experiences can sometimes increase their longevity in memory it can also be a source of misinformation about the original experiences, changing what we remember about them. That is, when memories are reactivated during conversation, subsequent recollections of these original experiences will include some of the original event and some of the subsequent conversation about that event (see subsequent section on "What Happens During Retention?").

5

THE NATURE AND NEUROSCIENCE OF AUTOBIOGRAPHICAL MEMORY

As noted throughout this book, memory is (re)constructive. That is to say that when we remember an event we have experienced, say going out for dinner, shopping in a supermarket, even witnessing a crime, the resulting mental representation that we experience as a memory is present in the brain in the form of a highly complex and extensive pattern of activation that unfolds and stabilizes (consolidates) over time. This is because *autobiographical memories* (memories for the events and knowledge of our lives) encompass different types of knowledge that are brought together in a constructive act of remembering. Let us briefly consider how this might work and what some of the consequences might be.

Imagine you are talking to an old friend and sharing some memories of the old days at college that you experienced together and your friend says:

> You know I really do remember that day, the last day of our finals, really clearly. I remember we both left the hall and almost skipped down the street. It was beautifully warm and we went and sat in the park and did some deep breathing. I thought, whatever the outcome, it's over now . . . and I had no idea what next.

As with virtually all autobiographical memories, this account contains some conceptual knowledge of the rememberer's life (the last day of finals) and some episodic knowledge (skipped down the street, beautifully warm, sitting in the park, deep breathing, specific thoughts). These latter details are almost certainly in the form of an *episodic memory* (a memory of specific experience) that most probably contains visual images and other content (e.g., recall of emotions and thoughts). An autobiographical memory is, then, usually a construction that features some conceptual knowledge and an episodic memory or memories (see Conway, 2009). It will thus entail activation of brain areas where these types of knowledge are stored, some bringing together of the various knowledge types, activation of areas in which visual images can be represented, and perhaps activation of some emotions. It will also involve activation of a retrieval process that accesses this knowledge (i.e., makes it active in the brain) and some sort of interlocking/monitoring of these dispersed but related activated regions. Thus, recalling even a simple long-held memory engages many regions of the brain, as we will see in the sections to follow, and it is never the case that bringing to mind an autobiographical memory causes only a minor and very delimited region of brain activation, as though retrieving a memory were like taking a book from a shelf. Memory is not like a library, but rather, it is a psychological process that takes time to execute and which centrally features the establishment of widespread transient but stable patterns of brain activation.

So, memory is (re)constructive and we will see just how (re)constructive shortly. However, first there is another aspect of remembering that is often overlooked and one that also contributes to (re)constructive memory processes, namely, inference. Just as when we perceive the world the brain makes (unconscious or non-conscious) inferences about that visual world, it does so too about the remembered past. For instance, in the example of the autobiographical memory detailed earlier, a whole range of inferences lies behind the memory account – that they were clothed, that it was summer, that the park was for recreation (and all the props and supports that implies), that they sat on a bench or maybe the grass, and so on. In other words, the memory is embedded in a mesh of schematic information about what usually happens when walking down a street, going to a park, experiencing relief after an arduous series of examinations, even sharing a moment with a friend. All of this knowledge becomes active too, mostly automatically and non-consciously, but sometimes it is consciously and intentionally inferred. We could ask the person doing the remembering: what shoes were you wearing? Most probably they could not answer (details such as these are not commonly remembered; e.g., Justice, Morrison, & Conway, 2013). However, and this is the central point, they might be very confident, even adamant, that they were wearing *some* shoes, but cannot recall which ones. This non-conscious and automatic contextualizing of memory makes remembering even more (re)constructive. The patterns of brain activation associated with these (re)constructed memories become even more complex, and, of course, open up the way for many memory errors. For instance, perhaps at the time, our rememberer was actually wearing sandals not shoes. Such inferential or contextualizing errors are most probably endemic when autobiographical memories are recalled. As we shall see shortly, the situation can be even worse than the mere possibility of just a few contextual errors. Neuro-imaging research shows us that remembering and imagining take place in the same neural networks. It is because of this that the probability of imaging something and then later remembering that imagining *as a memory* is itself not only possible, but highly likely.

The brain and imaging it in action

Before we can consider patterns of activation in the brain that underlie remembering it will be useful to consider the structure of the brain itself and some of the methods used to detect activation within it (those readers familiar with these topics may want to skip this section). The brain consists of three main regions: the brain stem and basal ganglia, the limbic system, and the neocortex. The limbic system (actually a complex set of neuronal networks and hubs some of which operate independently or in conjunction with other structures so the term "system" is a little misleading here) sits on top of the basal ganglia, and the neocortex is a layered sheet of cells folded around the limbic system, as shown in Figure 5.1.

In MacLean's (1990) triune brain model (originally developed in the 1960s), the basal ganglia and related structures are conceived of as the instinctual or emotional brain, sometimes referred to as the Reptilian Brain. It includes structures such as the caudate nucleus, nucleus accumbens, ventral tegmental area (primitive body image), among other structures. It regulates bodily functions and patterns of behavior in reptiles. In the human brain, its instincts are modulated through the

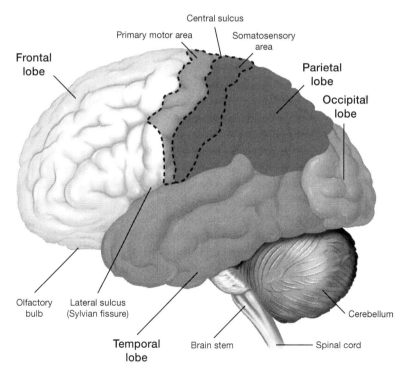

FIGURE 5.1 Diagram of the brain showing the frontal, temporal, parietal and occipital lobes, and other brain regions

From David Andrewes, *Neuropsychology: From theory to practice*, 2nd ed. (2015). Reproduced with permission from Taylor & Francis.

other two "brains." One of these other brains is the limbic system, viewed as the evolutionary old mammalian brain and is sometimes termed the "Emotional Brain." It includes the amygdala (fear), hippocampus (memory), hypothalamus (appetite), among other structures and mediates basic emotions and prosocial behavior including attachment, maternal nurturance, separation, distress, and playfulness. Finally, the last of these "brains" is the neocortex, the six-cell layered cortex wrapped around the ancient limbic system that mediates conscious thought, language, problem solving, reasoning, and advanced social comprehension (e.g., theory of mind). The triune brain model is no longer greatly used in neuroscience, in part because it has been found that these three very large brain areas contain structures that are found in many mammals of old or ancient lineages and so the mapping of brain structures in terms of evolutionary history is not so straightforward. Nevertheless, in terms of thinking about functions, the three different brain areas contained in the triune brain provide a handy heuristic.

The neocortex is subdivided on an anatomical basis into different regions known as lobes. These are the frontal, occipital, temporal, and parietal lobes (see Figure 5.2). Note that the neocortex itself is divided down the midline into two hemispheres, the left and right hemispheres, and lobes therefore have left and right locations; that is, they are *lateralized*.

The frontal lobe has many functions, some of the most important of which are: cognition, problem solving and reasoning, planning, motor skills, speech, impulse

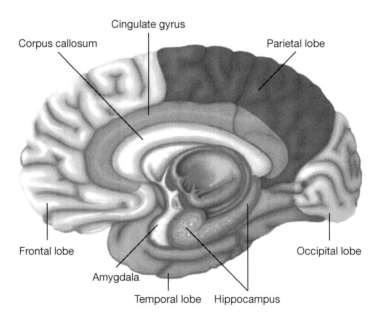

FIGURE 5.2 Diagram showing the different lobes of the brain.

From David Andrewes, *Neuropsychology: From theory to practice*, 2nd ed. (2015). Reproduced with permission from Taylor & Francis.

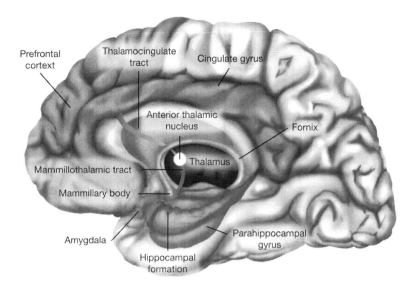

FIGURE 5.3 A sagittal view of the brain showing the hippocampus.

From David Andrewes, *Neuropsychology: From theory to practice*, 2nd ed. (2015). Reproduced with permission from Taylor & Francis.

control, regulating emotions, and sexual urges. The parietal lobe has several functions mainly including sensation, perception, and spatial reasoning but also encompassing speech and aspects of working memory. There are two temporal lobes, one located on each side of the brain. A major function of the temporal lobes is the processing of auditory sounds. Other critical functions include memory encoding and a structure within the temporal lobe forms a key component of what is known as the *medial temporal lobe* (MTL) memory system (see Figure 5.3). Finally, the occipital lobe, the smallest of the four lobes, is in the posterior region of the cerebral cortex, toward the back of the skull. The occipital lobe is the primary visual processing area of the brain. Of primary concern in the present chapter are the temporal lobe, the MTL, and the hippocampal formation. Although we will not go into the effects of brain damage in this chapter, we should note that damage to the hippocampus or related structures can lead to the impairment and even loss of the ability to encode new memories (known as *anterograde amnesia*). As well, following hippocampal damage, there is usually at least some loss of memories predating the brain injury (known as *retrograde amnesia*).

With some knowledge of brain regions and functions in mind, let us now turn to brain imaging techniques that have allowed us to develop an understanding of brain function that simply was not possible prior to their creation. The first of these is functional magnetic resonance imaging or functional MRI (fMRI) that measures brain activity by detecting changes associated with blood flow. This technique relies on the fact that when an area of the brain is in use, blood flow to that region also increases.

The primary form of fMRI uses what is termed the *blood-oxygen-level dependent* (BOLD) hemodynamic response. Thus, when a cognitive activity is in progress, say remembering how you celebrated your last birthday, those brain areas that mediate this activity will require more oxygen to function effectively and the BOLD response is a measure of the increased oxygenating blood flow to these areas. Of course, other brain areas that are not part of the process of, in this example, remembering, will not in most cases have an increased BOLD response. Thus, in order to "see" the brain activation, fMRI scans of the brain performing a control task are collected and their activations are subtracted from those collected when the task of interest, the experimental task, was being performed. The patterns of activation that remain visible after this contrast are unique to the experimental condition, in this example, remembering your last birthday.

Although there are many additional complications when using fMRI that this very cursory introduction has not dealt with, we simply wanted to provide the reader with a general picture of the technique. In passing, we note two important additional points: (1) choice of the comparison task is always problematic, and (2) because the BOLD response has to be averaged over many data points, the temporal resolution of fMRI is rather poor, being in seconds rather the milliseconds in which the brain works. On the other hand, fMRI has excellent spatial resolution and can identify brain regions and structures very precisely.

In contrast, electroencephalography (EEG) has a much finer, millisecond, temporal resolution but lacks the fine spatial resolution of fMRI. EEG is a technique used to gather data about electrical activity in the brain detected by electrodes placed on the scalp. When neurons, the main cells of the brain, "fire," they depolarize causing an electromagnetic signal. Neuronal networks that might, for example, be involved in remembering, consist of millions of neurons and many interconnections between neurons. When populations of such neurons become active this can be systematically detected at the scalp and, because of the strategic placement of electrodes, localized to the underlying brain regions (at least most of the time).

A particular type of EEG, known as event-related potentials (ERPs), has been useful in studying various aspects of cognition including memory. This is because in this technique, responses are time-locked to a particular event, say presentation of a stimulus on a computer screen, and changes in EEG wave forms can then be mapped from the stimulus onset to some predetermined point, usually a second or so after stimulus presentation. Unfortunately, this is not such a great technique for studying autobiographical memories as these nearly always take several seconds to be constructed in consciousness.

Another technique is sometimes used here and is called Slow Cortical Potentials (SCPs), a technique that tracks changes in EEG wave forms over longer periods of time. However, a problem with SCPs is that they can only measure with reference to a particular baseline and choice of a baseline is often difficult – rather like the choice of comparison task in fMRI. Nonetheless, construction of memories can be tracked, at the millisecond level, using SCPs in EEG.

All neuroimaging techniques have their advantages and disadvantages and future technological developments will no doubt greatly enhance our abilities to "see" what the brain is doing when carrying out tasks of interest, including remembering. For instance, the combination of fMRI and EEG might be one way to resolve the spatial-temporal resolution problem and there are, of course, many new techniques currently under development (e.g., multi-voxel pattern analysis – see Haxby, Connolly, & Guntupalli, 2014). However, as we will see next, the current techniques have taken the field a long way in understanding the brain networks underlying numerous forms of cognition including autobiographical memory.

The neuroanatomical basis of autobiographical memory

Initial neuroimaging studies of autobiographical memory date from the mid-1990s to the early 2000s (see Conway, Pleydell-Pearce, Whitecross, & Sharpe, 2002, and Maguire, 2001, for early reviews) but only began in earnest after that. There are at least two reasons for this. One is that it gradually became clear that using stimuli such as lists of words or pictures briefly studied before or during a scan did not engage the cognitive system to any great extent. Indeed, comparing the findings of these sorts of studies with the extensive and widespread disruption to autobiographical memory known at the time to occur following brain damage (see Conway & Fthenaki, 2000), it was clear that the neurological study of memory seemed to be missing important aspects. This was almost certainly because of the very low self-reference of the materials that were used as stimuli. However, lists of items (e.g., words or pictures) have one important advantage over autobiographical memories. That is, because these items could be strictly controlled for in terms of their specific properties (e.g., concreteness, familiarity, complexity), the experimenter could know (or so it was thought) what had been encoded and, therefore, what could potentially be recalled. In contrast, simply asking people to recall memories of events from their lives while they were in the scanner lacked any control over the encoding environment, and also required some degree of belief on the part of the experimenter that the participant in the scanner was *in fact* recalling memories.

The second factor was that, despite the lack of experimenter control, various groups nevertheless started to produce a series of important papers on the brain basis of autobiographical memory (Svoboda, McKinnon, & Levine, 2006, and Cabeza & St. Jacques, 2007, for reviews and the collection of readings in Addis, Barense, & Durate, 2015, for recent overviews). Next we consider the earlier work, and then turn to our current understanding of the neuropsychology of autobiographical memory.

The initial research into the brain basis of autobiographical memory used the hemodynamic method of fMRI (as well as Positron Emission Tomography, PET) and the electrophysiological method of EEG. The overall pattern of activations from several studies was one of left frontal activation coupled with activation of networks in the medial part of the brain. These latter networks included the retrosplenial and posterior cingulate corticies, the medial temporal lobes (hippocampal formation), temporoparietal junction, medial prefrontal cortex, temporopolar cortex, and cerebellum. Exactly in what order networks in these regions came on line was not known. However, this is a critical question because construction of autobiographical memories unfolds over a period of seconds, which in brain processing terms is a long period (compare, for example, word recognition times which are often less than 500ms or half a second). Evidence from an early SCP EEG study found that activation is first present in the left frontal lobes and only later in temporal regions (the medial temporal lobe memory system), and finally, when a memory was held in mind, activation was detected in the posterior regions of the right occipital lobes (primary visual processing areas) and posterior temporal lobes (Conway, Pleydell-Pearce, & Whitecross, 2001). Conway et al. (2001) proposed that the left frontal activation reflected the initiation and early processing of long-term memory search processes under frontal executive control. The temporal activation showed access to what they termed the *autobiographical knowledge base* (see Conway & Pleydell-Pearce, 2000) and finally the last stage (memory formation) was reflected in activation of networks located in posterior temporal and occipital areas. These later areas may mediate episodic memories that contain visual details of specific events (Conway, 2005, 2009). The construction of autobiographical memories is then a highly complex process featuring activation of many different brains regions: it is a process that is both topographically and temporally extended.

Svoboda et al. (2006), in their meta-analysis of 24 neuroimaging studies, found broad agreement for this general model based on these earlier studies and also were able to further specify and extend this model. Before turning to outcomes of these later studies we might note some of the shortcomings of the earlier studies that the later studies, using diverse methods, effectively obviated. The reason for noting these shortcomings is quite simply because they are interesting.

One problem was that of finding an appropriate baseline task. A number of the earlier studies used a baseline condition termed "rest." In this condition, the participant in the scanner was signaled to stop recalling memories and simply let their mind wander until signaled again for a further series of memory retrieval trials. But what is the participant actually doing in the "rest" condition? After all, one cannot simply switch one's mind off (even during sleep or other periods of unconsciousness). As noted by Andreasen et al. (1995; see too Conway et al., 2002), participants when in the "rest" condition were in fact daydreaming about future plans, recalling past memories, thinking about problems, and so forth. This, of course, is a problem as it means that when the brain activations are compared between autobiographical memory retrieval and rest it may be the case that one is subtracting out the exact activations one is looking for! Indeed, this is inevitable if during "rest" the participant is recalling past memories. However, as we will see in a later section (see The Default Network) although this was a problem for some of the early brain imaging studies of autobiographical memory retrieval it raised a very interesting issue in its own right, namely: what activations are occurring in the brain when attention is unfocused and a person is daydreaming or mind wandering? In other words, what does cognition default to when it is not task focused? Later brain imaging studies used control or baseline tasks that featured task-orientation often consisting of memory tasks but not ones that involved autobiographical memory. This allowed these studies to "see" much more accurately the activations uniquely mediating a particular task, such as construction of autobiographical memories.

A second problem with the earlier studies relates to how much time was to be allowed for a memory to be retrieved? This is a problem because retrieval times differ for each memory construction, some being quickly constructed and some that are constructed more slowly. In one early study, a relatively early cut-off time was used and because of that this study detected activation largely limited to left frontal networks, something that we now know mediates the early part of the retrieval process (Conway et al., 1999). Later studies avoided this problem by having participants hold a memory in mind for a period of time after it had been constructed (e.g., see Gilboa et al., 2004). A temporal problem that still remains is the poor temporal resolution of fMRI, making it difficult to image the sequence of processing as networks interlock over time in the formation of a memory.

In their meta-analysis, Svoboda et al. (2006) also identified what they termed a core network of brain activations, one that is present in the majority of studies, a secondary network that is detected less frequently, and finally, some activations that are seen in a single or only a few studies. The core autobiographical network of brain regions that are activated during memory construction are: the medial and ventrolateral prefrontal cortices (frontal lobes), medial and lateral temporal cortices (temporal lobes), temporoparietal junction, retrosplenial/posterior cingulate cortex, and the cerebellum (posterior regions). This network may come online sequentially with frontal networks first (search processes), followed by temporal networks, and then posterior networks. However, once activated, the whole complex autobiographical memory network will function simultaneously and interactively as information is activated in long-term memory, then evaluated and monitored by control processes, and then maintained as a stable mental representation.

The nature of these networks and their various functions in this overall autobiographical memory network are considered in detail in Svoboda et al. (2006). By way of summary, we might note that neural networks located in the frontal lobes serve many constructive and self-referential processes. Activation in the temporal lobes shows activation in the medial temporal lobe memory system and may reflect the creation of a stable mental representation that links to several other posterior brain regions. Probably most important with these networks is the establishment of a specific and detailed mental representation that will often include visual imagery – in short, the construction of an *episodic* memory.

Both Svoboda et al. (2006) and Cabeza and St. Jacques (2007) focus on networks that become active as memory specificity increases and as emotion intensifies. Emotional memories are rich in contextual details, have vivid sensory-perceptual properties, and, of course, when brought to mind, cause emotions themselves. One of the key important brain regions here is the amygdala, a mid-brain limbic system structure that interconnects heavily with the hippocampus to which it is adjoined. The amygdala is known to play a major role in the experience of emotions (especially fear) and as a memory is (re)constructed, activation of amygdala networks will stimulate the experience of memory-related emotions. Interestingly, hippocampal and other related networks may also mediate the experience of remembering. This is sometimes referred to as *recollective experience* which is the distinct feeling that a memory is a memory (see Gardiner & Richardson-Klavehn, 2000, for a review). Recollective experience contributes to the *feeling-of-rightness* (FOR) that accompanies a fully (re)constructed memory. The FOR, however, is mediated by monitoring executive processes in frontal networks. Finally, as explored in some depth in both review papers, there is extensive activation of posterior visual networks in the occipital, cuneus, and precuneus regions. This may represent the inclusion of episodic details, in the form of visual images, to the memory (re)construction (Conway, 2009). This model of brain regions mediating the construction of autobiographical memories is shown in Figure 5.4.

It should be born in mind that regions highlighted in Figure 5.4, although separable regions, do not function autonomously in the (re)construction of auto-

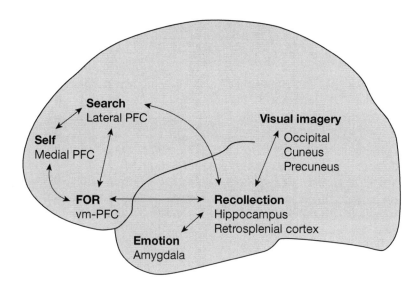

FIGURE 5.4 A basic description of key elements of the autobiographical memory retrieval network. This includes search and controlled processes (involving left lateral prefrontal cortex), self-referential processes (medial PFC), recollection (involving the hippocampus and the retrosplenial cortex), emotional processing (amygdala), visual imagery (occipital and cuneus/precuneus regions), and feeling-of-rightness (FOR) monitoring (ventromedial PFC).

biographical memories. Instead, they interlock in the process of memory (re)construction and act as a single superordinate network. Interestingly, we might note too that the regions shown in Figure 5.4 can also take part in other types of cognition and, therefore, in other superordinate networks (e.g., planning, decision making).

Finally, in closing this section, we briefly consider one important issue and that is the development of the autobiographical memory network. Is an infant born with this fully formed? If not, when and how does it emerge and what are the implications for child memory? For reviews of this area, which is a complex one with rapidly evolving research, the papers in Addis et al. (2015) and Ghetti and Bauer (2012) are highly relevant. For reviews of the development of memory more generally, Bauer (2007) and Howe (2011) provide comprehensive coverage (also see Chapter 4).

The general picture here is that as the brain continues to develop and mature neurophysiologically over the course of infancy, childhood, and into adolescence and early adulthood, it is inevitably the case that so too does the autobiographical memory network. Current research findings indicate that networks in the MTL may be fairly well developed by the age of about 12 months. However, further evidence indicates that the hippocampus undergoes neuronal development beyond this into the school years. Most striking however is the slow development of networks in the frontal lobes that continue neurological development into early adulthood (see an important report from the Royal Society, 2011, on Neuroscience and The Law). One of the major changes here is the (slow) pruning of neuronal connections via the process of programmed cell death (apoptosis). Essentially, neural networks in the frontal lobes are extensively over connected at birth and throughout childhood. Through experience, certain networks and pathways come to be used to some optimal extent whereas others have a lower baseline of activation. It is thought that it is these latter networks that are subject to apoptosis, triggered by their relative disuse. This has the beneficial effect of rendering processing in the surviving networks much more efficient and fluent. The down side is that the scope for change at the neuronal level is reduced. This is of interest because neurons are one of the few sets of cells in the body that do not divide. This makes a lot of sense if neurons represent knowledge gained from experience – if they were constantly replaced by cell division, presumably there would be no way to retain the represented knowledge. But does this mean that the shaping of neural networks, including those representing memory, can only take place by the type of neuronal pruning described above? Perhaps, but how neurons represent knowledge and memories is not known and there are some areas of the brain where new neurons are created (neurogenesis) throughout life, and these are in the hippocampus and olfactory bulb, with the former being crucial to memory formation (and quite possibly retrieval too).

The net effect of these developmental trajectories are that young children appear to have some relatively mature recognition abilities and experience familiarity when encountering some past event details. But they cannot recall contextual details, a function that emerges over the early years of childhood. Moreover, they do not have the frontal executive process of the adult memory system and so cannot construct memories with the rich conceptual structure and episodic details similar to those of adults. In addition, they do not have the cognitive feelings that guide and help monitor memory (mental) representations, such as FOR and recollective experience. Of some importance here is the development of conceptual control structures that organize information in long-term memory and, in so doing, channel search processes to sought-for-knowledge. For example, an important organizational structure known as the *life story* (Habermas & Bluck, 2000) does not develop until late adolescence. This, no doubt, has the effect of rendering searches of long-term autobiographical memory inconsistent and, perhaps, somewhat random prior to adolescence.

The evidence, then, from studies of post-birth brain development indicates that explicit, detailed, episodic memories from below about the age 5 to 6 years is probably less reliable than those found in adulthood. The behavioral evidence shows that the extent to which children can recall specific contextual details is limited with such details often being more fragmentary than those found in adult recall of specific events. This is not to say that children cannot provide accurate accounts of events they have experienced, but the ability to construct detailed memories of specific events from the past develops over childhood into early adulthood. It is not until the development of search, control, and monitoring networks in the frontal lobes is complete, in a person's early 20s, that a more complete autobiographical memory system is in place and operating at optimum effectiveness.[1]

Memory and the future

One of the many innovations introduced to modern memory research and theory has been a new focus of the relation of memory to the future. This was initiated by Tulving (1985) who, in 1972, had also introduced the whole notion of "episodic" memory. Tulving noticed that amnesic patients have great difficulty imagining future events. This suggested that a prerequisite for imagining the future was an intact autobiographical memory network. Following up on this subsequent research, other scientists examined the relation between the brain regions that mediate autobiographical memory and those that mediate the ability to imagine the future. The research of Schacter and his colleagues has led the way in this area (for a recent review, see McClelland, Schacter, & Addis, 2015). Remarkably, when people imagine the future the same brain network that mediates autobiographical remembering becomes active. That is, neuronal networks in the prefrontal cortex (frontal lobes), medial temporal lobes, and the posterior parietal cortex become highly active. In retrospect, this is perhaps not surprising – after all, when we imagine ourselves in the future we draw upon the past to do so. This may be why amnesic patients have such difficulty with what Schacter has termed *episodic simulation* (Schacter & Addis, 2009) or what is sometimes also referred to as *episodic future thinking*.

McClelland et al. (2015) reviewed the evidence showing that when an episodic simulation is made, rememberers first draw upon general personal knowledge before accessing specific episodic details. These are then bound together (probably in hippocampal networks) to form a transitory but stable mental representation that simulates a "memory" of a future event. Interestingly, children when asked to imagine the future appear not to be able to do so with any facility until about four or five years of age and older (e.g., Atance & Sommerville, 2014), paralleling the development of networks that underlie autobiographical memory. Imaging specific goals and the steps needed to be taken to achieve them also activates the autobiographical memory network and, moreover, imagining highly self-relevant goals activates this network, particularly the medial prefrontal and parietal regions more so than when imaging low self-relevant goals (D'Argembeau, Stawarczyk, Majerus, et al., 2010). In the Conway and Pleydell-Pearce (2000) account of autobiographical memory, goals play a central role in the organization of memory.

Imagining the future and remembering the past share a common, and complex, superordinate neuronal network consisting of various hubs distributed through our frontal, temporal, and posterior brain regions, including the MTL and hippocampus. Again, it is not known for certain what order such networks come on line when creating an episodic future simulation. However, an EEG study by Conway, Pleydell-Pearce, Whitecross, and Sharpe (2003) suggests that this might be similar to the construction of autobiographical memories, where the frontal networks are activated first, followed by more posterior networks very soon afterwards. Once all of these networks are activated, the mental representation is constructed. As Schacter (2012) points out, the ability to create simulations of the future is undoubtedly highly adaptive in an evolutionary sense. Being able to imagine what may take place in the future allows an organism to vicariously imagine ways of achieving the goal or plan managing strategies. One suggestion is that this ability to imagine may be particularly relevant to social interactions, past and future.

Despite this, there is a downside: because remembering past episodes and episodic future planning both take place in the same complex brain networks, the potential for them to become intermixed and even wholly confused is quite high. This is especially the case when the operation of frontal control processes is compromised in some way – that is, when they are not yet fully developed, they are in decline, or they malfunction due to some other factor (e.g., brain damage, substance abuse). However, whether the frontal control processes are compromised or not, distinguishing at the level of brain activations between remembering and imaging appears, at least with current technology, not possible in any definitive way.

The default network

When cognition is not task-focused, as mentioned earlier, and the individual is daydreaming, letting their mind wander (this is the "rest" condition in the early neuroimaging studies of autobiographical memory), then the frontal-temporal-parietal/occipital network we have already seen active in remembering and imagining again becomes active (Conway et al., 2016). Phenomenologically, this features planning, remembering, imagining, taking others points of view, making decisions, and many other higher order brain processes. This is now considered to take place in what is termed the *default network* (Buckner, Andrews-Hanna, & Schacter, 2008).[2] The default network is so termed because it is the network that comes on line when we are not engaged in some more focused task.

There are two broad subsystems of the default network.

1. The MTL memory system, consisting of structures such as the hippocampus, parahippocampal gyrus, retrosplenial cortex, and ventromedial frontal cortex. The main function of the MTL is in recalling past episodes and integrating knowledge to form a simulation of possible future experiences. Note that networks in the ventromedial frontal cortex mediate self-related processes and quite possibly are critical in determining the self-relevance of simulations of the future.
2. The prefrontal cortex (PFC), dorsal medial networks, temporoparietal junction, lateral temporal cortex, and temporal lobe. This subsystem appears to involve reasoning about self and others.

Both subsystems, MTL and PFC, converge on the posterior cingulate cortex and the anterior medial PFC, which act as hubs linking together the default systems from frontal through medial to posterior networks: a major superordinate brain network taking in vast areas of neocortex and sub-cortex (the limbic system).

Autobiographical remembering and imagining all take place in the default system, leading Conway et al. (2016) to refer to it as the *remembering-imagining system*. This brain relation between remembering and imagining, which at the level of neuronal networks are essentially the same thing, is of considerable significance when considering the *accuracy* of memories. It is clear that all memory constructions will contain details that are imagined and inferred, sometimes consciously as a person strives to remember a forgotten detail, but mostly non-consciously and automatically, as the brain "fills in" missing details. There is then an in-built mechanism for the generation of false memory details that, typically, would be plausible and highly schema-consistent with a memory construction. Perhaps even more problematic is that imagining in the default system may itself give rise to wholly false memories. This could occur simply because what was at first imagined is later recalled or reconstructed as a memory (i.e., its source is lost). This is a process that has been termed *imagination inflation* (Garry, Manning, Loftus, & Sherman, 1996) and the default network would seem to be an ideal brain system in which imagined memories can become actual "memories" (i.e., mental constructions that are recollectively experienced as memories).

Conclusion

Implications of the memory brain network for memory and law

We have seen that memory in terms of brain systems is a highly complex cognitive ability. In no respect can it be compared to other recording media such as books, videos, movies, or tapes. It is a purely *psychological process* that takes place in large, superordinate, and interlocked, memory networks. There are a number of important points for memory and the law that arise from our current understanding of the brain mechanisms of remembering and we close this chapter with the most important of these:

- Memory is a (re)constructive psychological process. It is not like other types of recording media to which it should not be compared. Because it is (re)constructive, all memories contain non-conscious inferences and guesses and, in this respect, all memories will contain information that is not derived from the original, direct experience.
- The brain regions relevant to autobiographical memory develop from the pre-birth years into early adulthood and decline in old age (over 70 years). Because of this, the memories of children are not like the memories of adults (see Chapter 4) and we should not expect them to show the same properties (i.e., recall of specific details with adult understandings).
- Remembering and imagining take place in the same complex brain system. Because of this, remembering and imagining are neurologically and psychologically intertwined and memories may, therefore, frequently contain imagined details (especially in children). Moreover, because both types of mental representation are created in the same neurological network, it is perfectly possible for events which have only been imagined to become remembered and experienced by the individual as "real" memories.

Notes

1. Although not covered here, it should be noted that the same brain network begins to degrade in old age, beyond about 70 years of age (e.g., see Rajah, Maillet, & Grady, 2015, for a recent review).
2. Note that there are many other researchers in this area but here we draw upon this one comprehensive review and on McClelland et al. (2015).

6

STRESS, TRAUMA, AND MEMORY

I can't stop remembering. I see it all so clearly. Like it happened just yesterday. But it was 5 years ago. It was bad enough that I was raped in the first place but to have to relive it over and over is just too much.

(Trauma survivor with PTSD; taken from Morgan & Southwick, 2014, p. 101)

Morgan and Southwick (2014) report on a case of a Muslim woman who had survived a horrific traumatic experience and who was subsequently diagnosed with post-traumatic stress disorder (PTSD). The woman was a primary witness for the 1998 International War Crimes Tribunal held in The Hague. A Bosnian-Croatian solider was tried for torture, inhumane treatment, and abetting the rape of the witness. Due to the traumatic and highly stressful event, the court believed that the witness would be able to confidently remember and identify her attacker. However, prior to the court commencing, the witness had provided a number of conflicting statements regarding the actions and appearance of the culprit. For example, shortly after the event in 1995, the witness described the defendant as being 5 foot 7 inches tall with short blond hair and blue eyes. At the trial in 1998, the accused was 6 feet tall with dark hair and brown eyes, yet the witness made a positive "in court" identification and described him as a "rather thin young man [who had put on some weight], rather strong jaw or teeth" who had, "chestnut to black hair," which was "cut short and combed up" (Morgan & Southwick, 2014). Of course, we would expect to see highly accurate and consistent descriptions given the striking vividness of the witness' own reports of the event. But in her statements, it appears that these central features of her abuser were inaccurate and had changed dramatically over the ensuing three years.

How could this be? There is somewhat of a lack of consensus regarding the effects of stress and trauma on memory. However, a long-standing belief among expert witnesses suggests that emotionally stressful events can in fact lead to a subsequent impairment in the ability to remember negative information related to that event. Kassin, Ellsworth, and Smith (1989) surveyed 63 eyewitness testimony experts and found a strong agreement that stress and event arousal had a negative effect on memory. In particular, 79% agreed that evidence from the research supports the statement: "Very high levels of stress impair the accuracy of eyewitness testimony." A further 71% of experts believed not only that there is scientific evidence that supports this statement, but that it was a sufficiently reliable fact that this point can be made without hesitation in the courtroom.

But were the beliefs of these expert witnesses correct? Where do we stand today? The answer is not a straightforward one. There is a lack of consistency, not only within the findings of the eyewitness literature, but also when comparing findings from the neurobiological domain. According to neurobiological research, memory for information encoded under stress tends to be superior to memory for information encoded in the absence of stress (see LaBar & Cabeza, 2006, for a review; Roozendaal & McGaugh, 2011). When confronted with a stressful situation, a physiological fight-or-flight response causes the release of adrenalin and noradrenalin, as well as the activation of the hypothalamic-pituitary-adrenal (HPA) axis which goes along with cortisol secretion. Additionally, this stress response facilitates the storage of memories related to the stressful situation by activating the amygdala which modulates the hippocampal region of the brain, known to be involved in memory formation (e.g., see Chapter 5 and Phelps, 2004; Schwabe, Joëls, Roozendaal, Wolf, & Oitzl, 2012; Wolf, 2009).

By comparison, in the past 30 years of research, behavioral studies examining eyewitness identification have shown a wide variety of findings. Some studies have shown that negative events are retained well (e.g., Bohannon, 1992; Brown & Kulik, 1977). Other studies have shown that negative emotional events are retained and recollected more poorly in comparison with neutral events (e.g., Loftus & Burns, 1982; Neisser & Harsch, 1990). Still other studies have demonstrated better recollection for central details of an emotional event at the expense of accuracy for peripheral details (Christianson, 1992). These different findings are likely due, in part, to the manner in which memory is tested and how stress has been manipulated. We have seen many approaches to the study of stress and trauma on memory in the forensic context. From the interviewing of witnesses or victims of real-life traumatic events (e.g., Brown & Kulik, 1977; Christianson & Nilsson, 1989; Yuille & Cutshall, 1986) to the laboratory and the use of simulated and staged events in which people are exposed to simulated crimes, accidents, and other highly emotional events (e.g., Clifford & Scott, 1978; Morgan & Southwick, 2014; Valentine & Mesout, 2009).

Despite these mixed results, it is clearly important to know just how heightened stress, the body's physical response to an emotionally charged situation, impacts the reliability of an eyewitness' memory. For example, witnesses of murder and victims of assault or rape are asked to recount vivid and detailed aspects of the crime, often repeatedly to various members of the law enforcement. These victims and eyewitnesses not only experienced a highly distressing situation at the encoding phase of the event, but in retrieving that information, they will also experience stress during recall. Research has examined how such emotional events are remembered by a victim, a bystander, or a perpetrator. That is, what specific details will be retained, and what will be lost? How malleable is the memory for this event? How do memories for emotional events compare to memories for non-emotional events? It is important to understand the effect of stress in laboratory studies and ensure that we can generalize these effects to real life instances of crime. What we have come to learn about the accuracy of emotional memories, and the potentially biasing effects of emotionally stressful events on memory, will be the focus of this current chapter.

Stress and eyewitness memory

In an infamous field study conducted by Yuille and Cutshall (1986), 13 of 21 witnesses to a shooting incident in Burnaby, British Columbia, Canada consented to take part in a follow-up research interview 4–5 months after the event. The original incident took place on a major thoroughfare in mid-afternoon in the community of Burnaby. One person was killed and a second seriously wounded. At the time of the incident police obtained statements in the form of a verbatim account recorded by an officer. The statement included, first, a description of the event in the witnesses' own words, and second, a series of responses to questions asked by the officer to elaborate on key aspects of the event. After four to five months, the witnesses were interviewed again by a researcher using the same procedure employed by the police. Although there were errors, witnesses were still able to exhibit high levels of detail after five months and the people who experienced more stress recalled more detail about the event. Five witnesses who had contact with either the thief, the store owner, or a weapon, reported extreme anxiety and stress and all five reported sleeping difficulties following the incident. The remaining eight reported low levels of stress or no stress at all. Yuille and Cutshall reported a reliable difference in accuracy between the high stress and low stress witness groups, with a mean of 93.36% compared with 75.13% during the police interview and 88.24% compared with 75.88% during the research interview. However, the effect of stress in this circumstance was confounded with the degree of involvement in the incident and therefore proximity to detail. Subsequent field studies have shown a more mixed picture of the effect of stress on eyewitness memory.

Other studies have found support for this early finding by Yuille and Cutshall (1986). For example, police trainees were found to have better accuracy and greater resistance to forgetting for eyewitness information when confronted with a high stress compared with low stress training simulation (Yuille, Davies, Gibling, Marxsen, & Porter, 1994). Trainees took part in a standard "stop and search" scenario where a witness informs the officer that a gentleman (suspect) had been acting suspiciously around cars in a parking lot. The interview with the suspect was manipulated to be highly stressful, where the suspect was uncooperative, abusive, and denied the allegations, or non-stressful, where the suspect was polite, cooperative, and answered all the police questions. When the trainees were interviewed about the simulation 12 weeks later, people recalling the stressful event were more accurate than those recalling the non-stressful event. However, Yuille et al. (1994) also reported that the police cadets in the high stress condition consistently provided less information than those in the non-stressful condition. Thus, greater accuracy in the detail recalled was accompanied by a reduction in the quantity of the information being recalled. Yuille et al. referred to a narrowing effect of attention. That is, witnesses focus directly on the source of stress, attending more to core details than peripheral ones – something we will come back to later.

Consistent with these enhanced effects of negative emotion on memory, another line of research has provided a reasonably consistent pattern when it comes to the emotionality of the information to be recalled. The majority of research on memory for emotional stimuli suggests that we remember negatively valenced and high arousal stimuli better than neutral, low arousal stimuli (Cahill & McGaugh, 1998; Dolan, 2002). However, there is also a paradoxical effect where there can be more false memories with that same negative material (Howe et al., 2010; Knott & Thorley 2014).

Although such studies suggest a certain advantage to the role of negative emotion and stress in eyewitness recall, other studies have produced far more mixed results. That is, some have shown no differences in recall of stressful events. For example, Hulse and Memon (2006) used virtual reality to simulate high and low stressful events. Police firearms officers had to complete a recall task for a "shoot" scenario in which they fired their weapon compared with officers in a "no shoot" scenario who did not open fire. Officers showed few differences in both accuracy and detail in subsequent recollections of the event. In contrast, field studies (e.g., Peters, 1988; Valentine & Mesout, 2009) have evidenced the opposite effect of stress on recall, with people in high stress circumstances remembering fewer details and being less accurate.

Although not specifically related to a forensic context, Peters (1988) found that participants who showed greater physiological activation while waiting to receive an inoculation showed stronger impaired eyewitness identification and recollection of the physical appearance of the nurse who gave the injection, in comparison to the identification of the experimenter who spoke to the participant shortly after the injection was given. Valentine and Mesout (2009) examined the ability of visitors to the London Dungeon to identify a target as a function of their state anxiety experienced while in the Horror Labyrinth. While in the labyrinth, an actor, dressed in a dark robe wearing theatrical make up, would step out in front of the participant and block their path. After 45 minutes, participants completed the state anxiety questionnaire followed by a memory questionnaire and identification task. High state anxiety was associated with reporting fewer correct descriptors of the target person, more incorrect details, and a dramatic impairment of correct identifications from a lineup. In fact, Valentine and Mesout reported that only 17%

of those with high anxiety correctly identified the person from a line-up compared with 75% who scored low for state anxiety. This finding is consistent with those findings of Morgan and colleagues (Morgan et al., 2004; Morgan & Southwick, 2014) who have provided robust evidence using a different methodology for the study of realistic, threat-to-life stress on eyewitness accuracy of soldiers at survival training school. The soldiers had been detained for 12 hours in a mock prisoner of war camp. Each soldier then underwent a high or low stress interrogation. They found that regardless of the method used to assess memory (i.e., live lineup, simultaneous or sequential presentation) eyewitness recall was less accurate for the high, compared with low, stress interrogations and this was accompanied by greater susceptibility to misinformation (Morgan, Southwick, Steffian, Hazlett, & Loftus, 2013).

A meta-analysis revealed that stress during encoding has negative effects on eyewitness identification performance (Deffenbacher, Bornstein, Penrod, & McGorty, 2004), with strong effects for target-present, but negligible effects for target-absent, lineups. However, a more recent study by Sauerland et al. (2016) highlighted that only six of the 22 eyewitness identification studies included in the meta-analysis displayed high ecological validity (i.e., employed a staged crime), only 10 included a suitable retention interval of at least 24 hours (others only used one to two hours – not a suitable enough time for the neurobiological effects of stress to take effect), and only seven included physiological measures of stress to verify whether the stress induction procedure succeeded in eliciting bodily stress responses. Worse, none of the studies included in the meta-analysis combined all three important elements. Sauerland et al. (2016) sought to correct this by including all three components in a single design. Specifically, they exposed a group of participants to a live staged crime, used a one-week interval between the event and the administration of the lineup, and measured participants' salivary cortisol levels. Although they still used a laboratory induced stress test to enhance levels of stress, this research still has higher ecological validity than its predecessors. Their findings showed that when attempting to identify the thief from target-present and target-absent lineups, there was no effect of high stress on memory performance.

So does negative emotion and stress enhance, impair, or have no effect on memory? Just from the key studies outlined above and the observations made by Sauerland et al. (2016), we can see that the answer to that question really varies depending on the way emotion is assessed (e.g., emotional saliency of the event vs. emotional distress of participants), the severity of that stress, the time between encoding and retrieval, and the kind of information being recalled (e.g., central vs. peripheral details of an event). Morgan and Southwick (2014) argued that although emotional events are remembered better than neutral events, there is a caveat – memory under highly stressful and potentially novel situations is vulnerable to error and inaccuracy and that memories formed under high stress may not contain the detail and precision needed for the judicial system. They argued that high levels of stress cause the release of norepinephrine that may actually exceed the optimal level needed for the formation of accurate memories.

There have been a number of explanations for the effects of heightened stress on eyewitness memory. In the first systematic review of stress on eyewitness memory, Deffenbacher (1983) concluded that stress affected performance according to an inverted-U function as described by the Yerkes-Dodson law. That is, performance improves with increases in arousal associated with the ascending arm of the inverted U and then impaired memory was associated with increases in arousal associated with the descending arm of the inverted U. Some 10 years later, Christianson (1992) argued that there was little research to show such a debilitating effect of stress on memory and instead, that memory for negative emotional events is better than that for neutral events. However, he argued that this was specific to the central details of the event. Negative emotion and stress cause a narrowing of attention to the central aspects of the event and allow for elaboration of those details, but this comes at the expense of peripheral details, where we become worse for accuracy and recollection of detail for negative compared with neutral events.

Although there is an abundance of research that supports such an explanation, including studies on weapon focus, not all research examining stress fit this model. In 2004, Deffenbacher and colleagues (Deffenbacher, Borstein, Penrod, & McGorty, 2004) argued for a more updated model for the effect of stress on eyewitness memory. They now distinguish between an *activation mode* of attention control, one that results in a defensive response and is likely to be induced in victims of crime, from an *arousal mode* of attention control, one that results in an orienting response. If the event results in the activation of the arousal mode of attention control, then memory will be enhanced for the central and important aspects of the event on which the response has been directed toward. If, on the other hand, a task elicits the activation mode of attention control, then memory will either be modestly enhanced or drastically reduced, depending on the relative amounts of cognitive anxiety (worry) and physiological activation (somatic anxiety) present (Hardy & Parfitt, 1991). As described in the catastrophe model of anxiety and performance:

> at relatively high levels of cognitive anxiety, continuous gradual increases in somatic anxiety (physiological activation) will at first result in continuous, gradual increases in performance, followed at some point by a catastrophic, discontinuous drop in performance.
>
> (Deffenbacher et al., 2004, p. 689)

Such an explanation can account for studies that show enhanced memory for central details due to an orienting response of the arousal mode of attention regulation, and the more severe effects found in the police interrogation literature, caused by very high levels of cognitive and somatic anxiety that cause a catastrophic drop in performance.

This theoretical model can account for many of the findings in the stress and eyewitness memory literature. However, whether results from laboratory studies provide an under- or overestimate of eyewitness memory performance, especially when eyewitnesses will ultimately vary in their state of heightened stress, is still an issue for concern for the eyewitness field. Deffenbacher's model requires additional scrutiny and further research is crucial to reconcile inconsistencies in findings and methodologies from previous studies. This is evident in a more recent replication of the Kassin et al. (1989) survey (Kassin et al., 2001). When questioned in 2001, only 50% of expert witnesses indicated that they would testify in court about the effects of stress on memory, compared with 75% in 1989 (Kassin et al., 2001). Thus, within the academic community, there is not enough consensus in the research to inform our judgment about the effects of stress and emotion on memory.

Confidence and memory for negative emotional events

So far we have considered the accuracy and detail of recollection as markers for the effects of stress and memory. Laboratory research allows for a controlled environment in which we can accurately assess these dependent variables. However, there is another dependent measure that has been assessed in relation to the effects of emotion and stress on eyewitness memory and that is confidence. We have seen that confidence in eyewitness statements rarely correlates with accuracy in identification. Indeed, confidence can be inflated by a number of factors throughout the legal process. "In wrongful convictions overturned by post-conviction DNA testing, witnesses have testified that they were '100% positive' of the identification, saying that they 'would never forget that face' – despite having identified the wrong person" (Innocence Project, 2009). As we will see (Chapter 7), confidence in eyewitness identification can be heavily influenced by bias in police interviews or lineup administrators. Simple statements such as "okay, good" or "Yes, that's who we thought it was" can increase confidence and even alter the recollection of the identification procedure, with witnesses often reporting certainty at the time of identification even though the record of the identification procedure may show they were initially hesitant or uncertain. Indeed, Thompson-Cannino recalls in the case against Ronald Cotton how her false sense of confidence increased over time (Thompson-Cannino, Cotton, & Torneo, 2009). Coupled with the strong evidence that shows that jurors (naïvely) assume confident eyewitnesses are reliable eyewitnesses, it is important to understand all factors that affect confidence statements in eyewitness accounts.

To consider the relationship between confidence and accuracy for traumatic and stressful events, we can turn to the so-called *flashbulb* memory literature. Brown and Kulik (1977) originally proposed that events which are emotional, surprising, and consequential result in highly detailed memories that are almost akin to a photograph of the original event. Such detailed memories could be extremely accurate due to the activation of a presumed special and distinct neural mechanism that leads to a "print now" command when we encounter a shocking event (Brown & Kulik, 1977). Since 1977, we have seen the alleged creation of such memories for shocking public events, including the Challenger explosion (Neisser & Harsch, 1992), the death of Princess Diana (Kvavilashvili, Mirani, Schlagman, & Kornbrot, 2003), and the 9/11 terrorist attacks (Hirst et al., 2009). Although frequently described as being rich and vivid in detail, these memories often lack consistency and accuracy. In fact, emotion has been shown to enhance a subjective sense of remembering as well as an overall confidence in the accuracy of memory performance but not necessarily memory itself (Sharot, Martorella, Delgado, & Phelps, 2007; Talarico & Rubin, 2003). Not surprisingly, then, the enhanced subjective experience for emotional and traumatic public events is not often accompanied by enhanced accuracy of these memories (Christianson & Engelberg, 1999; Hirst et al., 2009).

Such investigations of memories for traumatic public events highlight the consequence of the impact of emotion on people's beliefs about the accuracy of their own recollection. This enhanced subjective judgment of memory accuracy has also been demonstrated in the laboratory. For example, Rimmele, Davachi, Petrov, Dougal, and Phelps (2011) presented participants with emotional and neutral scenes and manipulated the inclusion of an object in each scene. Participants were later tested on a scene recognition test and an object recognition test. They were asked to make remember/know decisions for each scene and object recognized. A remember response reflects a sense of recollective experience of the event and a know response reflects a sense of familiarity in the absence of any recollective experience (Rajaram, 1993). Results showed that for scene memory, recognition and overall subjective ratings of remember responses were higher for negative compared with neutral scenes. In contrast, performance for the more detailed memory of objects from each scene was lower for negative compared with neutral scenes despite no difference in subjective recollective experiences. Thus, the impaired recognition for more specific details from the scene, but enhanced memory for the overall scene itself, supports previous studies that show that emotion benefits memory for the central details of a stimulus with a corresponding deficit in memory for contextual items (Kensinger, Piguet, Krendl, & Corkin, 2005). Furthermore, Rimmele et al. (2011) observed a similar dissociation reported in the flashbulb memory studies. Here, confidence (or in this case, an enhanced experience of remembering) in memory accuracy was high and memory for specific details was relatively poor.

So far we have seen that understanding the role of stress and emotion in determining the reliability of memory for the legal field is an extremely challenging one. This is because summarizing the research in this field in a comprehensive manner for the legal system cannot be easily achieved. There are a number of factors that have led to varying results and although we are beginning to see an emerging pattern, there are still a number of uncertainties. Moving forward, it is important that the research in this field adopts a more systematic methodology to allow replication and development. What we can take away from this is that we are likely able to remember traumatic and stressful events reasonably well. However, we may be poorer at remembering peripheral and specific details, these memories can still be subject to distortion, what we remember may depend on how we engage with and process the information, and we may have a higher (and unfounded) degree of confidence in the accuracy of the details that we do remember.

Children and memory for traumatic events

So far we have dealt with adults' recollections of traumatic and stressful events. The way in which stress and trauma can influence children's thinking about and memories for certain events in their life has been, and still is, a major and often controversial social, legal, and scientific issue. This section will focus specifically on stress, trauma, and children's memory. Due to the high profile day care child abuse cases of the late 1980s and early 1990s, there has been increased attention to children's memory skills and their credibility as eyewitnesses (see Chapter 8, and Goodman, 2006, for historical reviews). This of course has serious consequences in the legal field and understanding what influences children's memory accuracy, and developing methods to support children's memory recollection, has been the focus of much research in the eyewitness memory field. We will explore these factors in more detail in our later chapters. However, here it is important to consider the effects of emotion, stress, and trauma on children's eyewitness memory recollections.

Studying children's memory for ecologically valid as well as stressful events to simulate a forensic event poses a moral and ethical issue. We cannot deliberately expose children to high levels of stress and particularly not to traumatic events. Rather than trying to replicate a valid forensic situation in the laboratory, researchers have examined children's memory for medical procedures and injuries. Over the last 20 years this has proven to be a successful method for investigating eyewitness memory in children for naturally occurring and ecologically valid events. For example, Howe and colleagues (Howe, Courage, & Peterson, 1994, 1995) conducted a series of studies recruiting children from a hospital emergency room. Children were aged between 18 months and 5 years. In a follow up interview conducted in their homes within two to three days of treatment, children's memory for the accident and the emergency room treatment was examined. Additional interviews were conducted after six months and following a one-year delay. Free recall as well as open-ended cued recall techniques were used to elicit details of central and peripheral information. Howe et al. (1994, 1995) found that although details peripheral to the event diminished over time, the core or central aspects of the event were well remembered even after a one-year interval. Similar findings have been reported by Peterson and colleagues (see Peterson, 2012, for a review) in a large body of work examining delays of six months (Peterson, 1996; Peterson & Bell, 1996), one year (Tizzard-Drover & Peterson, 2004), two years (Peterson, 1999; Peterson, Moores, & White, 2001; Peterson, Pardy, Tizzard-Drover, & Warren, 2005), and five years (Peterson & Parsons, 2005; Peterson & Whalen, 2001). In her review, Peterson reported that older children had more complete recall than younger children and that although accuracy remained high, it did deteriorate with time. Central components were recalled significantly better than peripheral components for 2-year-olds as well as 3–4-year-olds, but no differences were found for older children.

Research has also examined the accuracy of children's recollection when they were later given incorrect and misleading information after the injury. Although we have devoted Chapter 8 to examining children's suggestibility and proneness to false memories, errors can also occur for highly emotional and traumatic events just as they do for more mundane events due to the reconstructive nature of memory. Howe et al. (1995) reported that a subset of children who had gone on to experience additional emergency room visits included details from these experiences when providing their report of the initial event, often blending these experiences into a single report. In a forensic setting, a naïve interviewer would not have been able to separate the information from the different experiences and hence not detected the error in remembering. Similar intrusion findings have been reported by a number of researchers conducting similar emergency room studies as well as examining other medical procedures (e.g., Bruck, Ceci, Francoeur, & Barr, 1995; Stuber, Nader, Yasuda, Pynoos, & Cohen, 1991). Indeed, Peterson (2012) only examined recollections from the injury event because this would be considered a more unique event in comparison with the visit to the emergency room which, if visited previously and subsequently to the event in question, would contain many similar components across visits. Thus, she argued that the injury event provides a clearer picture of how memory reports change. Of course, unlike examining the treatment for the injury where witnesses could verify what happened during treatment, studying the injury event itself can be problematic if there were no witnesses to verify what happened during the incident.

It is important to point out that children are able to remember real-life traumatic events in great detail, even over long periods of time. More central details are better recalled than peripheral, and older children will remember more than younger children. Due to the reconstructive nature of memory, there will be errors but as we will see in Chapter 8, younger children tend to produce less information when using open-ended questions, and errors will then increase dramatically when questions become more closed-ended (e.g., "Was the man wearing a hat on his head?" rather than "What was the man wearing") (Fivush, Peterson, & Schwarzmueller, 2002).

So far we have examined recollection of highly emotional events, but we have yet to consider the extent to which stress influences the accuracy of children's recall. Other naturally occurring traumatic events have been utilized to examine children's memory skills, with a particular focus on the effect of children's emotional reaction to recollection of the event itself. We have seen earlier that stress has inconsistent effects on the level of recall and accuracy in adults' memory skills, although there is some consensus that the level of stress and how we react to that stressor can alter performance. There is even less clarity on the effects of stress on children. One of the main issues facing researchers is, of course, how do you define a high stress group in children and how is stress operationalized? There have been several methods developed to assess children's stress levels. These include, for example, self-report measures, ratings of stress level provided by the parents or doctors, objective stress ratings based on specific behavioral indices such as crying and painful expression, and physiological measures such as heart rate, skin conductance, and hormonal (e.g., cortisol) levels. Research has shown that when compared, these measures of stress do not correlate highly with one another (Eisen, Goodman, Ghetti, & Qin, 1999; Ornstein, 1995; Parker, Bahrick, Lundy, Fivush, & Levitt, 1998), and they tend not to predict differences in memory performance. Although recreating extremely high levels of stress in the laboratory is not ethical, it is nevertheless important to understand how stress impacts memory, and what, if any, differences exist developmentally.

To do this, researchers have typically examined the effects of stress on prolonged memory for naturally occurring traumatic events and disasters. One of a few studies that has systematically examined the relationship between stress level in children and memory for an event was conducted by Bahrick, Parker, Fivush, and Levitt (1998). They examined how stress affected 3- to 4-year-old children and their memories for Hurricane Andrew, a storm that hit Florida in 1992 and devastated the coastal area. Children were placed into low, moderate, and high stress groups based on the amount of damage to the family's home. Children were placed in the low stress group when the family had prepared for the hurricane and had little property damage. Children were placed in the moderate stress group if their family's property had sustained substantial damage to the exterior of their home, but not the inside of the house itself. Finally, if they suffered severe damage to their house they were placed in the high stress group (also see Fivush, Sales, Goldberg, Bahrick, & Parker, 2004).

In interviews conducted two to six months after the event, children were asked to recollect details about the preparation for the storm, the storm itself, and the aftermath of the storm. Open-ended questions and non-directive prompts were used until children could no longer provide any further information. In contrast to the research reviewed earlier with adults (e.g., Yuille & Cutshall, 1986), Bahrick et al. (1998) reported that children's recall was related to the amount of stress they had experienced. Children who were in the moderate stress group recalled more than children in the high stress groups. However, in a follow-up interview six years later (Fivush et al., 2004), children were able to recall the core aspects of the event and there were no differences in the amount of recall among the children from the three stress groups. In fact, children reported twice as much detail as they did in the original interview, although this was attributed to the children's age and the ability to provide a more developed verbal report due to their increase in their language skills. Although recollection did not differ as a function of stress, Fivush et al. (2004) did report that there were signs of the effects of stress on memory six years on. Specifically, they reported that children originally placed in the high stress group needed more prompts and cues to recall as much information as the children from the two lesser stress groups. They argued that children who experience high amounts of stress at the time of the storm were still able to recall the same amount of detail but that stress interfered with the ability or willingness to retrieve information for recall. As a form of avoidance, the highly stressed children did not want to respond freely about their experiences because they found it stressful to recall the event.

Other studies have reported similar results. Wolitzky, Fivush, Zimand, Hodges, and Rothbaum (2005) found that children who were less anxious about a cancer-related medical procedure included more internal state language, demonstrating their cognitive and emotional processing during their retelling of the event. In both of these events, children who were less stressed and less anxious were able to express their thoughts and emotions concerning the event better than children who were more anxious and stressed. Again, this may be an avoidance tactic used to prevent the reliving of traumatic experiences. These findings provide some indication that not only is the amount of recall affected by stress, but also what children will focus on when reporting traumatic experiences. Children who experience high stress conditions are capable of recalling details of the event, but how much they recall may be dependent on the interview techniques used to elicit that information. The legal system may need to tread a fine line, however, between providing non-directive cues to help children who may be using avoidance tactics to speak openly about an event, and more leading questions that may elicit errors in recall. After all, such recollections, like all recollections, are subject to reconstructive memorial processes.

So far we have only considered recollections of natural disasters and traumatic medical experiences. However, research has also examined recollections of abusive experiences and the long-term effects of those experiences on memory accuracy. Accounts of childhood sexual abuse tend to be fairly durable, with the ability to recall core details lasting many years. Alexander et al. (2005) examined the predictors of memory accuracy and memory errors 12 to 21 years after documented abuse occurred in children aged 3- to 17-years of age at the time of the abuse. Individuals with more PTSD symptomatology had better encoded and rehearsed central details of their abuse experience that allowed for the mainten-ance of accurate memory over the long term compared with victims who had fewer PTSD symptoms. Alexander et al. argued that for high PTSD sufferers, CSA was a highly emotional event and the emotion-related semantic network that resulted may have facilitated memory retention (see also Howe & Malone, 2011). Those with fewer PTSD symptoms associated with the abusive event may have actively avoided discussing the abusive event, leading to poorer long-term mem-ory. Alexander et al. concluded that memory for emotional events and trauma-related information is generally well retained and that this better retention is correlated with the degree of PTSD symptomology (also see Paunovic, Lundh, & Oest, 2002).

In addition to these differences due to PTSD, Alexander et al. also found that accuracy rates for documented abuse were reasonably high. Specifically, they found that even after some 12 to 21 years since the abuse occurred, 72% of what was recalled was correct. Of the 28% that was not correct, 14% were errors of omission (forgetting) and the remaining 14% were errors of commission (false memories). Interestingly, the more severe the abuse the more accurate the memory.

Despite certain inconsistencies in the methodological procedures and measures of stress utilized, it is tempting to conclude that the evidence from this body of literature suggests that children's memory for traumatic events is more durable than for more mundane events. Indeed, it would appear that memory is better for central compared with peripheral details, and older children remember more than younger children, although with age, recollections become more detailed, due to the development of better encoding, storage, and retrieval skills (Howe, 2011). However, it is important to point out that contrasts between memory for traumatic and non-traumatic events has typically been conducted between participants rather than within the same individual. It is only by contrasting memories for these different types of events within the same person that we can really discover whether these types of memory differ independent of individual differences in general memory and language skills.

There are only a handful of studies that have compared both traumatic and non-traumatic memories within rather than across individuals. For example, Fivush, Hazzard, Sales, Sarfati, and Brown (2003) examined children's (5 to 12-year-olds) memories for traumatic events (e.g., serious illness or death, violent altercations, parental separation) and non-traumatic events (e.g., vacations, parties). They found no differences in the length of narrative produced by the children as a function of event type. Although there were no quantitative differences, there were qualitative differences in what was being remembered. Specifically, for non-traumatic events, children included more descriptions of people and objects involved in those events than in the traumatic events. For these latter events, they included more descriptions of their' and others' emotional and cognitive states during the event. Thus, although narrative length might not differ, the content of the narratives does differ for children's memory of non-traumatic and traumatic events.

Others have found that narratives about traumatic experiences can be longer than those for non-traumatic experiences. For example, Sales, Fivush, and Peterson (2003) examined mother–child conversations about positive (e.g., vacation) and traumatic (e.g., emergency room treatment) events and found that the latter narratives were longer than the former ones. Interestingly, and also unlike the Fivush et al. (2003) findings, Sales et al. (2003) found that talk about emotions was greater for positive than traumatic events. One reason for the differences between these studies might be the different ages of the children in the different studies. Specifically, children in the Sales et al. study were aged between 3 and 5 years old whereas those in the Fivush et al. study were 5- to 12-years old.

Finally, Bauer, Burch, van Abbema, and Ackil (2008) examined children's repeated recall (over time) of a traumatic and a non-traumatic event. The traumatic event was a tornado that devastated the small (population 9500), rural town of St. Peter in Minnesota in 1998. The tornado had winds exceeding 200 miles per hour and cut a destructive path through the town that was 1.25 miles wide. The tornado took the life of one 6-year-old who was well known to most of the participants in the study, damaged 75% of the town's homes, and completely destroyed (or made irreparable) 28% of the homes (see Bauer et al., 2008). The effects on the town were long lasting and included loss of power for at least a week, 2100 children were out of school for over a week, and once back in school children of all ages attended the same school in shifts for the remainder of the academic year.

Bauer et al. (2008) conducted two interviews of mother–child pairs about the tornado and a non-traumatic event (e.g., a birthday party), one 4 months after the storm and the other one 10 months after the storm. The two non-traumatic events were unrelated to the tornado although one had taken place prior to the tornado and the other one had taken place after the tornado. They found that conversations about the tornado at both 4 and 10 months were twice as long as those about the non-traumatic events and the length of the conversations about the non-traumatic events did not differ. Of course, as Bauer et al. point out, one reason why conversations about the storm might have been longer is that there is simply more to talk about. Moreover, longer conversations do not necessarily mean that memories are richer for those events. When Bauer et al. controlled conversation length, although the content of the conversations differed as a function of event type, children's contributions to the conversations did not differ in level of detail as a function of event type.

So, if memories for traumatic events are more durable than those for more mundane events, and as we have seen not all studies have shown this, then what would be the cause? Researchers have considered the importance of adaptive significance. For example, Foa and Rothbaum (1998) argued that the preservation of such memories will help ensure the organism's future survival as they will need to remember to avoid similar threatening events in the future. Autobiographical memory research also shows that any experience that is distinctive and personally significant will be better remembered (Brewer, 1986; Conway, 1996; Howe, 1997). Such explanations of distinctiveness have also been replicated in the laboratory (Howe, Courage, Vernescu, & Hunt, 2000). Indeed, findings support the idea for considerable continuity between memory processes that govern recollection of traumatic experiences and those that govern laboratory-based memory experiences (Howe et al., 2011).

Trauma-related psychopathology and cognitive functioning

Much of the research we have covered so far considers eyewitness testimony and memory accuracy of non-abused children who have experienced an emotionally negative or traumatic event. However, there is some research that has examined how experiences of maltreatment and the consequences of long-term abuse affect children's eyewitness memory and suggestibility. For example, there is a growing body of research that has looked at maltreated children's memory in laboratory-based studies. In one such study, Baugerud, Howe, Magnussen, and Melinder (2016) used a false memory task (the DRM paradigm) to examine differences in true and false memory rates for emotional and neutral word lists in maltreated and non-maltreated children (see also Howe, Cicchetti, Toth, & Cerrito, 2004; Howe et al., 2011). Non-maltreated children showed better true memory performance compared with maltreated children regardless of list type. However, for false memories, although maltreated children did not differ in comparison with non-maltreated children for neutral lists, they produced significantly more false memories for emotional word lists. Goodman et al. (2011) found a similar result with higher false recall for trauma-related words in maltreated adolescents. Baugerud et al. (2016) argued that maltreated children could be more prone to false memories for negatively valenced materials because they are more sensitized to the negative information which may heighten arousal. Unfortunately, these children are also more familiar with negative emotional stimuli, thus enhancing the ease with which these negative words are activated and ultimately wrongfully recalled. These studies are important to the understanding of maltreated children's basic memory processes. However, it is also critical to consider how maltreated children will perform in more applied eyewitness situations.

Eisen, Qin, Goodman, and Davis (2002) highlighted the importance of examining children in eyewitness memory studies with a history of maltreatment. This is particularly relevant given that such children would be highly likely to be interviewed in a forensic setting. Accuracy in such reports would be crucial given the legal and social service implications. It is important to ensure the credibility of the witness and be aware of any cognitive factors in maltreated children that may cause inaccurate representations of abusive events or possibly even implicate adults who were innocent of any action. Likewise, we need to be aware of how maltreatment and long-term exposure to traumatic events influence forgetting and know just how much information we should expect an abused child to provide. Indeed, trauma theorists who examine memory accuracy in the adult population have shown significant relationships between dissociation, known to be a clinically relevant factor in the history of abuse and trauma, and suggestibility. Perhaps as Putnam (1997) argued, the lack of confidence in memory caused by dissociation (a protective coping mechanism to avoid thinking about the event) leaves the individual open to suggestion, something which can serve to help fill in the gaps of their own autobiographical memory.

Supporting evidence for this has come from studies that show positive correlations between dissociative experience scores and imagined events (Heaps & Nash, 1999) as well as errors on misleading questions (Merckelbach, Muris, Rassin, & Horselenberg, 2000). Interestingly, no differences are evident for memory performance when misinformation is not explicitly provided (van den Hout, Merckelbach, & Pool, 1996). Despite these findings, limited research has investigated the relationship of trauma-related psychopathology, such as dissociation and PTSD, with memory performance and suggestibility in children. Furthermore, research has suggested that maltreatment experiences can have adverse effects on memory via physiological mechanisms (Bremner, Krystal, Southwick, & Charney, 1995; Rausch, 1996; but see De Bellis, Hall, Boring, Frustaci, & Moritz, 2001) and cause delays in cognitive development (e.g., Eigsti & Cicchetti, 2004; McFadyen & Kitson, 1996), which all have negative "knock-on" effects for children's memory accuracy (e.g., Henry & Gudjonsson, 2003).

In one of a few studies that has examined trauma related psychopathology in children, Chae, Goodman, Eisen, and Qin (2011; see also Eisen, Goodman, Qin, Davis, & Crayton, 2007; Eisen et al., 2002) investigated memory accuracy for a social interaction with an unfamiliar adult in maltreated children aged 3- to 16-years old. Children were divided into five abuse classifications based on the Child Protective Services records and the hospital unit assessments. These included a sexually abused group, a physically abused group, both a sexually and physically abused group, a neglected group, and a control (not maltreated) group. Four days after the social encounter children were interviewed. The memory interview included a free recall period, followed by a series of misleading and non-misleading yes/no questions. Measures of individual differences in psychopathology including dissociation as well as PTSD, depression, anxiety, and general cognitive functioning were also recorded. Results showed that physically or sexually abused children scored highest on dissociation measures compared with neglected children and children with no reported abuse history. Overall, older children showed greater accuracy with fewer errors. Abuse classification status did not significantly predict memory performance or suggestibility but suggestibility was highest among children who scored high on dissociative measures. Other measures of psychopathology, including PTSD, did not uniquely contribute to children's memory accuracy. Chae et al. (2011) concluded that children with a high self-report of trauma symptoms and who scored high for dissociative tendencies have greater difficulty in remembering previous events. This could be due to poor source-monitoring performance or, similar to findings with adult sufferers, subject to response bias tendencies or greater suggestibility (e.g., Eisen & Carlson, 1998). Cognitive functioning, as measured by short-term memory tests, intelligence, and verbal skills, significantly correlated with memory performance and susceptibility to suggestibility. Those children with higher cognitive functioning scores were better able to provide more correct details to the free recall questions and produced fewer errors when asked misleading questions. Similar to children with no history of maltreatment (e.g., Chae & Ceci, 2005), children with poorer short-term memory skills appear to lack efficient memory monitoring strategies and become less certain of their own recollections, thus becoming more susceptible to misleading information. Further, those with limited verbal skills may find it more difficult to describe their experiences or understand the questions being asked.

It appears from this research that, in general, maltreated children are as accurate in their memory performance as children with no recorded or known maltreatment. However, work by Eisen and colleagues has shown that children who score high on trauma related psychopathology scales, and those with delayed cognitive functioning, are more susceptible to suggestion and to misleading information and are more likely to produce memory errors. These findings, and those from the laboratory (e.g., Baugerud et al., 2016), should be carefully considered when the legal professions conduct interviews and evaluate the reliability of eyewitness testimony from maltreated children. However, in general, the relationship between emotion and memory in terms of developmental changes has been under-investigated and further research in this area needs to focus on developmental differences in the effects of emotion, stress, and psychopathology as a result of child abuse to allow for a more complete understanding of the effects of these factors on memory reports.

Conclusion

This summary of the evidence examining the effects of stress and exposure to negative events on eyewitness memory illustrates the considerable progress that has been made over the last 40 years. However, it also highlights some of the serious inconsistencies in these findings. Although there are a number of studies that we have not covered in this chapter, their inclusion would not change the conclusions we have reached. Indeed, one of the major problems with all of this research is that there are a variety of inconsistencies across studies, ones that are confounded by the implementation of diverse methods used to manipulate stress, what type of event is being studied, variations in the types of questioning used to elicit memory, and lack of standardization of the delay between initial exposure to an event and when questioning takes place. Taken together, with the possible caveat that results of laboratory studies may overestimate eyewitness memory performance, especially when eyewitnesses are in a state of heightened stress (Ihlebaek, Love, Eilertsen, & Magnussen, 2003), there is still a lot for the field of science to uncover in order to be able to fully inform legal professionals about the role of stress and emotion on eyewitness memory. Although there is considerable neurobiological evidence attesting to the impact that stress and trauma can have on the encoding, storage, and retrieval of event memories, the behavioral evidence is not as clear cut. Thus, although emotion and stress can have a powerful influence on eyewitness memory, its influence may be greater on the neural systems underlying memory than on the behavioral expression of those memories.

7

EYEWITNESS IDENTIFICATION

Theory, evidence, and procedural implications

On September 18, 2003, Calvin Willis was released from prison after serving over 21 years for a crime he did not commit. In 1982 Willis was tried and convicted for the rape of a 10-year-old girl in Shreveport, Louisiana. In June 1981, an intruder entered a home where three girls – aged 10, 9, and 7 – had fallen asleep. Two of the girls had fallen asleep on the couch, the third in bed. The intruder carried the nine-year-old to the bed, where her seven-year-old sister was sleeping. The 10-year-old victim awoke and saw a man standing above her, naked except for a cowboy hat. The attacker choked her and hit her head against the wall. The victim was able to escape and ran from the intruder, but was caught in the front yard. She was kicked in the stomach and lost consciousness. Her two younger sisters heard the noises but remained in the bedroom. Their mother did not return to the house until the morning.

What led to the conviction of Calvin Willis? When the police began their investigation, the interviews of the three girls produced inconsistencies in their statements. The nine-year-old girl could not identify the perpetrator's face but described his shoes, which were shaped like cowboy boots. At trial, the girl identified Willis by his boots, though her testimony of what the boots looked like differed from the boots Willis was arrested in two days after the crime. She testified that she did not see the attacker's face. The seven-year-old girl had been asleep but awoke when she heard the victim's cries and the attacker's threats to kill her. She identified the voice as that of Calvin Willis, whom she had spoken with once. One police report said the 10-year-old victim did not see her attacker's face. Another report – which was not introduced at trial – said she identified Calvin Willis, who lived in the neighborhood. The girl's mother testified that Willis had been in her house before, he was known to wear a cowboy hat, and she had seen him in boots similar to those described by her daughter. The police testimony also differed with regard to the photographic evidence. An investigator testified that she showed the victim a lineup that included Willis' photograph because the victim had said that Calvin was the attacker. Her mother provided the last name of Willis. The victim's mother testified that Willis' name did not come up before the lineup. Upon further questioning, however, she testified that the victim had said Calvin did it before they were taken to the police station and that he had been wearing a cowboy hat and cowboy boots. The victim testified that she was told to pick the man in the photographic lineup that did not have a full beard. She also testified that she did not pick anyone from the lineup and that Willis' picture was not part of the array. The victim never made an in-court identification of Willis but stated that Calvin was standing above her when she awoke. Willis was convicted by a jury and sentenced to life in prison. In 1998 his case was accepted by the Innocence Project and a post-conviction DNA test of the rape kit and a pair of boxers left at the scene of the crime excluded Willis as the perpetrator of the rape that occurred in 1981 and ultimately led to his sentence of life without the possibility of parole (see "Innocence Project – Calvin Willis," 2003).

Eyewitness testimony that directly implicates an alleged perpetrator is compelling evidence in any trial and a single witness' identification can often be enough to obtain a conviction. However, eyewitness misidentification is one of the greatest causes of wrongful convictions worldwide. Recall that the Innocence Project and Innocence Network UK projects (non-profit legal clinics founded in 1992 by Barry C. Scheck and Peter J. Neufeld in association with the Benjamin N. Cardozo School of Law at Yeshiva University and in the UK, more recently, by Dr. Michael Naughton of Bristol University in 2004) are litigation and public policy organizations, as well as University run projects, dedicated to exonerating wrongfully convicted people through DNA testing. A report published by the Innocence Project (Innocence Project, 2009) stated that over 230 people, serving an average of 12 years in prison, have been exonerated through post-conviction DNA testing in the United States alone. Of those wrongfully convicted, over 75% involved eyewitness misidentification (179 people).

This report highlights a number of other worrying statistics. For example, of those 179 individual cases, 38% were based on multiple eyewitness misidentifications of the same innocent suspect. Fifty-three percent involved cross-racial misidentifications. In 50% of the misidentification cases there was no further corroborating evidence and the eyewitness testimony was the central evidence used against the defendant. Worse, in 36% of these cases, the real perpetrator was identified through the post-conviction DNA test, and in just fewer than 50% of these cases, they had gone on to commit additional crimes of rape and murder. Unfortunately, most crimes, even today, do not include DNA-rich biological traces, and the reliance on eyewitness testimony has not been diminished by the development of forensic-DNA testing (Wells & Olson, 2003). Eyewitness testimony is still among the most prevalent and persuasive pieces of evidence used in the courtroom. As Davis and Loftus (2012, p. 2) note, "The U.S. legal system currently allows conviction of criminal charges based solely on the testimony of a single eyewitness. It is therefore of considerable importance to ask whether the eyewitness accuracy is sufficient to warrant a conclusion of guilt beyond a reasonable doubt."

Similarly, in the United Kingdom, the reliability of eyewitness identification has been attracting concern from the legal professions for at least 100 years (Valentine, Darling, & Memon, 2006). Valentine et al. (2006) refer to the 1904 trials of Adolf Beck, who, on two separate occasions, was wrongfully convicted of jewelry theft based on mistaken identification. In both trials, Beck was identified by multiple eyewitnesses even though both crimes were subsequently found to have been committed by William Wyatt. In 1904 the committee of enquiry led directly to the establishment of a Court of Appeal. Further concerns about wrongful convictions in the United Kingdom based on eyewitness misidentification led to a government enquiry in 1976 led by Lord Devlin (Devlin, 1976). The report led the English Court of Appeal to establish a requirement that in cases of disputed identification, the trial judge is required to caution the jury members about the issues surrounding eyewitness identification and that the judge should highlight that confidence in identification does not necessarily lead to accuracy in identification (*R. v. Turnball,* 1977).

Eyewitness identification procedures used in the United States and United Kingdom have some important differences. In the United States, live lineups and identification from arrays of photographs are both frequently used to collect formal eyewitness identification, whereas traditionally, in the United Kingdom, formal eyewitness identification evidence has typically been obtained from live/video lineups unless the suspect is not available and in which case still images may be used (Police and Criminal Evidence Act or PACE, Code D, 2011). Regardless of the differences in procedures adopted to ascertain eyewitness identification, there are a number of factors that will affect the reliability of these identifications in both cases.

When criminal conviction is based on eyewitness identification there are two substantial issues. First, what is the accuracy of human memory and under what circumstances can we provide sufficiently reliable evidence? Second, in the court, what ability do the observers have in judging the accuracy of witnesses' memories and in using this judgment to reach appropriate decisions? Although we will address the latter in the coming chapters, considerable research has examined the limits of human memory and the conditions under which distortions can frequently occur. The end goal is to understand the conditions that lead to the most accurate eyewitness testimony and to develop instructions for judges and juries that help in the assessment of the accuracy of a particular eyewitness' statement. Based on this research we can inform the legal system regarding some basic limits of performance and we can aid in preventing identification conditions that may hinder accuracy further. However, as Davis and Loftus (2012) warn, there is much evidence to suggest that, even under the best conditions, eyewitness accuracy may still not be sufficient to allow for convictions based solely on the testimony of one or more eyewitnesses. It is important to understand the limits of memory, limitations that include not just factors that affect an eyewitness' suggestibility (also see Chapter 8), but also those factors that affect our perceptual capacities. We turn to an exploration of these factors in the next section.

Factors that influence eyewitness identification

Research conducted in the field of psychological science on eyewitness memory over the past 100 years (see Clark, Moreland, & Gronlund, 2014; Loftus, 1979; Munsterberg, 1908) has helped develop procedural reforms that have been embraced by leading national justice organizations including the National Institute of Justice (NIJ) and the American Bar Association. Guidelines for understanding and assessing the reliability of eyewitness identification have been set out in influential legal decisions (*Manson v. Braithwaite, 1977; Neil v. Bigger screen, 1972*) and the procedures that have been recommended are designed to increase the accuracy of eyewitness identification measures. Such recommendations include better procedures for constructing lineups, presenting individuals in lineups sequentially rather than all at once, refraining from post-identification feedback that may influence the witness' decision and confidence, and informing the witness of the culprit's potential absence from the lineup. It is important to note that although the NIJ provided detailed instructions for eyewitness identification procedures to the approximately 18,000 state and local law enforcement agencies across the United States, only a few states have engaged in these improvement efforts and implemented these new procedures. Consequently, in America, eyewitness identification policies remain fragmented by jurisdiction (National Research Council, 2014).

In the United Kingdom, there have been recent developments in England and Wales (although this does not apply to Scotland and Northern Ireland) in Code D of the Police and Criminal Evidence Act of 1984, which was revised in 2011, and the current code of practice refers to the importance of the similarity of the foils in the lineup, that the witness be advised that the person they saw may or may not be present, that they do not need to make a positive identification, and that video identification is preferred over the use of live identification. Despite these revisions, there are still a number of important factors that can affect the accuracy of the eyewitness. Indeed, work continues to be done to understand the effects of these factors on eyewitness identification and to recommend additional reforms in the legal system that adequately address these potential consequences.

In order to address these questions, researchers in the field of eyewitness testimony consider two categories of variables that affect the accuracy of eyewitness identification. Introduced in the 1970s (Wells, 1978), *estimator variables* often refer to the limits of human memory (factors that affect encoding or retrieval of the event), which we have no control over, and *system variables* (or procedural variables), which can be controlled by the criminal justice system which could influence eyewitness decisions. This partitioning of variables that influence identification accuracy led to a steady flow of experimental work over the next 40 years that revealed weaknesses in both the memories of the eyewitnesses but also, and most importantly for the applied nature of this research, in the methods through which the justice system extracts those memories.

Estimator variables

Estimator variables tend to be associated with factors that affect the eyewitness or factors that are operating either at the time of the criminal event (factors that may influence the encoding of the event) or the time between witnessing an event and the identification process (length of retention interval). Research has shown that eyewitnesses level of stress or trauma at the time of the incident can effect recollection (see Chapter 6) but also, the level of light that could affect visibility and the clarity of a perpetrator's features, the physical distance between the witness and the perpetrator, distinguishing features of the perpetrator, simple disguises the perpetrator may be wearing (Cutler, Penrod, & Martens, 1987), whether the witness is aware a crime is taking place (Leippe, Wells, & Ostrom, 1978), age of the witness, particular biases in own-race identification, and the presence or absence of a weapon (Loftus, Loftus, & Messo, 1987). We will focus on just a few of these factors below.

Age

Extensive research has examined the age of the eyewitness. Typically, very young children and the elderly have been shown to perform significantly worse than young adults. In a review conducted by Fitzgerald and Price (2015) they report that, without question, the most influential finding in the child eyewitness identification literature is that children are more likely to choose an innocent lineup member from culprit-absent lineups. Pozzulo and Lindsay (1998) reviewed nine studies that compared children's and adult's culprit-absent lineup results. Correct rejection rates were lower for all young child age groups (4, 5–6, 7–8, and 12–13 years) compared with young adults.

The difficulty with such a task is likely due to several issues. First, children are sensitive to the social demands of the lineup task. That is, children tend to give the answer the interviewer wants to hear (Bruck & Ceci, 1999). Although it is not a suggestive or leading question, if an authority figure is presenting photographs for a lineup, the child will assume that the culprit is present and they must pick the "right" picture (Lowenstein, Blank, & Sauer, 2010). More recent studies have included an instruction that warns children of the possibility that the culprit may not be in the lineup, but even with this caution, children are less likely to reject the innocent members of the lineup (Keast, Brewer, & Wells, 2007).

Second, children have not developed the cognitive skills needed to produce an appropriate response to reject a culprit in a culprit-absent lineup. A recall-to-reject strategy is needed in such cases. This is a far more difficult task than making a familiarity decision. In developing a recall-to-reject strategy, the child needs to be able to recall contextual details such as where and when the person was encountered before being able to make the appropriate response (Gross & Hayne, 1996). To correctly identify that the culprit is absent, the witness must bring to mind the culprit and then make comparisons of this representation with each member of the lineup. Recall-to-reject is a harder cognitive task than recognition based on familiarity and may pose too great a task for young children.

Other issues include the inability to withhold an inappropriate response due to response inhibition immaturity in children (Nigg, 2000). That is, children are inclined to choose an innocent person in a lineup because they have an inability to stop themselves from responding positively. Yet other researchers (Davies, Tarrant, & Flin, 1989; Diamond & Carey, 1977) propose that children use less appropriate face-processing strategies such as a feature-by-feature-based approach (extracting distinctive features such as eyes and nose for face recognition) instead of a holistic-processing strategy (the ability to construct a perceptual integration of all facial features to identify the face) (although not all research has shown this to be the case, see Crookes & McKone, 2009). There are clearly several explanations for children's increased likelihood of falsely identifying an innocent member of a lineup and it almost certainly involves a combination of the factors listed above.

There is an additional finding in the child eyewitness identification literature which is at first glance somewhat surprising. Where culprit-present lineups are used, children aged five years and older often make correct identifications at rates similar to those for young adults. Indeed, the evidence appears strong for this claim. In one meta-analysis (Pozzulo & Lindsay, 1998), all of the children except 4-year-olds were as likely to correctly identify a culprit in culprit-present lineups as adults, and that 5–6-year-olds produced a higher correct identification rate than adults. However, Fitzgerald and Price (2015) have argued that although this research demonstrates that children can achieve similar correct identification rates to those of adults, these reports of equivalent performance may not be indicative of equivalent ability. That is, the likely reason for children's poor performance in culprit-absent and good performance in culprit-present lineups is a general tendency to respond with a yes. We refer to this in the cognitive literature as a liberal response bias (Green & Swets, 1966). Such an explanation has not received full attention because it has become common practice to not report rejection rates for culprit-present lineups (see Fitzgerald & Price, 2015). In their more recent meta-analysis taking into account post 1998 age-related identification studies with children, Fitzgerald and Price (2015) used grouped data from culprit-absent and culprit-present lineups to produce signal detection measures. As predicted, young adults were better than children at discriminating the guilty from the innocent suspects in the lineup. At a practical level therefore, young children's sensitivity to the presence or absence of the culprit in a lineup raises doubts about children's ability to make correct identifications and rejections during trial.

At the opposite end of the age spectrum, research into older adult eyewitnesses has received considerably less attention. However, the research that has been conducted has typically shown a similar pattern to that of children. That is, older adults have higher false identification rates in culprit-absent lineups and similar levels of correct identifications in culprit-present lineups (see Bartlett, 2014). Similar to the child witness literature, both cognitive and, to a lesser extent social, factors have been suggested to explain the greater propensity to choose an innocent person in the culprit-absent lineups. However, the underlying social influence factor differs for older adults compared with children. Although research has been limited in this area, what research there is shows that rather than compliance with an authoritative figure, older adults are particularly motivated to "help" with police investigations and that it is this tendency to help that may be the critical factor that biases lineup choice (e.g., Sporer & Martschuk, 2014). One of the other main concerns with older adults is their memory for the target. Age-related memory deficits in older adults are well known but these can be minimized with environmental or contextual support (Anderson & Craik, 2000), including context reinstatement or pre-identification practice trials that reduce older adults' misidentification rates (Wilcock & Bull, 2010; but see Memon, Hope, Bartlett, & Bull, 2002). Interestingly, for intervention work, sequential presentation of lineup members has been shown to reduce older adults' misidentification rates but also reduce correct identification rates (e.g., Memon & Gabbert, 2003). Although a pattern reported with the general use of sequential presentation (see later for a discussion of the different types of lineups), the effect is more exaggerated with older adults. In sequential presentation, each face is viewed separately and an absolute decision has to be made for each. In their study, Memon and Gabbert (2003) found that for correct target identification, the corresponding proportions were .09 (9) and .31 (25) for young and old participants, respectively. Although target position in the sequence may be an important factor, they argued that the older adults may find it more difficult to ignore "familiar" foils when asked to make an absolute decision for each face.

Own-race bias

Another important estimator variable that has been examined extensively over the past 25 years is cross-racial identification. Research has shown a robust effect where people show better recognition for faces of their own racial group compared with faces from a different racial group (own-race bias, Meissner & Brigham, 2001). An effect unknown at the time, but one that played a crucial role in the famous "Quincy Five" case. In 1971, five black men were arrested for the murder of Thomas Revels. Despite the lack of any physical evidence, the positive identification from five white eyewitnesses was enough to convict them of the crime. They were only exonerated when the real perpetrators were found and convicted based on latent fingerprint evidence (see Meissner & Brigham, 2001).

Own-race bias is now a widely recognized phenomenon within the legal system. The Innocence Project (2009) has reported that in 53% of wrongful convictions caused by misidentification, the witness and the perpetrator were of different races. Cross-racial misidentifications in the DNA exoneration cases involve an African-American or Latino defendant 99% of the time. Most now agree that own-race bias (also known as the cross-race or other-race effect) occurs reliably in a number of cultural and racial groups (Kassin et al., 1989).

In the laboratory, the own-race bias effect has shown robust findings. In 2001, Meissner and Brigham conducted a meta-analysis of 39 research articles and showed that hits and false alarm rates were consistent with an own-race mirror-effect pattern. That is, own-race faces produced a higher proportion of hits and a lower proportion of false alarms compared with other-race faces. A number of different theoretical frameworks have been developed to explain the cognitive and social mechanisms that may explain this phenomenon. Early theoretical explanations included physiognomic differences between races and later, interracial contact and the involvement of a perceptual learning mechanism (for an interesting discussion of how other-race bias effects may have their origins in infancy, see Anzures et al., 2013).

McClelland and Chappell's (1998) model of recognition memory provides a framework that is consistent with the above findings. In this model, individuals store features of a given stimulus in memory and these features are updated in the representation each time the individual encounters that stimulus. With regard to the own-race bias effect, individuals store own-race faces more accurately and efficiently with respect to the appropriate featural and configural information represented in memory. This is likely the result of prior experience with own-race faces that allows us to attend to invariant aspects of the face. Other-race faces are encoded in a less efficient manner in which fewer cues are selected for storage (see Meissner & Brigham, 2001, for a full review). One particularly important finding from this meta-analysis indicated that, when responding to other-race faces, participants increasingly adopted a more liberal response criterion as the length of time between study and test increased. Thus, participants required less evidence from memory (e.g., familiarity or memorability of the face) to respond positively that they had seen an other-race face. Given that the length of time between viewing a suspect and being asked to identify that person can vary dramatically (from days to weeks or even years), the legal community needs to be aware of these effects of time (for a meta-analysis concerning the importance of time in eyewitness identification, see Deffenbacher, Bornstein, McGorty, & Penrod, 2008; also see Dysart & Lindsay, 2007).

There are often a number of estimator, or event-related or person-related estimator, variables that the legal system cannot control. Any changes in policy concerning the interviewing of eyewitnesses will not make identifications any more accurate because these factors cannot be altered or eliminated. What is important is to educate the legal system and jurors about the research concerning these factors and to make them aware of the limitations they pose on eyewitness accuracy. To see how these factors are important, consider the following case from the Innocence Project (2009):

Case: *Larry Fuller*
Sentence Served: *19.5 years*
Conviction: *Aggravated rape*

If these shortcomings in eyewitness identification had been understood, maybe Larry Fuller would not have been arrested and convicted for aggravated rape in 1981. He served a 19.5-year sentence before being exonerated by DNA testing. Although the case was further compromised by procedural errors, there were a number of estimator variables that the police should have taken into account when the witness made their identification.

First, the victim initially informed the police that she could not provide a description of the perpetrator because of the limited lighting. The attack took place in the victim's bedroom at 6 a.m., 45 minutes before dawn. Second, the perpetrator carried a knife that he used to cut her hand, neck, and back, causing a possible weapon focus effect[1]. Finally, the victim was Caucasian and the perpetrator was African-American. The police and the legal system should have paid more attention to these factors and heeded caution in the arrest and subsequent conviction of Larry Fuller.

In the initial investigation, the police showed the victim six photos and although the victim stated that the photo of Fuller looked a lot like the guy, she could not make a positive identification. After the initial police interview, a report was issued stating that the investigation should be "suspended" because the victim "was unsure of the suspect at the time." What followed ultimately led to the wrongful arrest and prosecution of Larry Fuller. Despite this initial report, the police remained focused on Fuller. In a follow-up interview the police showed the victim a second photo array consisting of three Polaroid pictures. Fuller's photo was the only one that was repeated from the original array. Of particular interest was the fact that this second Polaroid was taken one week after the attack and Fuller had a full beard. The victim said her attacker did not have facial hair but still positively identified him. Fuller was arrested and the case went to trial, where the prosecution told the jury that the victim had "never wavered" in identifying him. The jury deliberated for 35 minutes before returning a guilty verdict. As we will see, juries are often informed that the eyewitnesses who testify express complete confidence that they had chosen the perpetrator. This is likely seen as powerful evidence at the time of the trial. However, they are often not informed that initial confidence is very often low and that there are frequently expressions of uncertainty. Although it is still possible to make a positive identification under the circumstances the victim faced in this case, a number of procedural errors further compromised this case.

As we have seen throughout this book, we do not capture a perfect, error-free memory trace of a witnessed event. What we perceive and subsequently remember can be heavily influenced by a number of factors including biases, cultural factors, emotions, prior experiences of the world, delay, and of course, ordinary limits of human memory and perception. However, even in the most ideal of situations, accuracy can be hindered merely by the fact that the appearance of the face at both initial exposure (during the crime itself) and subsequent identification procedures will differ. That is, unlike standard lineup target identification procedures used in the laboratory, in real life, we do not see the same identical presentation of the face at both study and test. Although reviewed extensively elsewhere (see Bruce, 2009), there is a wealth of research that shows that any variation between the exact appearance of the target during initial exposure and subsequent identification tests leads to a decline in performance. These differences can arise because of simple issues such as having two different photos of the same individual, differences in the media used to present the face at exposure and test (live vs. photo, live vs. film, etc.), or differences in viewing angles and lighting. On its own, this poses a serious concern given the fact that an eyewitness to a real-life crime will never see an identical presentation of the suspect from that which they saw during the crime itself. Together these, as well as other factors, limit human cognition and these limits compromise performance in eyewitness identification. As we will see next, in addition to these limitations, suggestion and the exposure to new information may influence and distort what the individual believes she or he has seen (National Research Council, 2014).

System variables

A growing body of applied research has also shown us that key system variables, such as lineup procedures (e.g., how the lineup is structured, how witnesses are instructed prior to viewing the lineup) and the collection and use of witness confidence statements, can have a marked influence over the validity and accuracy of eyewitness identifications. Whereas understanding estimator variables can, at best, help instruct the legal community about the fallibility of memory, understanding system variables and the development of procedures to overcome bad practice can help prevent inaccurate identifications from occurring in the first place (Wells & Olson, 2003).

Lineup composition

Lineup composition is a primary issue in the eyewitness identification literature. A suitable lineup should contain a single suspect alongside a number of filler or foil members. In the legal context, the police will be uncertain about the suspect's guilt or innocence. Laboratory replication of this scenario therefore requires two types of mock lineups: target present (guilty suspect/culprit is present in the lineup) and target absent (culprit is absent and thus the suspect is innocent).[2] By using both types of mock lineups we can consider procedural manipulations that can not only decrease the likelihood of false identification of the innocent suspect but also what factors may decrease the likelihood of correct identification of a guilty suspect (Clark & Godfrey, 2009).

So, what criteria should the police use to select the lineup fillers? Of course, for applied research, experimenters can use their knowledge of the culprit's identity to select fillers in a systematic fashion to see which features are important for identification purposes. However, for the police, often the identity of the culprit is not known. Instead, a suspect is taken as the central tendency and the lineup is made of fillers with similar characteristics to the suspect. Some researchers argue that this is not the most ideal method for lineup composition. Using the suspect as the central tendency can create a "backfire effect" as they may have an increased chance of being identified as the culprit if they were the original reference point to create the fillers (Clark & Tunnicliff, 2001). Instead, Wells and colleagues (Wells, Rydell, & Seelau, 1993; Wells, Seelau, Rydell, & Luus, 1994) suggested a fit-to-description strategy where fillers are selected based upon the eyewitnesses' verbal descriptions (also see Malpass, Tredoux, & McQuiston-Surrett, 2007). This method has been shown to work well (e.g., see Tunnicliff & Clark, 2000) but it is not without its flaws and oftentimes this approach does not increase identification accuracy (Clark & Godfrey, 2009; Valentine, Darling, & Memon, 2007). Indeed, biases still remain against the innocent with this method when the verbal description is sparse (Clark & Tunnicliff, 2001). To date, there is still no consensus on how best to select fillers for lineups. However, the evidence does indicate that a more accurate identification should come if the lineup contains multiple fillers who are reasonable competitors for the culprit and thus the suspect does not unduly stand out (see Gronlund, Goodsell, & Andersen, 2012).

This final point is an important one. Research suggests that the police suspect should not unfairly stand out. Unfair lineup procedures may make the witness more likely to identify the police suspect. Again, we only need to refer to the Innocence Project cases (see *www.innocenceproject.org*) to find evidence of this effect. For example, Leonard Callace was identified in a police lineup for the sexual assault of an 18-year-old nursing home aide in 1985. The description given to the police at the time of the assault was of a man with reddish-blond afro style hair and a full beard with a cross tattoo on his left hand. Although Callace had a trimmed beard, he had long hair and a small cross on his right hand. In the lineup he appeared with five men who only had moustaches. Callace was picked from the lineup and served six years in prison before being exonerated by DNA evidence.

In one of a number of studies on this subject, Colloff, Wade, and Strange (2016) examined the importance of preventing suspects with distinctive features from standing out in lineups. Previous research has shown that suspects who stand out (have visible tattoos, piercing, scars, distinctive facial hair, etc.) are prone to be selected. However, is this a result of the unfair lineup that ultimately biases the witness to choose the police suspect or because unfair lineups make it more difficult for witnesses to determine whether the lineup contains the actual culprit? Colloff et al. (2016) examined whether unfair lineups reduce the ability of a witness to distinguish between innocent and guilty suspects as well as their ability to judge the accuracy of their own identifications. Colloff et al. used standard target-present and target-absent lineup procedures and varied the foils/suspect photographs so that a distinctive feature of the suspect was left alone (unfair lineup) or was hidden and similarly covered for all foils (fair lineup). Unfair lineups increased the willingness of the witness to identify the suspect but also impaired their ability to distinguish between lineup suspects who were guilty or innocent and accurately judge the trustworthiness of their identification decision. Because unfair lineups affect the ability to distinguish between innocent and guilty suspects, police need to consider how distinctive suspects may stand out and the biasing effect this can have on witness identification of the police suspect. Colloff et al. concluded that the police need to apply fair lineup techniques to improve accuracy in identification.

Live vs. video vs. photo lineups

In addition to live lineups that we have just discussed, eyewitness identification can also take place using photographs or videos. In the United States, photo lineups are used approximately three times more often than live lineups (Wogalter, Malpass, & McQuiston, 2004). Here, witnesses are typically presented with six photos arranged in two rows of three photos each and are asked whether the perpetrator is shown in one of these photographs. When photographs are used, the suspect may stand out visually simply because the image is larger or different in lighting or color. These incidental differences in the pictures themselves are known as the "oddball bias" (also see, e.g., Flowe & Humphries, 2011). Of course, avoiding oddball effects is relatively straightforward and can be accomplished by making the photographs uniform with pictures being the same size, using the same background, and so forth. Indeed, sometimes these problems can be avoided by taking the photographs from booking photos or from drivers' licenses.

By contrast, live lineups are more frequently used in the United Kingdom with identifications often taking place in what are known as "identification suites." Here, eyewitnesses are exposed to an "identity parade" where suspects are paraded in front of witnesses for identification. More recently, in many jurisdictions in the United Kingdom, eyewitnesses are shown a video lineup in which suspects appear in a series of videos that have been produced using VIPER (Video Identification Parade Electronic Recording). Here, suspects appear individually in the video for about 15 seconds and are shown from a number of angles (i.e., looking directly into the camera as well as turning to the left and right so their profiles can also be viewed).

The question as to which of these procedures is best for accurate identification of the perpetrator is still not known. Indeed, findings from studies comparing these procedures are mixed. For example, Valentine and Heaton (1999) found evidence suggesting that live or video image lineups produce more accurate identifications than photo lineups. This may be because the former are more dynamic representations whereas the latter are static representations. This explanation is consistent with the literature on face recognition. Specifically, face recognition is superior when presentation is dynamic because this provides the witness with sufficient information that they can construct a three-dimensional representation of the suspect (O'Toole, Roark, & Abdi, 2002). As well, eyewitnesses get to view the suspect from multiple angles, including left and right profiles, something that may reduce mistaken identifications (Bruce, Burton, & Hancock, 2007). Interestingly, although dynamic identification procedures may aid adult eyewitness identification as well as that of older children (i.e., children aged 13 to 15 years) (Havard, Memon, Clifford, & Gabbert, 2010), it may not improve young children's (i.e., children of 6–7 and 9–11 years of age) identification of suspects (Beresford & Blades, 2006; Skelton & Hay, 2008).

Although there is also evidence that electronically presented lineups are better than live lineups, this difference may have more to do with the lineup composition than the medium of presentation (Valentine, Pickering, & Darling, 2003). Specifically, the construction of video lineups can be better controlled because the police can draw on a large database of suspects whereas live lineup composition is determined by convenience sampling. That is, people are recruited for the lineup simply because they happen to be around at the time the lineup is being presented to the eyewitness. In these circumstances, the relationship between fillers and the suspect is not as well controlled as when video lineups are used.

Simultaneous vs. sequential lineups

After constructing the lineup and determining the medium by which it is to be presented, the next question is how the suspects should be presented? Considerable research has investigated two primary means by which lineups should be conducted. The simultaneous lineup occurs when all members are presented at once and the eyewitness makes one decision (which, if any of these individuals, is the perpetrator?). This has been the standard method. However, researchers have argued that this method tends to induce relative judgements (Lindsey & Wells 1985; Wells 1984) where eyewitnesses compare lineup members with one another and choose the person who most resembles the perpetrator. Although most lineup procedures in the United States (Wogalter et al., 2004) and the United Kingdom (Valentine et al., 2006) use the simultaneous method, there is a movement toward conducting sequential lineups. In the United States, state and local jurisdictions in five states have moved to using this technique and a survey of police officers in Ontario, Canada (see Beaudry & Lindsey, 2006), found that 56% of lineups conducted between 2002–2004 were sequential. In a sequential lineup, lineup members are presented one at a time. The eyewitness must make a decision about each ("yes" or "no": this is the perpetrator) before moving on to the next one. The lineup terminates when the eyewitness gives a "yes" response.

An important difference between these two procedures is that the witness in the sequential lineup condition does not typically know how many individuals will be viewed (Gronlund et al., 2012). This means that whereas only one decision is needed in the simultaneous lineup and the eyewitness knows how many individuals need to be considered, in the sequential lineup, the eyewitness needs to make a series of decisions and if each decision is a "reject" then the witness will go through the lineup not having chosen anyone when it terminates (Gronlund et al., 2012). Interestingly, the current PACE code of practice in the United Kingdom does not allow any advantage of sequential presentation to be realized because it requires witnesses to view the entire lineup twice before making any decision (Valentine et al., 2006). Nevertheless, the advantage of this lineup procedure was first discovered in a study by Lindsey and Wells (1985). Here participant-witnesses viewed a mock crime and were later asked to pick the perpetrator out of a target (perpetrator) present or a target absent lineup (the perpetrator is replaced with an innocent suspect). To examine lineup procedures, the lineup members were presented simultaneously (six lineup members at once) or sequentially (viewed an unknown number of lineup members one at a time). Lindsey and Wells found a large decrease in the false identification rate in the target-absent condition for the sequential lineup compared with simultaneous lineup (from .43 to .17) but also a slight decrease in the correct identification rate when the perpetrator was present (from .58 to .50). This last finding is one of the reasons why the move to sequential lineups has its critics.

Clark (2012) carried out a meta-analysis of 51 studies using the standard 2 (sequential vs. simultaneous) x 2 (perpetrator present vs. absent) designs. Both correct and false identification rates were significantly reduced by the sequential lineup. Thus, sequential lineups cause us to be significantly more conservative. This technique reduces the false identification rate, meaning an innocent suspect in a perpetrator absent lineup is less likely to be put at risk. However, the cost to this benefit is that there is a reduced willingness to choose from the sequential lineup at all, resulting in a reduced correct identification rate. Of course, research in this area is by no means conclusive. Work continues to investigate the sequential lineup advantage, or indeed, if the sequential lineup advantage even exists (Gronlund, Carlson, Dailey, & Goodsell, 2009). It might be the case that rather than changing our identification process from relative to absolute judgments, a sequential lineup just raises the criteria for making a positive identification.

Post-identification feedback

The Oregon Supreme Court has recognized at least one of the important system variables that can influence the reliability of eyewitness evidence:

> Confirming feedback, by definition, takes place after an identification and thus does not affect the result of the identification itself. It can, however, falsely inflate witness confidence. . . . As a result, the danger of confirming feedback lies in its potential to increase the *appearance* of reliability without increasing reliability itself.
>
> (*Oregon v. Lawson*, 2012, p. 21)

This decision highlights two key factors. First, it confirms that certainty of the eye-witness identification is changeable; that is, a witness' initial confidence level may be low, but with positive post-identification feedback, this can alter. Second, this over-stated confidence can have subsequent consequences during the trial when testimony of the witness will portray a misleading level of certainty, convincing the jury of the reliability of the identification. Indeed, by the time of the trial, the witness takes the stand and provides very convincing testimony that a jury will often not question.

Case Example: *Ronald Cotton*
Sentence Served: *10.5 years*
Conviction: *Rape, Burglary*
(Taken from Innocence Project 2009)

Ronald Cotton was sentenced to life plus 54 years and spent over 10 years in prison before his exoneration through DNA testing in 1995. Cotton was misidentified by Jennifer Thompson-Cannino, a rape victim in North Carolina. Positive post-identification feedback led to an increased false sense of confidence. The victim was shown a photo array and a subsequent live lineup. Different foils were used in each presentation while Cotton remained present in both. After the photo array, the investigators told the victim, "You did great." After identifying Cotton the second time in the live lineup the investigator told her, "We thought that might be the guy. It's the same person you picked from the photos" (Thompson-Cannino, et al., 2009, p. 37).

During the trial, Jennifer Thompson-Cannino testified that she was absolutely certain that Cotton was her assailant – even after being presented with a person at the second trial who it was later discovered was the real perpetrator:

> Ron was the only person who had been in both the photo and the physical lineups, making his face more recognizable to me. And then the police told me that I had identified the same person in the physical lineup whose photo I had selected, so by the time I went into court, everything added up for me: I was defiantly confident that Ronald Cotton was the one.
>
> (Thompson-Cannino et al., 2009, p. 271)

As we have seen, post-identification feedback simply means that the *appearance* of memory reliability has been influenced by the lineup administrator (Wells, Steblay, & Dysart, 2015). Over 15 years of research has shown that positive confirm-ation of lineup identification ("Good, you identified the suspect") can have a powerful impact on the retrospective judgments of an eyewitness following a lineup decision. Confidence of identification includes both inflation in the believed quality of identification process (certainty and ease of the identification) as well as the viewing experience for the crime event (how good the view was, how much attention was paid to the event; see Wells & Bradfield, 1998).

Post-identification feedback can have serious consequences on the reliability of the eyewitness testimony. However, there are procedures that can reduce and even prevent contamination during the identification process. Retention interval between the time of the crime and the time the eyewitness identifies the suspect is one such factor. However, perhaps more important is the use of the double-blind lineup procedure. The double-blind lineup was first introduced over 25 years ago as a way to prevent lineup administrators from influencing eyewitness identification decisions (Wells, 1988). Indeed, the American Psychology-Law Society (Division 41 of the American Psychological Association) has endorsed the use of double-blind lineups in a 1998 "white paper" (Wells et al., 1998). Double-blind lineup procedures are based on the well-known experimenter-expectancy effect (e.g., Rosenthal, 1964; Rosenthal & Rubin, 1978). For example, when used in clinical trials, some patients will receive the active medication, while others will receive a placebo, but neither the researchers nor the patients know who is receiving the drug and who is receiving the placebo. In an eyewitness identification setting, neither the eyewitness nor the administrator of the lineup knows which persons in a photo array, video file, or live lineup are the suspects and which ones are the fillers. Thus, this procedure prevents a lineup administrator from either intentionally or unintentionally influencing a witness' selection (National Research Council, 2014).

In addition to the use of a double-blind procedure, the National Research Council (2014) also recommended that law enforcement agencies document the initial confidence judgments when making the initial identification and that it be reported during trial. We have seen that the confidence of the eyewitness can be misleading quite simply because memory is malleable and can be subject to distortion. Indeed, a detailed analysis of DNA exoneration cases reveals misidentifications that were virtually always made with high confidence in a court of law (Garrett, 2011). Despite what we know about the weak or non-existent link between confidence and accuracy in these cases (Krug, 2007), jurors still tend to give more weight to the testimony if the eyewitnesses report that they are very sure of their identifications. Courts are going some way toward dealing with this issue. For example, in 2011, the New Jersey Supreme Court ruled that the jurors must be provided with the following instructions regarding confidence and accuracy:

> You heard testimony that (insert name of witness) expressed his or her level of certainty that the person he or she selected is in fact the person who committed the crime. As I explained earlier, a witness's level of confidence, standing alone, may not be an indication of the reliability of the ID. Although some research has found that highly confident witnesses are more likely to make accurate identifications, *eye-witness confidence is generally an unreliable indicator of accuracy*.
>
> (New Jersey Model Criminal Jury Charges, 2012, pp. 4–5)

Although these juror instructions are necessary to understand the limitations of human memory, Wixted, Mickes, Clark, Gronlund, and Roediger (2015) argue that they fail to draw any distinction between the confidence initially expressed at the time of the first identification versus the confidence expressed months or years later during the trial. Indeed, evidence suggests that initial identification confidence can be far more reliable than subsequent confidence judgments and if the jury had knowledge of the initial confidence and the subsequent shift in confidence in the courtroom, this may have prevented many wrongful convictions.

Garrett (2011) analyzed trial materials for 161 DNA exonerees who were misidentified. He found that in 57% of these trial transcripts (92 out of 161 cases) the witness reported that they had not been certain at the time of the initial identification. Findings from empirical research support the strong relationship between accuracy and initial identification confidence. That is, identifications made with low confidence are associated with low accuracy (typically 40% correct or lower), whereas identifications made with high confidence are associated with high accuracy (typically 80% or more; see Brewer & Wells, 2006; Horry, Palmer, & Brewer, 2012; Keast et al., 2007, for examples).

These trends occur not only in laboratory-based studies using mock witnesses and lineups but also in studies of actual eyewitnesses identifying perpetrators of real crimes. For example, Wixted, Mickes, Dunn, Clark, and Wells (2016) examined the reliability of eyewitness identifications from actual police lineups conducted in the Robbery Division of the Houston Police Department. The results confirmed the laboratory research and showed that when fair lineups are used in a double-blind fashion, eyewitness confidence was a reliable indicator of identification accuracy.

Based on these (and other) findings, Wixted et al. (2015, p. 516) made the following recommendation:

> Jurors should consider the level of certainty expressed by an eyewitness during the initial identifications (at which time confidence is likely to be a *reliable* indicator of accuracy) while disregarding the level of certainty expressed at trial (because, by then, confidence may no longer be a reliable indicator of accuracy).

Indeed, Wixted et al. (2015) concluded that, in their view, when it came to initial confidence ratings at the time of identification, the best scientific evidence suggested that low confidence implies low accuracy, and high confidence implies high accuracy. However, confidence must only be assessed and used at the time of initial identification, using appropriate lineup procedures, and not during court (also see Wixted et al., 2016).

Conclusion

It is important to remember that eyewitness identification is an important tool for the legal community. However, as Davis and Loftus (2012) argue, when it comes to what the law asks of witnesses, much of this is beyond the limits of the human cognition. When it comes to the ability to identify a once-seen unfamiliar stranger, what are the limits of witness identification performance? And what are the limits of memory's resistance to distortion? As we have seen in this chapter, the malleable nature of memory, perception, and confidence, the limitations in our ability to recognize faces and individuals, and the current law enforcement procedures for eyewitness identification can all result in mistaken identifications. We can improve eyewitness accuracy of identifications but this involves new law enforcement training protocols, standardized procedures for administering lineups, and improvements in the handling of eyewitness identification in court (National Research Council, 2014). We, as scientists, must play our part in this by extending the research on eyewitness identification to continue to (1) examine new and different estimator and system variables that may affect accuracy and (2) make laboratory studies more readily applicable to actual practice and policy. Of course, reaching a goal of evidence-based policy and practice will require collaboration from both the research community and the legal field, in the setting of research agendas and agreement on methods for acquiring, handling, and sharing of data. In this respect there is still significant work to be done (see National Research Council, 2014, for a review).

This is not to say that considerable progress has not already been made. Indeed, if we knew then what we know now, Calvin Willis, like so many others, might not have been convicted of rape and sentenced to life without parole. Similarly, Al-Megrahi, a Libyan convicted of the Lockerbie bombing in 1988, may not have gone to prison. It is with this infamous case that we shall end this chapter.

Full details of the eyewitness evidence can be found in the police reports, trial court opinion, and appellate court opinions (see *Megrahi v. Her Majesty's Advocate*, 2002), with a full review published in a special issue of *Memory* by Loftus (2013). To summarize, in 1988 a Pan Am Flight exploded over Lockerbie, Scotland, killing 270 people. It was not until 12 years later that Al Megrahi stood trial and was convicted of the crime. His conviction was based largely on the testimony of a man named Mr. Gauci, a Maltese shopkeeper that Al-Megrahi allegedly purchased clothing from that was later found in the suitcase that contained the explosives.

The police first interviewed Mr. Gauci on September 1 1989, 9 months after the clothing purchase. Mr. Gauci was able to provide a detailed account of the man who purchased these clothes and two weeks later went to police headquarters to try to make a photofit likeness of the shopper, followed soon after by an artist sketch. Over the following year, Mr. Gauci viewed a series of photographs in an attempt to identify the shopper. It was not until February 1991 when Mr. Gauci made a first tentative identification of Al-Megrahi. Here, Gauci chose Al-Megrahi's photograph from one of 12, stating that although he looked like the shopper, he did not appear to be old enough. This first identification occurred more than two years after the clothing purchase. Subsequent viewings of Al-Megrahi, one during a lineup in April 1999 and then at the trial in 2000, led Gauci to state on each occasion that he thought it was him, and that Al-Megrahi resembled the man a lot.

Loftus (2013) highlighted a number of factors that led to serious concerns about the reliability of this eyewitness identification and subsequent testimony. One important issue concerns exposure time and the length of the retention interval prior to eyewitness identification. Specifically, Gauci first identified Al-Megrahi some two years after the clothing purchase. This is an extraordinary length of time to remember the face of a stranger during what is arguably a short and considerably mundane meeting (i.e., a clothing purchase). Research from the face recognition literature shows particularly poor performance over long time periods (e.g., Brigham, Maass, Snyder, & Spaulding, 1982). We also know from the memory distortion literature that not only does memory fade, but it also becomes increasingly vulnerable to post-event information. That is, new information can become incorporated into the witness' memory and can cause alteration and distortion (for a review, see Frenda, Nichols, & Loftus 2011). Loftus (2013) also underscores the fact that Gauci made a tentative identification in February 1991, but identified Al-Megrahi from a lineup in April 1999. A few months prior to this line-up Gauci was exposed to a photo of Al-Megrahi which appeared in *Focus* magazine. Loftus speculated that this photo, and other similar photographs, may have acted as post-event information which could have influenced Gauci's memory for the shopper who came to purchase clothes in 1988. Indeed, research supports this form of photo-bias. Brown, Deffenbacher, and Sturgill (1977) found that participants in a line up who had never been seen before were mistakenly identified 8% of the time. However, if a mugshot had been seen prior to the lineup, mistaken identity increased to 20%. This type of photo-biased identification could have occurred in Gauci's case.

Other factors known to influence eyewitness testimony can be found in the police and trial reports as discussed by Loftus (2013). As we have seen, confidence makes an eyewitness' identification more impressive to the trier of fact. However, research has shown that confidence and accuracy are often weakly correlated following initial identification. In the reports, as time goes on, Gauci's confidence increases. In the original photo identification, Gauci gave a tentative response and stated Al-Megrahi looked similar to the man in his shop. However, at trial, Gauci more confidently identified Al-Megrahi in court stating that "He is the man on this side" (*Megrahi v. Her Majesty's Advocate*, para [40], 2002). There are a number of other factors, including cross-racial identification and critical changes in Gauci's testimony, all of which lead us to wonder about the validity and reliability of Gauci's eyewitness testimony. As Loftus concludes, "My examination has led me to seriously wonder: Is the Lockerbie bomber still out there?" (Loftus, 2013, p. 589).

Notes

1. Extensive research has shown that the presence of a weapon draws the attention of eyewitnesses. This can lead to poor recall and recognition of the culprit in subsequent lineups. In one of the earliest studies of weapon focus, Loftus et al. (1987) explored how the presence of a weapon influenced picture-viewing behavior. In two identical

experiments gaze was measured while participants viewed one of two scenarios: Slides depicted a man (the target) approaching the front of a fast food restaurant where he displayed either a gun (the weapon condition) or a check (the control condition). The man then received money and left. Participants in the weapon condition fixated for longer duration on the gun than participants who were in the check condition. In a subsequent lineup, participants in the weapon condition were less accurate than those in the cheque condition at identifying the target (Loftus et al., 1987). There have been two explanations for this effect. The arousal/threat hypothesis suggests that in the presence of a weapon, its threatening nature elevates physiological arousal. This results in a fixation on the source of the arousal/threat at the cost of the peripheral stimuli (Easterbrook, 1959). Other research has shown that, rather than increased levels of arousal with attention narrowing, unusualness may influence attention. That is, surprising or unexpected objects attract attention, drawing the observer's gaze more readily than objects expected given the scene's content (Loftus & Mackworth, 1978).

2. Note that the term *culprit* refers to the person who actually committed the crime and the term *suspect* refers to the person the police think committed the crime.

8

SUGGESTIBILITY AND INTERVIEWING

In 1988, Kelly Michaels (*State v. Michaels*) was accused of sexually abusing twenty preschool children at the Wee Care Nursery in Maplewood, New Jersey. The abuse allegations came to light when a former pupil of the school who attended Michaels' class went for a routine check-up. The pediatrician used a rectal thermometer to take the child's temperature and on doing so the child remarked "That's what my teacher does to me at school" (Manshel, 1990, p. 126). On the advice of the doctor, the mother contacted the state's child protective agency. The child was interviewed by an assistant prosecutor and while using an anatomical doll the child inserted his finger into its rectum. The child went on to divulge information regarding two other boys at the nursery who had the same thing happen to them. When later interviewed, both denied this had happened to them, but one boy did say Michaels touched his penis.

Following these initial interviews, the Wee Care Nursery School informed parents of all the children at the nursery of the alleged events and held a meeting with these parents to discuss the issues surrounding the common occurrence of child sex abuse. A social worker at the meeting urged the parents to examine the children for any signs of abuse, including genital soreness, nightmares, bed-wetting, and any negative changes in behavior (Ceci & Bruck, 1993). Social workers and police investigators extensively interviewed the children of the Wee Care nursery. Over several months, new allegations emerged. Eventually, when the case went to trial, Michaels was accused of the sexual abuse of twenty children over a seven-month period. Michaels was accused of horrific acts, including licking peanut butter off children's genitals, playing the piano in the nude, and raping the children with a variety of objects including knives, forks, spoons, and Lego blocks (Ceci & Bruck, 1993). There were no adult eyewitnesses, there was no medical evidence of sexual abuse, the parents had not seen any physical signs of abuse, and emotional disturbances only materialized after the children began being interviewed. However, prosecutors argued that children's reports had to be authentic because the children would not otherwise have the knowledge to be able to describe the abuse and events that Michaels was accused of (Ceci & Bruck, 1995). She was eventually convicted of 115 counts of sexual abuse but after five years in prison, the New Jersey Supreme Court overturned the decision and Michaels was released.

The Wee Care Nursery case is one of the most widely documented in the scientific community surrounding child eyewitness testimony. At the time the defense tried to argue that the children's reports were the direct result of the repeated and suggestive interviewing of biased social workers and police investigators who were in the blind pursuit of what they believed to be justice. Indeed, the effect of interviewer bias and the failure to test alternative explanations for children's behavior and their answers was rife across the interviews with the children from the Nursery. But, at the time, little to no expert evidence was available to substantiate the claims that such questioning would lead to entire false reports. It was not until the appeal case that the court received an Amicus Brief, produced by Bruck and Ceci and members of the scientific community (1995). The report highlighted the dangerous effects that interviewer bias and suggestive interviewing can have on children's memory. The Appellate Division reversed the convictions based, in part, on this Amicus Brief.

The difficult truth here is that the sexual victimization of children typically occurs behind closed doors, often with no witness. Frequently, there are no physical signs of abuse (although this is not always the case, see McGough, 1993), so we rely on children's reports elicited by the police or social workers. The Wee Care Nursery case was just one example where reports of horrific and ritualistic long-term abuse were made with no medical evidence or adult eyewitnesses for corroboration. Nevertheless, such allegations were believed by the social workers and police officers in these cases simply because it was believed children would not, and could not, make up such allegations. Because there was no direct evidence to support the claim that the leading and suggestive interview questions could result in false recollections, inevitably, many of these allegations ended in convictions. It is important to note here that researchers in this field uphold the statement that most child sexual abuse cases in the legal system are based on true claims, but there are important issues surrounding interview techniques and types of questions that can affect the reliability of children's testimony. This is the problem that we focus on in this chapter.

In general children's autobiographical recall can be considered accurate for a wide range of life events. However, these recollections can be greatly distorted when interviewers are biased in their questioning and details are elicited during suggestive interviews. This poses significant problems particularly when interviewing young children. Children of preschool age typically give only sparse information to open-ended questions or when asked to provide a free narrative of an event. Thus, interviewers will often resort to yes/no questions, or forced-choice questions to elicit more information. We now know, from the wealth of research conducted in this area, that children's answers to such questions can be quite inaccurate (e.g., Brady, Poole, Warren, & Jones, 1999; Peterson & Bell, 1996). We also know that younger, compared with older, children are often misled by suggestive and leading questioning (Ceci & Bruck, 1993) and are likely to change their answers if the same question is repeated (e.g., Poole & White, 1991). The exponential growth in research examining the suggestibility of children's memory has highlighted the various internal and external factors that lead to errors in children's reports. In this chapter, we will review some of this research with the focus being predominantly on the factors that cause errors in children's reports. We do so to illustrate what can happen if interviewers use various techniques that are known to be leading and suggestive in nature. We then consider research that has attempted to identify non-suggestive interviewing techniques, ones that have led to the creation of preferred interviewing strategies for children and were developed by the National Institute of Child Health and Human Development (NICHD; see Lamb, Orbach, Hershkowitz, Esplin, & Horowitz, 2007). The main focus of this chapter will be the effects of interviewing and suggestion on children's memory, but we will also consider the research examining the effects of suggestion and interview styles on older adults' recollections.

Memory evidence from children remembering childhood events

The biases and beliefs of the interviewer can have devastating consequences for children's eyewitness statements and ultimately on their recollection of events. The interviewers in the Michaels case did not consider that the bizarre behaviors and answers could have meant that the children were confused, that they were just repeating something that had previously been said to them, they were just pretending, or that they had not understood the question. The interviewers continued with a particular line of enquiry even after the child had said the event did not occur. Using bribes, threats, and repetition of questions, the interviewers persisted until they heard what they wanted to hear. One of the important claims made by the prosecution was that children of this age range would not be able to describe sexual experiences without having been exposed to them. But paramount to these investigations was the repeated questioning from therapists, police, and social workers across numerous different interviews. These questionings would repeat information about unusual bodily experiences and highly sensitive personal interactions they believed had happened (White, Leichtman, & Ceci, 1997). There is compelling evidence of the negative effects of this biased and repetitive questioning, as well as the need for a more careful consideration of the child's possible misunderstanding of the questions being asked. Below is an extract from the interview transcripts of the Wee Care Nursery case. Despite initial denial, the preschooler begins to accept the suggestions of the interviewer and provide increasingly bizarre replies:

Child: I forgot what happened, too.

Interviewer: You remember . . . Your penis was bleeding. Tell me something
   else: was your hiney bleeding, too?

Child: No.

Interviewer: Did [defendant] bleed, too?

Child: No.

Interviewer: Are you sure she didn't bleed?

Child: Yes . . . I saw her penis, too.

Interviewer: Show me on the [anatomical] doll . . . you saw that? Oh.

Child: She doodied on me . . . She peed on us.

Interviewer: And did you have to pee on her at all?

Child: Yeah.

Interviewer: You did? And who peed on her, you and who else?

Child: [Child names a male friend].

Interviewer: Didn't his penis bleed?

Child: Yes.

Interviewer: It did? What made it bleed? What was she doing?

Child: She was bleeding.

Interviewer: She was bleeding in her penis? Did you have to put your penis
   in her penis? Yes or no?

Child: Yeah . . . And I peed in her penis.

Interviewer: What was that like? What did it feel like?

Child: Like a shot.

Interviewer: Did [friend] have to put his penis in her penis, too?

Child: Yes, at the same time.

Interviewer: At the same time? How did you do that?

Child: We chopped our penises off.

> (pp. 45–50; Superior Court of New Jersey, Appellate
> Division, from *State of New Jersey v. Margaret Kelly
> Michaels*, appendix, Vol. 1, Docket No. 199–88T4)

The development of today's interview protocol for questioning children will
mean that such inexplicable questioning is now uncommon but this excerpt
illustrates that biased repeated questioning can lead to bizarre and elaborate replies.
Cognitive factors, including poor memory organization leading to faster fading of
information, as well as social factors, including the interviewer's perceived status,
causes the increase in uncertainty in children's memory, something which in turn
leads them to be more vulnerable to suggestion.

   Not only is this evident in excerpts from high profile court cases, but it has also
been found in experimentally controlled laboratory studies. White et al. (1997)
examined the effect of suggestions provided to interviewers prior to questioning children aged three to five years old on their descriptions of a past event.
Children took part in a modified game of *Simon Says*. Working in pairs, children
took turns carrying out actions on themselves (e.g., "rub your stomach") or

watching (or experiencing) benign physical touches carried out by the researcher (e.g., "touch your partners' foot"). Thus, children had experienced an event where they had been physically touched (or not), carried out unusual or usual actions, and acted or observed another child act (touching their partner or observing them being touched). One to two months after the event each child received two interviews, one conducted by an interviewer that had been briefed with accurate information and one who had been briefed with inaccurate information. Inaccurate information included "normal" false details (actions that had occurred but the recipient of the action changed, e.g., the researcher touched the child rather than the child touching the researcher) and more "bizarre" inaccurate information (unusual actions including children licking the researcher's elbow, putting marbles in the researcher's ear, etc.). Results indicated that younger children agreed to actions taking place that were inaccurate more often than older children. Children of all ages agreed more readily with questions about unusual than usual actions and these bizarre misleading questions preferentially elicited commission-elaboration responses (inaccurate elaboration errors prefaced by "yes" or "no" answers – e.g., "did you kiss the researcher," would elicit a response such as "no, she kissed me"). Finally, younger children's reports declined in accuracy over time (White et al., 1997). As the researchers concluded, this study provided a conservative test of suggestibility to biased repeated questioning over just two interviews. A response like this last one could be the sort that would spark a formal enquiry into the child's claims. It is the repeated exposure to these leading questions through the course of parental questioning, therapeutic work, and police investigation, as well as the shared concerns of the parent or caregiver being conveyed to the child, that is critical to the issues of testimonial accuracy that we face in such situations.

Biased repetitive questioning is just one investigative technique that can cause errors in children's recollections of an event. In what follows, we will consider several other suggestive techniques highlighted in the Wee Care Nursery case and consider the specific research that has examined the effects of these techniques in experimentally controlled conditions. The Amicus Brief for the case of State of New Jersey v. Michaels cites interviews with the Wee Care children and provides examples of the suggestive and faulty interview techniques that undoubtedly led to the false allegations unearthed in this case. We will review several of these here, drawing on both the examples from the case itself and subsequent experimental research that highlights the techniques involved (see Bruck & Ceci, 1995 for the full reprinted Amicus Brief). Ceci and Bruck (1995) and, later, Schreiber et al. (2006) identified several techniques used by the interviewers. These include, but are not limited to: the introduction of suggestive information to the interview; positive (and negative) reinforcement, including praise, promises, disagreement, and disapproval; the use of conformity pressure; and, finally, speculation about supposed events and the use of anatomical dolls.

In the excerpt below, we can see evidence of the interviewer's bias in their questioning. They introduce suggestive information and maintain one line of enquiry without investigating an alternative hypothesis. The interviewer ignored the bizarre or inconsistent statements, never questioned what the child may have meant, and finally provided suggestive information including, "So she made you eat the peanut butter and jelly and the orange juice off of the vagina too?":

(In this section, the interviewer is using anatomically detailed dolls and different utensils with the child.)

> Interviewer: Okay, I really need your help on this. Did you have to do anything to her with this stuff?
> Child: Okay. Where's the big knife at. Show me where's the big knife at.
> Interviewer: Pretend this is the big knife because we don't have a big knife.
> Child: This is a big one.
> Interviewer: Okay, what did you have to do with that? What did you have to . . .
> Child: No. . . . take the peanut—put the peanut butter.
> Interviewer: You put what's that, what did you put there?
> Child: I put jelly right here.
> Interviewer: Jelly?
> Child: And I put jelly on her mouth and on the eyes.
> Interviewer: You put jelly on her eyes and her vagina and her mouth?
> Child: On her back, on her socks.
> Interviewer: And did you have to put anything else down there?
> Child: Right there, right here and right here and here.
> Interviewer: You put peanut butter all over? And where else did you put the peanut butter?
> Child: And jelly?
> Interviewer: And jelly.
> Child: And we squeezed orange on her.
> Interviewer: And you had to squeeze an orange on her?
> Child: Put orange juice on her.
> Interviewer: And did anybody—how did everybody take it off? How did she make you take it off?
> Child: No. Lick her all up, eat her all up and lick her all up.
> Interviewer: You had to lick her all up?
> Child: And eat her all up.
> Interviewer: Yeah? What did it taste like?
> Child: Yucky.
> Interviewer: So she made you eat the peanut butter and jelly and the orange juice off of the vagina too?
> Child: Yeah.
>
> (Bruck & Ceci, 1995, pp. 277–278)

Positive (and negative) reinforcement can strongly influence children's behavior. Below we see excerpts from the transcripts where children were offered popsicles for the incriminating statements and promises to end the interviews ("we can finish real fast if you just show me what you showed me last time"). Positive reinforcement plays on the child's need for acceptance and praise ("Thanks for telling me," "you talk better than the younger kids"):

> Interviewer: That's why I need your help, especially you older kids . . . because you can talk better than the younger kids . . . and you will be helping to keep her in jail longer so that she doesn't hurt anybody. Not to mention that you'll also feel a lot better once you start.
>
> (Bruck & Ceci, 1995, p. 283)

> Interviewer: We can finish this real fast if you just show me real fast what you showed me last time.
> Child: No.
> Interviewer: I will let you play my tape recorder. . . . Come on, do you want to help us out? Do you want to help us keep her in jail, huh? . . . Tell me what happened to (three other children). Tell me what happened to them. Come on . . . I need your help again, buddy. Come on.
> Child: No.
> Interviewer: You told us everything once before. Do you want to undress my dolly?
> Interviewer: Let's get done with this real quick so we could go to Kings to get popsicles. . . . Did (defendant) ever tell you she could get out of jail?
>
> (Bruck & Ceci, 1995, p. 298)

The powerful nature of reinforcement has been demonstrated in experimental research. For example, Garven, Wood, and Malpass (2000) examined the effects of reinforcement and co-witness information on children's recollections of a classroom visitor. During story time, children were introduced to a visitor named Paco Perez. He gave children a sticker on their hand and handed out treats. After 20 minutes, he left. Children were interviewed about mundane as well as fantastical events using various control and suggestive techniques. For reinforcement, the interviewer praised children when they answered yes to a question and showed disappointment if the child answered no. For co-witness information, the interviewer told the child what other children had supposedly said. One particular technique incorporated both co-witness information and reinforcement. This is illustrated from the extract below (taken from Garven et al., 2000, p. 41):

> Interviewer: . . . The other kids say that Paco took them somewhere on a helicopter [Co-witness Information]. Did Paco take you somewhere on a helicopter?
> Child: No.

> Interviewer : You're not doing good. Um-uh (negative) [Reinforcement]. The other kids say that Paco took them to a farm [Co-witness Information]. Did Paco take you to a farm?
>
> Child: Yes.
>
> Interviewer: Great. You're doing excellent now [Reinforcement]. The other kids say that Paco showed them the animals on the farm [Co-witness Information]. Did Paco show you the animals on the farm?
>
> Child: Yes.
>
> Interviewer: Great. You're doing excellent [Reinforcement]. One last question. The other kids say that Paco took them on a horse ride [Co-witness Information]. Did Paco take you on a horse ride?
>
> Child: Yes.

As in the above example, the use of reinforcement dramatically increased the rate of making false allegations about fantastical events. Co-witness information on its own yielded weaker effects. Although other previous research has shown a stronger co-witness effect (Leichtman & Ceci, 1995), Garven et al. (2000) argued that the co-witness may need to be an authority figure or close friend, or that it is most effective after repeated recall attempts, something we will return to later in this chapter. Garven et al. (2000) further reported that children tended to repeat the false allegation during the second interview, even without any further reinforcement, and that many children, even when challenged, upheld the allegation and insisted it was an event that had happened to them. This demonstrates the serious consequences of carryover effects. Just one interview with reinforcement (both positive and negative) that leads to a false allegation will cause that false allegation to remain and be reported in subsequent interviews. Indeed, children who received reinforcement techniques at the first interview and were later re-interviewed two to three weeks later without reinforcement produced the same fantastical error rates as children who received reinforcement at both interviews. Furthermore, in response to a challenge (which is analogous to cross-examination), if a child made a false allegation after reinforcement, then the probability that the child would later claim that the allegation they made was based on a personal account rather than from a second hand source was 25% of all misleading mundane items and 30% of all fantastic items. Often these allegations, even when challenged, contained elaborate narrative event sequences, usually characteristic (it has been argued) of children's true statements (Faller, 1988; Raskin & Esplin, 1991). An example can be seen from Garven et al. (2000, pp. 16–17, Appendix), where a six-year-old girl provides an unusual but logical narrative of a false event:

> Interviewer: You said that Paco took you to a farm. Did you see that or hear about it?
>
> Child: I see that.
>
> Interviewer: Can you tell me more about the farm?

Child: Yeah, it had lot of animals. I could ride on them, I could take milk out.

. . . [Later in the interview when asked about the helicopter]

Child: The helicopter almost crashed but it was a mountain and it was blocking us.

Interviewer: Oh.

Child: So we got out of the way and went across it.

We can see here, from both the experimental evidence and evidence from the interview transcripts of the Wee Care Nursery case, that any type of promising, implying, or punishment during the substantive part of an interview should be avoided. Such reinforcement can swiftly induce children to make false allegations. Of course, it is important to note here that there is a difference between this type of reinforcement and what Garven et al. (2000) refer to as "social support" that can be beneficial when building a rapport between the interviewer and child (Goodman, Bottoms, Schwartz-Kenney, & Rudy, 1991) to aid the more substantial section of the interview.

Throughout the interview transcripts of these abuse cases we also see evidence of repeated questioning. The most often repeated questions used close-ended prompts (yes/no answers only) and are typically suggestive in nature. Such repetition often leads to changes in the child's original answer. The reason for this is an obvious one. Young children are more likely to believe that they are being asked the same question again because the first answer they gave must have been wrong. Alternatively, a child's answer may change because any previous suggestion by the interviewer may now be incorporated into their memories. For example:

Interviewer: When Kelly kissed you, did she ever put her tongue in your mouth?

Child: No.

Interviewer: Did she ever make you put your tongue in her mouth?

Child: No.

Interviewer: Did you ever have to kiss her vagina?

Child: No.

Interviewer: Which of the kids had to kiss her vagina?

Child: What's this?

Interviewer: No that's my toy, my radio box. Which kids had to kiss her vagina?

Child: Me.

(Bruck & Ceci, 1995, p. 283)

Again here, the interviewer not only repeats the suggestive line of questioning but encourages the child to use imaginative thought when asked to conduct sexualized demonstrations with an anatomical doll. That is, they were asked to think about how a certain event could have happened and show the interviewer by demonstrating the act with a doll. This alone has been shown to be a dangerous suggestive technique (for reviews, see Bruck & Ceci, 1995; Howe & Knott, 2015) in part because the child is asked to picture or imagine an event happening that may have never have happened. This form of self-generation leads to errors in later recall because children (and adults) make source errors that events actually happened when in fact, they were ones they had only thought about. These errors in source monitoring not only occur in forensic interview settings but are also quite common in experimentally based research in both adults and children (e.g., Otgaar, Candel, Merckelbach, Wade, 2009; Wade et al., 2002).

Worse, the use of anatomical dolls, although beneficial when overcoming language barriers or embarrassing conversations for children, can lead to an increase in errors when suggestive questions are used. Experimental research has found that the use of anatomical dolls to act out a recently experienced medical procedure led to increased errors particularly in 3- to 4-year-olds (Goodman, Quas, Batterman-Faunce, Riddlesberger, & Kuhn, 1997). In the Wee Care nursery case, interviewers used the doll to show and talk about touching of genitals which made it seem acceptable to act out sexualized behaviors as if it were a game. Children will of course be curious to explore a novel doll with cavities that they will not have seen before:

> Interviewer: Can you think of a way somebody might have used this to hurt little girls?
> Child: (indicates the tummy)
> Interviewer: Where else do you think a little girl could have gotten hurt with a wooden spoon?
> Child: The belly button.
> Interviewer: Where else do you think a little girl might get hit with a wooden spoon? How do you think Kelly used this fork to hurt little girls?
> Child: Belly button.
> Interviewer: Where else? (finally after many more persistent questions)
> Child: Bottom.
>
> (Bruck & Ceci, 1995, pp. 292–293)

Of course, the issue of repeated questioning during an interview is a difficult one. Interviewers often want to repeat a question to clarify details previously mentioned. However, as we have seen above, children may believe that the interviewer is unsatisfied with their account or the child may change details in their accounts to be consistent with what they believe the interviewer wants to hear and thus, produce responses that are inconsistent. Of course, this will lead to concerns about the child's credibility as a witness. These effects of repeated questioning have been demonstrated not only in field-based studies as we have just seen, but also in experimental research (Howie, Kurukulasuriya, Nash, & Marsh, 2009; Melinder, Scullin, Gravvold, & Iversen, 2007). For example, Howie, Nash, Kurukulasuriya, and Bowman (2012), using a laboratory-based procedure, found that children of four to eight years of age were sensitive to adult dissatisfaction and interpreted their repeated questioning as an implicit suggestion to change their answers. This was even more apparent when followed up with a challenge (e.g., "Are you sure about that?"; also see Endres, Poggenpohl, & Erben, 1999).

Andrews and Lamb (2014) studied the effects of repeated questioning in a forensic setting by examining transcripts of forensic interviews with 115 children aged between three and twelve years, interviewed between one day and eighteen months after allegedly experiencing a single incident of sexual abuse. Andrews and Lamb first investigated the use of repeated questions in the forensic interviews. All but ten interviews showed that children were asked repeated questions. The type of questions most often repeated were closed-ended (e.g., "Did you see his penis?", "He forced you to do that, didn't he?") at 69.7%, with fewer open-ended questions (e.g., "Where were you when that happened?") at 30.3%. Furthermore, open-ended questions appeared to be used more often when questions were repeated for purposes of clarification, whereas closed-ended questions were used to challenge a child's previous response. In terms of the effects of children's responses, their analysis indicated that suggestive repeated questions were more likely to elicit contradictions than any other type of prompt, with open-ended invitations providing the lowest. Overall, the findings from these forensic interviews support previous experimentally based research and indicate that children are more likely to change their answers when questioned repeatedly using suggestive prompts (Andrews & Lamb, 2014).

Although Garven et al. (2000) reported weaker effects of co-witnesses on recall accuracy compared with reinforcement, a number of studies have shown strong effects of conformity to peer pressure. As we have already seen, this form of suggestive technique involves telling the child (or even adult) witness that the other witnesses (peers or adult figures) have already said the event has happened. Such a technique can make the child feel forced to "go along" with what has already been said (Leichtman & Ceci, 1995).

> Interviewer: Anyway, I'm wondering if you can tell me some things of how Kelly was touching some of your friends in the way that you didn't like too much. And all the other friends I talked to told me everything that happened. 29C told me. 32C told me. 14C told me and now it's your turn to tell me. You don't want to be left out, do you?
>
> Interviewer: All your friends that I mentioned before were telling us that Kelly, the teacher we are talking about, was doing something they didn't like very much. She was bothering them in kind of a private way and they were all pretty brave and they told us everything, and we were wondering if you could help us out too, doing the same thing.
>
> Interviewer: I will get you the badge if you help us get this information . . . like all your other friends did.
>
> Interviewer: Why don't you tell me or show me what she was doing, okay? Just like all your other friends. 8C showed me and 2C showed me.
>
> (Bruck & Ceci, 1995, pp. 284–285)

The suggestive effects of such a technique have been supported by a number of laboratory studies. For example, Leichtman and Ceci (1995) found that when a teacher emphasized incorrect behavior stereotypes of a visitor to a preschool this, plus suggestive questioning, led to the highest number of false reports regarding the events of the school visit, with young children producing the most errors.

The effects of co-witness information have also been explored with adult witnesses. Shaw, Garven, and Wood (1997) examined the effect of a witness' statement immediately after receiving information about what a co-witness had said. Participants completed a questionnaire about the then recently completed O. J. Simpson trial. Co-witness information came in the form of bogus feedback about the responses made by other participants. Results showed that if participants received incorrect information about a co-witness response, they were more likely to give the wrong answer compared with a no co-witness condition. Paterson and Kemp (2006) found a similar effect when participants were shown a crime video and exposed to incorrect post-event information via either a co-witness discussion, indirect co-witness information, leading questions, or media report. Both co-witness discussion and indirect co-witness information led participants to report incorrect information in their report more than any other method.

Although, of course, with all of these experimental studies we must be cautious when generalizing to actual witnesses in the legal system. However, it does seem clear that for children (and adults), co-witness information can have an immediate effect on a witness' memory report. In fact, Shaw et al. (1997) highlighted those the effects of incorrect co-witness information were consistently larger than that of correct co-witness information on later witness memory reports. Although current UK Police and Criminal Evidence (PACE) regulations state that police should tell witnesses not to discuss the actual identification procedure, published data has shown that this is not actually the case. Indeed, co-witness discussion appears to be quite common in cases where there are multiple witnesses. Skagerberg and Wright (2008) investigated the frequency of co-witness discussion in sixty witnesses at the Force Identification Unit in Brighton, UK. Co-witness discussions were reported by 88% of the sample with 58% of the multiple witnesses reporting discussing the crime and suspect details with at least one other co-witness. We cover the effects of collaborative remembering in Chapter 10, however it is important to note that although co-witness discussion could lead to more information being remembered, such discussions can result in inaccurate memories and transfer of misinformation from one witness to another.

We have considered several suggestive interview techniques that have been shown to compromise the accuracy of young children's witness and victim reports. In cases such as the Wee Care nursery scandal, these suggestive interview techniques were used extensively, along with biased interviewers that led to a devastating effect. Although research has shown that young children (three to four years of age) are the most suggestible age group, there is also evidence that older children (six and upwards) can also demonstrate errors in recollection with the use of suggestive interviewing techniques. For example, 7- to 10-year-olds still produced 30%

incorrect responses to appearance related misleading questions when interviewed about a mock theft of a bike (Roebers, Bjorklund, Schneider, & Cassel, 2002) and misled children (3- to 12-year-olds) were more likely to make errors in a forced-choice task compared with children who had not been misled (Ceci, Ross, & Toglia, 1987). Moreover, as we saw in Chapter 2, even adults are prone to errors when various suggestive interview techniques are used (e.g., Loftus & Pickrell 1995; Wade et al., 2002). However, despite the wealth of evidence that indicates children can make false claims about events that happened to them, children can also report accurately. The answer to the question of "how accurate can they report?" depends on exposure to, as well as the type of, suggestive interviewing techniques. As Bruck and Ceci (1995, p. 436) conclude, "the reliability of young children's reports has more to do with the skills of the interviewer than to any natural limitations on their memory."

An interview technique to make children more credible witnesses

We have seen from the above research and interview transcripts that preschool children are especially vulnerable to suggestion, manipulation, and coercion. Of course, this is not to say that children are incompetent and incapable of acting as a witness, but rather, it indicates that the competency and capability of the interviewers requires attention when eliciting accurate details of witnessed events. Since the publication of the seminal research by Ceci and Bruck (1993, 1995), researchers in this field have examined ways to improve the quality of interviewing to both maximize the informativeness of children's testimony while simultaneously reducing the risk of errors. This requires the careful consideration of investigative procedures that are employed as well as an appreciation for the capacities and tendencies of young children (Lamb, Sternberg, & Esplin, 1995). Indeed, the work of Michael E. Lamb and colleagues (e.g., see Lamb, Hershkowitz, Orbach, & Esplin, 2008) over the past 25 years has focused not on the incompetence of children or their immature characteristics that lead to such substantial errors in their witness statements, but rather, the capacities that children do have that allow them to participate constructively within a legal setting. Below, we will briefly examine the developmentally sensitive techniques that should be used in interview situations to help young witnesses function as well as possible and that prevent situations that undermine children, making their testimony, in effect, worthless.

Professional guidelines place particular emphasis on child-directed interviewing with a view to limit the extent to which the interviewer can influence the children's response. Several interview protocols have been developed to support forensic interviewing techniques for eliciting accurate statements from younger children (see Brown & Lamb, 2009). The Cognitive Interview, originally developed for use with adults, has now been adapted for use with children of varying ages (see LaRooy, Brown, & Lamb, 2013). The Cognitive Interview technique is not without its critics, with methodological issues believed to cause large individual differences in baseline interviewer skills and thus the quality of the interview

(Memon & Higham, 1999). That said, in laboratory-based studies with children, these adaptations have proven useful in increasing detail without compromising accuracy (e.g., Akehurst, Milne, & Köhnken, 2003; Larsson, Granhag, & Spjut, 2003; Milne & Bull, 2003). Narrative Elaboration Training (NET) was also developed by Saywitz and colleagues (Saywitz & Snyder, 1996) to help children develop their narrative description of events. The children first practice (with feedback) reporting on past events before focusing the interview on the target event. The technique elicits open-ended and specific prompts, but also the use of visual cue cards to guide the narrative (categories relating to location, action, participants). Laboratory-based studies have shown that children are able to provide more information, without increasing error, especially in relation to the visual cue cards (Brown & Pipe, 2003; Peterson, Warren, & Hayes, 2013).

These various techniques have several common components. Most importantly, information is elicited using open-ended prompts and interviewers first build rapport and explain interview ground rules before the interview "proper" begins. Unfortunately, however, as research has shown (Davies, Westcott, & Horan, 2000), there was no real consistency to the use of these age-appropriate questioning techniques across interviewers, even after extensive training. Therefore, researchers at the National Institute of Child Health and Human Development (NICHD) developed a flexible interview protocol that operationalized the professional recommendations from past research. Lamb and colleagues (Lamb et al., 2007; Orbach et al., 2000) developed a protocol with explicit instructions to guide the interviewer from the initial rapport building stages to the substantive interview. Here, the early stages allow the child to become accustomed to the open-ended interview style. The interviewer will establish a rapport with the child using invitation style questions such as, "Tell me about things you like to do," that are followed up with either cued invitations or directive questions such as, "tell me more about [activity the child has mentioned]" or "when did that happen?" (Lamb et al., 2007, p. 12). The child becomes acquainted with the interview style during this initial rapport-building phase.

Once the child is comfortable with the interviewer, there is a training phase. Here the child is prompted to describe a recently experienced "non-critical" event. This further familiarizes the child with the interviewer's open-ended narrative prompts which will be followed up with cued invitations for specific details and directive style investigative utterances. The final phase of the interview will be the substantive phase where the interviewer moves on to the critical event. Before substantive events are discussed, interviewers encourage children to talk only about events "that really happened." If the interviewer says something wrong, the child is instructed to correct the interviewer and if they do not understand a question they should request explanations or clarification. A similar format is then used to elicit information about the critical event(s) with the interview beginning with a series of open-ended questions related to the allegation followed by directive prompts that target specific issues (for more detail see Phases of the NICHD protocol from Lamb et al., 2007).

The flexibility of the NICHD protocol has allowed forensic investigators to conduct successful age-appropriate interviews with children. Moreover, field studies have shown that when trained using the NICHD protocol, interviewers are more likely to follow best practice recommendations. That is, there is increased use of open-ended prompts to tap recall of event memory and less use of forced choice and suggestive questions, techniques that are more likely to tap recognition memory which can lead to increased errors. This protocol has been used successfully within the UK (Lamb et al., 2009), Israel (Orbach et al., 2000), USA (Sternberg, Lamb, Orbach, Esplin, & Mitchell, 2001), and Canada (Cyr & Lamb, 2009), with the majority of children in all of these studies providing substantially more forensically relevant details to open-ended prompts than children interviewed by the same interviewers prior to training.

Research using the interview protocol is still ongoing and the protocol itself continues to develop. For example, Malloy, Katz, Lamb, and Mugno (2015) suggested that interviewers should be trained in the development of the children's requests for clarifications. That is, they should ensure that children know when to ask for clarification and interviewers should know the most appropriate way to deal with a clarification request. In an analysis of 91 interview transcripts, Malloy et al. (2015) found that young children made few requests for clarifications and that when they were made, interviewers often rephrased the question, but at other times provided an explanation or simply reiterated it with little change. This occurred regardless of the child's age.

Of course, there are important issues relating to reasons why a child may not ask for clarification. For example, young children have poor comprehension monitoring. Also, they may not feel comfortable admitting they do not understand a question or they may feel pressured to answer every question regardless of whether they comprehend it. Although the NICHD protocol helps prepare children to make clarification requests, Malloy et al. (2015) suggested that interviewers could benefit from specific training to deal with responses to clarification requests. This is especially important given that 16% of the interviewer's interventions led to uninformative responses from the children.

It is also often difficult in field studies to test the accuracy of the information elicited using the NICHD protocol because interviewers rarely know exactly what happened. Using an event that was known to the researchers, Brown et al. (2013) directly evaluated the accuracy of information elicited from children in response to various techniques used within the NICHD protocol. This included both open-ended prompts (e.g., "tell me everything that happened . . .") and focused invitation prompts (e.g., "tell me more about . . .") that were compared with focused option-posing and suggestive prompts (e.g., "tell me about the lady that came in," when there had been no mention of the lady). To do this, children were interviewed about two events that had happened four to six weeks earlier; the target event (a photography session) was an event that happened to them and a false event (in this case, a class trip to a fire station) that was fictitious. It is important to make these direct comparisons to ensure that a protocol designed to increase a child's

TABLE 8.1 Scripted prompts for target and false event

Target event	False event
I heard that a few weeks ago someone took you from your class on your own to have a picture taken. I wasn't there but I'd like to know all about what happened. Tell me everything you remember about having your picture taken. Try not to miss anything out. I want you to tell me as much as you can.	I heard that a few weeks ago you and your class took a trip to the fire station. I wasn't there but I'd like to know all about what happened. Tell me everything you remember about what happened when you went to the fire station. Try not to miss anything out. I want you to tell me as much as you can.
It's important for me to know all about what happened if you had your picture taken. Tell me all about that.	It's important for me to know all about what happened if you went to the fire station with your class. Tell me everything you remember about that.
Did someone take you from your class so you could have a picture taken?	Was there a class trip when you put on the fireman's uniform?
I heard that you went to (location of event) and had your picture taken. Tell me all about that.	
I heard that you had your picture taken in a costume. Tell me all about that.	
I heard that you got to wear a pirate's costume. Tell me all about that.	

Adapted from Brown et al. (2013).

event narrative would not also increase the amount of detail of a narrative about an event that never occurred. This has real-world context if you consider the Wee Care nursery case and the fact that the interviewers were questioning children about an allegation which the interviewer did not know was true or false. Children received practice of event recall using open-ended or directive yes/no questions before being interviewed about the target and false events with that same style of questioning technique. Table 8.1 shows the scripted prompts for the false and target event taken from Brown et al. (2013).

Their findings indicated that children were generally highly accurate regardless of prompt type. However, two additional outcomes of interest bear mentioning. First, children who provided narrative accounts of the false event were also less accurate in their event details of the target event. Second, children who received practice recall of an event using directive and yes/no questions were least accurate when questioned about the false event first.

The NICHD protocol is a child forensic interviewing protocol that remains a "work-in-progress" (Hershkowitz, Lamb, & Katz, 2014). The above mentioned recent studies demonstrate potentially important implications for the development of enhanced training and the need for care that should be taken during the rapport building and training phases. Nevertheless, the protocol has demonstrated its versatility in different interviewing situations including when children are witnesses rather than victims (Lamb, Sternberg, Orbach, Hershkowitz, & Horowitz, 2003) or are the alleged perpetrators of crimes (Hershkowitz, Horowitz, Lamb, Orbach, & Sternberg, 2004). Moreover, the protocol's versatility extends to children of different ages (4- to 8-year-olds, Lamb, Sternberg, Orbach, Esplin, et al., 2003) and to children with intellectual disabilities (Brown, Lewis, Lamb, & Stephens, 2012). It has been shown to be successful in helping interviewers conduct high quality interviews that aid children's ability to produce detailed narratives that are high in accuracy. As Brown et al. (2013) conclude, there is no perfect interview technique. Some children (like adults) may be reluctant to disclose information, and some, given the very nature of memory, will provide false details and events. But for now, the NICHD protocol should be seen as a method of best practice that has been empirically driven and based on a sound scientific rationale.

Suggestibility in older adults

The majority of this chapter has been concerned with children's susceptibility to suggestion. However, a small but growing body of research is examining the vulnerability of older eyewitnesses to suggestion. Of course, people (children, adults) of all ages have demonstrated susceptibility to suggestion. Under "optimal" conditions, we are all capable of false recollections in the presence of implicit or explicit suggestions. However, here we are interested in whether age differences in adulthood lead to increases (or indeed decreases) in our susceptibility to suggestion.

We know from previous research that older adults face age-related deficits in many cognitive functions including memory (Craik & Jennings, 1992; La Rue, 1992). Similarly, we have seen that source-monitoring decreases with age (Hashtroudi, Johnson, & Chrosniak, 1989). This has been evidenced in a number of experimental contexts. For example, older adults have difficulty distinguishing whether an item on a word list was internally generated or externally presented (Rabinowitz, 1984), whether information was presented in a video or in a photograph (Schacter, Koutstaal, Gross, Johnson, & Angell, 1997), and whether a statement was given by one person other another (Ferguson, Hashtroudi, & Johnson, 1992). These skills are particularly important when establishing the accuracy of eyewitness memory. If older adults have impaired memory and source monitoring capabilities, they may be more vulnerable to suggestive questioning than younger adults.

In fact, several studies have shown that older adults are more susceptible to misinformation than younger adults. For example, Cohen and Faulkner (1989) presented older (mean age, 70.4 years) and younger (mean age, 34.9 years) adults with a ten-minute video depicting a crime and provided misleading information on critical aspects of the crime. Older adults made more errors and were more misled than younger adults, but showed no differences in the memory for control details (where there was no misleading information). Several other studies have since found similar results (Loftus, Levidow, & Duensing, 1992; Mitchell, Johnson, & Mather, 2003), although others have failed to find any age differences (Bornstein, Witt, Cherry, & Greene, 2000; Gabbert, Memon, & Allan, 2003).

Using a more ecologically valid paradigm, where the participant is involved in the event rather than simply an observer of the event, Mueller-Johnson and Ceci (2004) enlisted 113 young (mean age, 20.2 years) and old (mean age, 76.4 years) adults to take part in an event that included a shoulder and back massage and then several relaxation tasks including the use of a massage tool, stress ball, and various aromatherapy oils. After two and three weeks the participants were interviewed either suggestively or neutrally about the event. Suggestions and misinformation related to various aspects of the event, including the time when they were touched. For example, "When the massage therapist massaged your hands and arms, did she talk to you then?" (Mueller-Johnson & Ceci 2004, p. 1116). At the final phase, participants were all interviewed in a neutral manner with standard free-recall, unspecific prompting, and open-ended specific questions. Findings from this study showed that older adults produced more false memories in relation to the suggestive questioning from the initial interview than the younger adults. Twenty-nine percent of older adults were misled about where they had been touched which was nearly double the rate of younger adults. When older adults included suggestions in their reports, their confidence did not decrease as was the case with younger adults.

Although little research has investigated the effects of suggestibility on older adults' memory, this particular study, using a participant-based paradigm, has demonstrated a decrease in accuracy and a greater willingness to accept false information through suggestive questioning. Due to inconsistent findings in the few studies that have been conducted, further research is needed. No matter, these findings have important implications for the legal field. Both for seniors who become witnesses to crimes or accidents and the growing public awareness of elder mistreatment, understanding and evaluating older adult testimony is imperative. Just as for children, interviewers of older adults need to be aware of the possible effects of suggestive interview techniques on their witness/victim statements.

Conclusion

The overarching goal of the research conducted in this field is to examine the nature of children's narratives that are elicited under conditions of high interviewer bias, suggestive questioning, and a number of other specific conditions that may alter the accuracy of what is being remembered. These include interviewer techniques that tend to increase or decrease the accuracy of eyewitness memory narratives, such as repetitive questioning, repeated interviewing, and the effects of peer and co-witness pressure. Unless the interviewer was also an eyewitness, they are not privy to the events of an attack or sexual assault and thus we cannot accurately determine whether a single detail or an entire narrative provides an accurate account of an experience or whether it is the result of repeated erroneous suggestions. Bruck, Ceci, and Hembrooke (2002) quite aptly argued "suggestive interviewing is a double-edged sword" (p. 551); whereas it can increase agreement about the recounting of an event across witnesses and can increase the output of low probability details, because this can occur for both true and false narratives (albeit more often for false narratives), it means it is impossible to make an accurate judgment of the witness' narrative elicited using these suggestive interview techniques. In the laboratory, we have full control over and knowledge of the witness' experience. In the real world we do not.

However, there is light at the end of the tunnel. We have learned that we can lessen the adverse effects of suggestibility by changing the interview technique itself. For example, we know that for children, their eyewitness reports will be less distorted after one interview than after several (Bruck & Ceci, 1995). New interview protocols have been designed to reduce the use of leading questions, from repeating close-ended yes/no questions, and from the use of positive/negative reinforcement. Of course, this does not mean that all interviewers are aware of or use these techniques when eliciting information from eyewitnesses. Therefore, the courts still need to understand the complexity of the situation surrounding the effects of suggestibility on memory reports. From the countless studies conducted over the years we have seen that results vary greatly and even within studies, individual differences can cause considerable variability in the usefulness of these techniques. Indeed, the most highly suggestive interview, one that contains considerable misleading information, may not distort an eyewitness' memory. On the other hand, some eyewitnesses may incorporate suggestions very easily, even following a single, short interview. There were, and still are today, numerous obstacles that face interviewers and the police who investigate suspected child maltreatment cases. Suggestive interview techniques can make non-abused children look like abused children. These techniques were used in the Wee Care case and others like it. There was, and still is, no scientific test to determine whether children's reports are accurate. If there were incidents of sexual abuse, these dangerous interview techniques make it impossible to ever know who the perpetrators were and how the abuse occurred.

9

MEMORY DEMANDS ON JURORS IN THE COURTROOM

Jurors are faced with a rather daunting task, namely, to decide the guilt or innocence of a complete stranger based largely on their memory of the evidence presented at trial. Not only must this decision be just, fair, and right, but it comes after listening to and processing copious amounts of evidence and legal submissions, much of which is not familiar to jurors. As Johnson (1993, p. 605) so aptly put it:

> The rules and procedures used to govern the conduct of jury trials reflect a great deal of faith in jurors' ability to understand and retain information over long periods of time, often with much intervening information. Jurors are expected to operate as passive recipients of information presented by the parties, and generally are prohibited from taking notes, asking questions, or using other potentially memory-enhancing tools. In addition, little opportunity is provided for review or elaboration of the concepts presented. From this impoverished learning environment, jurors are expected to recall the evidence and testimony presented at trial, recall the judge's instructions about the law applicable to the case, and reach a rational conclusion regarding the proper verdict in the case. Clearly the procedures governing the jury's task during the trial belie the (naïve) belief that large amounts of novel and often complex information can be retained and integrated over a substantial period of time.

Given that trials can last not just for days but oftentimes weeks, or even months, retaining what has been said can be a monumental task. As seen in the quote from Johnson (1993), jurors are not routinely allowed to make notes and even when they do, these notes are frequently not allowed in the deliberation room. Reasons why notes are not universally accepted include concerns that by taking notes, jurors can get distracted from the trial itself and miss crucial evidence (see *Matthews v.*

Commonwealth Edison Co. in Robbennolt, Groscup, & Penrod, 2014) or that the juror with the most complete set of notes (be they accurate or inaccurate) may wield considerable influence in subsequent decision making (see *United States v. Darden* in Robbennolt et al., 2014). Although research on note taking will be reviewed later in this chapter, suffice it to say that critical decisions about guilt or innocence are typically made based on what can be remembered in the absence of memory aids. As with all of human memory, forgetting is commonplace and much of what is said during the trial is not well remembered. Indeed, misremembering trial information is not uncommon, with jurors frequently forgetting critical details of the case or remembering them inaccurately (e.g., Bodenhausen, 1988; Bourgeois, Horowitz, FosterLee, & Grahe, 1995; Fitzgerald, 2000; Kassin & Wrightsman, 1979; Pennington & Hastie, 1988; Pritchard & Keenan, 1999). Below, we consider two models of how jurors remember trial evidence, the story model and the comprehension-set model.

How jurors remember: the story model

For many jurors, the meaning and content of the evidence is unfamiliar and this stretches their interpretive abilities and increases memory load. In order to reduce this memory load, jurors frequently resort to forming schemas for the evidence (Pennington & Hastie, 1988). That is, in order to reduce the burden of trying to interpret and remember so many facts as a trial unfolds, jurors create what are known as scenarios or schemas, memory "structures" that serve to summarize the meaning of the facts of the case (for a review, see Hastie, Penrod, & Pennington, 1983).

Indeed, one of the most familiar models of how jurors reduce their memory load during a trial is called the *story* model. Originally proposed and tested by Pennington and Hastie (1988, 1990, 1992, 1993; also see Huntley & Costanzo, 2003), the story model describes the process by which jurors bring their biases to bear on trial evidence, construct a schema concerning that evidence, and use that schema to decide the guilt or innocence of the defendant. For example, Pennington and Hastie (1988) asked jurors to describe the process they used to determine the verdict in a specific case. Their descriptions (stories) of the evidence had remarkable overlap among those who came to the same verdict. That is, those who found the defendant guilty had many similar story elements as did those who found the defendant not guilty. Moreover, when jurors were given a recognition test for the evidence presented in the case, memory was better for items that were story-consistent than information that was inconsistent with their schema.

According to the story model, jurors construct a number of stories to begin with but as the trial proceeds, they select one story that provides the best "fit" to the evidence (for an overview, see Pennington & Hastie, 1993). Of course, attorneys can influence which story fits best in their opening and closing arguments. A good example of this can be found in the trial of O. J. Simpson (e.g., see Gates, 1995). Here, the prosecution created a story about spousal abuse, jealousy, and an escalation of domestic violence to an extreme level, murder. The defense, on the other hand, created a story about a corrupt police force that planted and mishandled evidence, all in the aid of victimizing a black man. When trial evidence was presented, jurors constructed their own stories by including the facts of the case that best suited one of the two frameworks presented at the beginning of the case (see Mendoza-Dinton, Ayduk, Shoda, & Mischel, 1997). Of course, the story model is relevant not just to criminal cases, but has also been applied to civil cases including those to do with sexual harassment (Huntley & Costanzo, 2003).

Although constructing a schema to reduce memory load during a trial may be helpful in retaining the central meaning of the trial evidence, schemas can also serve as a major source of evidence distortion. This is because they are summaries of the evidence and tend not to preserve factual details of the case. Thus, jurors attempt to understand the bottom-line meaning of the evidence, rather than remembering individual facts, and those meanings are the memories that they primarily rely on when deliberating on verdicts (Hans & Reyna, 2011). These summaries, although helping to preserve the meaning of the evidence presented, can also lead to the creation of meaning-consistent false memories for the facts (i.e., produce memory illusions for "facts" that are not in evidence). If these meaning-consistent false memories are used to reason about the facts from the case, then verdicts might be formed based on memories for facts that were not actually in evidence (Reyna, Hans, Corbin, Yeh, Lin, & Royer, 2015).

How jurors remember: the comprehension-set model

Another approach to understanding how jurors reduce memory load is provided by the comprehension-set processing model (Costabile, 2009; Costabile & Klein, 2005). Here, jurors do not develop meaning summaries as the trial progresses but, rather, they focus on trying to understand each item of information presented in a trial one at a time. Any global integration and evaluation of the trial information (including the extraction of meaning-consistent schemas) is deferred until a judgment is explicitly required (i.e., during jury deliberation) and is computed based on the information most readily accessible in memory (Lichtenstein & Srull, 1987; Wyer & Srull, 1986). What this suggests is that jurors should not be particularly vulnerable to creating false memories for meaning-consistent evidence that has not been presented, at least not until memories of that evidence are retrieved during verdict deliberation.

To see how this model works, consider a study by Mallard and Perkins (2005). Participants were presented with a trial transcript about a case where the defendant was accused of murdering his ex-wife and her lover. The transcript contained both admissible (incriminating letter) and inadmissible (incriminating wiretap) evidence from the same witness (presented on separate pages in the transcript). If participants integrated the evidence into a single schema, then when they were told to ignore the inadmissible evidence provided by that witness, they should also ignore the admissible evidence that came from the same source (witness). However, participants behaved in a way indicating that they treated each piece of evidence from the same witness independently and were able to ignore just the inadmissible evidence. This finding is consistent with the comprehension-set model inasmuch as jurors appear not to be integrating trial evidence even when it is presented by the same witness.

Similarly, in an earlier study, Devine and Ostrom (1985) examined information integration in a criminal trial setting where multiple witnesses (sources) provided multiple pieces of information. They presented mock jurors with a trial transcript in which the identity of the witnesses was either made salient (e.g., witnesses were questioned one at a time) or the topic of the evidence was made salient (e.g., all witness statements about a specific topic [e.g., motive for the crime] were presented together). Regardless of salience, mock jurors remembered the same number of facts, but the information remembered had different meanings depending on the initial focus (person or topic). That is, for the person-oriented condition, judgments were made about each particular witness and these judgments could taint how the facts are remembered. This suggests that how testimony is presented at trial can affect the way in which that information is interpreted and integrated (see later discussion in this chapter) and that trial structure can impact on a juror's ability to integrate information into a coherent story prior to the deliberation process. As Costabile (2009, p. 321) suggests:

> "if unable to successfully integrate evidence into a coherent understanding of trial proceedings, even the most dedicated jurors must base their verdicts upon the evidence brought to mind during juror deliberation – enhancing the reliance on salient or striking trial testimony and potentially reducing the impact of relevant but pallid witness statements."

Other factors affecting what jurors can remember

Stereotypes

In addition to these specific concerns that arise during the presentation of courtroom evidence, jurors' memory is subject to other biases. For example, jurors bring with them not only the ability to form schemas, but also come well-equipped with various stereotypes. Indeed, Bodenhausen (1988) examined the role of stereotypes in juror deliberation and found that jurors' verdicts tended to be consistent with their stereotypic biases about defendants. It is difficult to avoid stereotypes as they tend to prejudice one's interpretation of the evidence outside of our awareness. What this means is that trial testimony can be (mis)interpreted without us even knowing it in ways that are consistent with a juror's stereotype.

For example, consider gender stereotypes. Oftentimes the same evidence can be evaluated differently depending on whether the defendant is male or female. In one study, Strub and McKimmie (2016) examined gender stereotypes by co-varying the gender of the defendant (male or female) with the defendant's traits (masculine or feminine). Participants read a fictional transcript of a murder case and then gave a verdict. Male defendants were more likely to be found guilty than female defendants, but female defendants were viewed less favorably when they were described in more masculine than feminine terms.

Courts are often aware of stereotypes related to gender (also see McKimmie, Masters, Masser, Schuller, & Terry, 2013) or race (e.g., see Clark et al., 2013), among others (e.g., juvenile offender type, see Haegerich, Salerno, & Bottoms, 2013). It is because of this awareness that judges often admonish jurors to avoid being influenced by these personal biases. However, research suggests that despite these admonishments, stereotype biases are difficult for jurors to avoid (Haegerich et al., 2013). In fact, once jurors' stereotypes have been activated, judgments of guilt are far more likely to occur than when these biases have not been activated (Haegerich et al., 2013). Indeed, much like judges' instructions to forget inadmissible evidence (see later in this section), once this bias is activated and the evidence has been processed through the veil of this stereotype, it is extremely difficult if not impossible to "delete" this interpretation from the juror's perception of the evidence in the case (for an exception, see the later section on *Note Taking*).

Pretrial publicity

Another influence that is extremely difficult to eradicate in jurors' interpretation and processing of evidence is pretrial publicity. Pretrial publicity simply refers to information (usually from print, broadcast, and electronic mass media – e.g., television, newspaper, radio, magazines, the Internet) gleaned by jury-eligible individuals prior to the trial that may unduly influence their interpretation of trial evidence. Indeed, studies have shown that pretrial publicity biases jurors' interpretation of trial evidence even when they have received warnings from the judge to avoid such biases (e.g., Kassin & Wrightsman, 1988).

To see how pretrial publicity about a case can influence a juror's memory for, and interpretation of, the evidence, Kramer, Kerr, and Carroll (1990) exposed mock jurors to either neutral or prejudicial newspaper articles about a criminal case prior to the mock trial itself. Although all participants were instructed to base their verdicts solely on the evidence itself, pretrial publicity increased guilty verdicts by 15% (from 33% to 48%). Similarly, Honess, Charman, and Levi (2003) found that mock jurors who recalled more pretrial publicity were also more confident that the defendant was guilty.

That jurors' verdicts are influenced by pretrial publicity has been confirmed using meta-analytic techniques. In one particularly critical meta-analysis, Steblay, Besirevic, Fulero, and Jiminez-Lorente (1999) examined 44 studies with nearly 6000 participants. What makes this meta-analysis important is that the studies that were examined had employed a variety of different methodologies to estimate the effects of pretrial publicity on juror verdicts. As the authors anticipated, jurors who were exposed to negative pretrial publicity about the defendant were more likely to reach a guilty verdict than jurors who had not been exposed to this pretrial publicity (Steblay et al., 1999).

Of course, a critical component to pretrial publicity is its emotional content (e.g., see Ruva, Guenther, & Yarborough, 2011). Normally such pretrial publicity casts a negative bias on the defendant and this can play a role in how jurors interpret the trial evidence. We will have more to say about the emotional nature of the trial evidence and how it may be tainted by emotional pretrial publicity later in this chapter. For now, it is simply important to note that emotion plays a central role in the retention of pretrial publicity and can taint how trial evidence is interpreted (Ruva & Guenther, 2015; Ruva et al., 2011).

Finally, the question arises as to how pretrial publicity affects jurors' memory and decision making. Admittedly, these effects, like those associated with stereotypes, may occur outside of jurors' awareness. But how can this be when jurors should be aware that the source of these biases are external to the trial evidence?

One answer to this conundrum can be found in the literature on *source memory*. Here, jurors simply misattribute information acquired through pretrial publicity to information they acquired during the trial itself. In other words, information in memory loses its "source"; that is, the juror no longer remembers whether the information being retrieved occurred before the trial started and they were selected as a juror or whether it occurred during the trial as part of the evidence they acquired as a juror. In support of this idea, Ruva, McEvoy, and Bryant (2007) found that although mock jurors had good memory for both pretrial publicity and information presented at trial, they mistakenly (and very confidently) believed that the pretrial information had been presented as part of the trial evidence. Indeed, the longer the delay between acquiring information through pretrial publicity and the trial itself, the more likely it is that these source confusions will occur (e.g., Ruva & McEvoy, 2008).

Recency effects

Memory for evidence is also subject to recency effects. For example, jurors' memory is better for more recently presented evidence than evidence presented at the beginning of the trial (Costabile & Klein, 2005). This is important because if the critical evidence is presented first, then jurors either might not understand that this is the critical evidence, as comprehension of the nature of the proceedings has not developed yet or, worse, jurors may not remember this critical evidence because people tend to be poorer at remembering early-presented information. For example, Costabile and Klein (2005, Experiment 3) found that participants who read critical evidence late in a mock trial experiment were better at recalling that evidence (90%) than participants who read this evidence early in the mock trial (62%). This recency effect is well established in the memory literature and is of concern when considering the pivotal role that trial structure can play (i.e., the defense typically presents evidence later in the trial than the prosecution) in subsequent memory for the evidence. Indeed, across all of their experiments, Costabile and Klein (2005, p. 56) found that "incriminating evidence is more likely to lead to a guilty verdict when it is presented late in the trial than when it is presented early." Using their comprehension-set model, they attribute this decision-making effect to the jurors' memory for the evidence. Specifically, "later evidence was more likely to be remembered by the juror, and thus, more likely to influence juror verdicts" (Costabile & Klein, 2005, p. 56).

Directed forgetting of inadmissible evidence

Although the admissibility of evidence in a trial is most often determined in the absence of the jury, there are occasions in which jurors are unexpectedly exposed to inadmissible evidence. This can happen when, for example, a witness says something during their (cross)examination that violates the rules of evidence. In such cases, the judge can take one of two courses of actions. The first option is for the judge to declare a mistrial and order a new trial with new jurors at a later date. Of course, this delays the course of justice so in many cases the judge will take the second option, namely, to instruct jurors to disregard what was said.

If the judge takes this second option, the question arises as to how well jurors can intentionally forget (disregard or ignore) evidence that has been heard in the courtroom. There is a substantial body of memory research which suggests that it can be very difficult to intentionally forget information that has been presented. Successful forgetting of evidence can depend on a number of factors including how the to-be-forgotten information was encoded as well as the type of instruction to forget that was given (for a thorough review, see MacLeod, 1998).

In one study, referred to earlier in this chapter, Mallard and Perkins (2005) examined the intentional forgetting of inadmissible evidence when that evidence was strongly related to the other evidence jurors were expected to retain. Specifically, they examined whether mock jurors could "forget" the inadmissible testimony of a witness whose other testimony was admissible. To do this, they presented mock jurors with a summary of a murder trial in which an incriminating and admissible letter was presented. This was followed by wiretap evidence which was presented by either the same or a different witness who produced the letter, and the wiretap evidence was subsequently ruled as either being admissible or as inadmissible (due to its unreliability). The results showed that mock jurors were able to disregard the wiretap evidence when it was ruled as inadmissible regardless of whether that witness also produced the admissible and incriminating letter evidence.

Of course, there are also paradoxical effects of attempting to forget evidence. This is especially true when that evidence is emotionally charged (e.g., see Edwards & Bryan, 1997; Wegner, 1989) or concerns long-held stereotypes (e.g., Macrae, Bodenhausen, Milne, & Jetten, 1994). That is, attempts to suppress thoughts about previously presented (emotional) evidence or to ignore long-held stereotypes, like trying not to think of a pink elephant when instructed to do so, are doomed to failure (for a review, see Kassin & Studebaker, 1998).

Returning to the matter of inadmissible testimony, some studies have failed to reveal any effects on mock jurors' verdicts due to instructions to disregard testimony. That is, participants instructed to disregard (e.g., wiretap) evidence performed no differently from those not instructed to disregard the evidence (e.g., Carretta & Moreland, 1983). Worse, some studies have found a "boomerang" effect of in-admissibility instructions such that mock jurors' attention was inextricable drawn to the inadmissible evidence, making such evidence more salient during the delib-eration process (e.g., Pickel, 1995; Wolf & Montgomery, 1977). Thus, although there are some studies that show that inadmissible evidence can, under very special circumstances, be successfully ignored by mock jurors during deliberation, the great majority of studies show that these instructions are usually ineffective (for a similar conclusion, see Golding & Long, 1998).

Emotion and juror memory

Although memory (and cognitive) demands on jurors' processing of the evidence are palpable, there is an additional complication. Specifically, evidence that is pre-sented, particularly in criminal trials, is frequently emotional in nature (see Chapter 6 for a more general discussion of emotion and memory). Emotional evidence (e.g., cases that involve violence, cruelty, brutality, tragedy) can affect not just the mood of jurors (which can affect what gets encoded in memory; e.g., see Bland, Howe, & Knott, 2016; Zhang, Gross, & Hayne, 2017), but can also affect the reliability of memory for the evidence (see Phelps, 2012). For example, Semmler and Brewer (2002) examined the influence of mood and emotion on processing of trial evidence. They presented mock jurors with a case concerning a motor vehicle accident involving a car and a fuel truck. The car hit the trailer of the fuel truck, resulting in the death of the driver and injury to one of two children. The results showed that when mock jurors heard testimony that induced sadness (e.g., the truck driver suffered mental anguish after the accident) they were more accurate at the detection of inconsistencies in testimony. Although anger was not directly manipulated in this study, in participants who did evince anger (as measured by mood scales), their processing of evidence was impaired (for more on the role of emotion in memory, see Chapter 6).

Questions in the legal system have arisen concerning how best to address these issues as, clearly, juror attention to, and memory for, the evidence is viewed as quint-essential to just and fair decision-making during jury deliberations. In what follows, we consider one way in which jurors have been permitted external memory aids, namely note taking. We examine different types of note taking and the impact that has had on both memory accuracy and decision making during deliberation.

External memory aids in the courtroom: note taking

A number of courts around the world have considered the merits of two different issues surrounding note taking: (1) whether jurors should be allowed to take notes during the trial itself and (2) whether those notes should be consulted during the deliberation phase of the trial. Concerning the first issue, recall that the main question of interest to the judiciary is whether note taking during the trial will cause jurors to miss crucial evidence. For the second issue, the critical problem is whether the juror, who has what appears to be the most comprehensive set of notes, will rule the day when deciding the verdict of the trial. We discuss each of these issues, as well as how best to structure notes, in the remainder of this section.

Should jurors be allowed to take notes during the trial? Although permitted in some, many courts have been reluctant to allow note taking not just because such behavior may divert attention away from the ongoing presentation of evidence, but because jurors may differ in their literacy levels, disadvantaging some jurors while advantaging others (for a comprehensive review of case law concerning this matter, see Larsen, 1996). Empirical research on this matter has involved both field and laboratory studies. For example, in one field study conducted by Flango (1980), jurors in a criminal and a civil trial were required to take notes and were compared with jurors in standard criminal and civil trials where no notes were allowed. Although note takers put more emphasis on the defense's case than those that did not take notes, no other differences were obtained. This study, along with other field studies (Heuer & Penrod, 1988, 1994; Sand & Reiss, 1985), found that although most jurors perceive their notes to be helpful inasmuch as they serve to refresh their memory about the case, it did not influence jurors' comprehension of the evidence (see Penrod & Heuer, 1996, 1997). Of course in field studies, a number of controls are missing including random assignment of cases, trial length, and difficulty of the evidence being presented. All of these problems make it difficult to interpret research outcomes.

By contrast, in better controlled experimental studies involving mock jurors, note taking has been found to improve both memory and comprehension. For example, Rosenhan, Eisner, and Robinson (1994) randomly assigned 144 jury-eligible college students and jurors to either a note-taking or a no-note-taking condition and showed them a 75-minute video simulation of a civil trial. When recall was assessed immediately after the simulated trial, the results showed that those who took notes exhibited better memory for the evidence than those who did not take notes. Similar improvements in memory for evidence has been found in a number of other experimental studies with mock jurors (e.g., Fitzgerald, 2000; ForsterLee & Horowitz, 1997; ForsterLee, Kent, & Horowitz, 2005; Hope, Eales, & Mirashi, 2014; Horowitz & Bordens, 2002; Horowitz & ForsterLee, 2001). Thus, when better controlled experimental studies are conducted, the evidence seems clear that note taking does enhance jurors' memory for the evidence.

Of course, deciphering which parts of the evidence are the most important is a difficult task for many jurors. Indeed, as trials are a new experience for most jurors, they may not be savvy enough to know the best way to take notes (see Matthews, Hancock, & Briggs, 2004). Not only is this a case of knowing what the key pieces of evidence are, but it can also be a question of metamemory – that is, knowing how your own memory works (or fails to work) in order to take the best notes to refresh one's memory during deliberation.

In many of the experimental studies just discussed, jurors simply took what are called "freestyle" notes. That is, they were provided with blank paper and allowed to write down whatever they thought was relevant to the case. Although memory performance was better for the note takers, during the memory test, mock jurors were allowed to consult their notes. This is equivalent to allowing jurors to use their notes during deliberation and raises the issue as to whether memory enhancement was due to the taking of notes (facilitation during encoding of the evidence), having the notes during the memory test (facilitation during retrieval), or both. The answer to this question is not just of interest from a theoretical perspective but also for pragmatic reasons. That is, even in circumstances where judges permit note taking, this does not automatically mean jurors can bring their notes with them during deliberation. In fact, quite often a juror's notes are confiscated prior to entering into deliberations. This is because, as mentioned earlier, the fear is that the juror who is viewed as having the most complete set of notes (whether they are or are not and regardless of their level of accuracy) will often have a greater say in determining the verdict. Thus, if notes provide the most benefit during retrieval, then note taking during the trial will be of little benefit if judges ban the use of those notes during deliberation.

One study that has addressed this issue was conducted by ForsterLee, Horowitz, and Bourgeois (1994). Here, in the note-taking condition, mock jurors were further divided into two groups during the retrieval phase – notes accessible and notes inaccessible. As it turned out, there were no memory differences between these two conditions and both remembered more than those who did not take notes. Thus, at least from this study, it does not seem that access to notes during deliberation alters what can be remembered and that the memory advantage occurs during the encoding phase. This is consistent with a large body of evidence from the education literature which shows that note taking does enhance students' memory for lecture material (for meta-analyses, see Kobayashi, 2005, 2006).

Given the rather extensive research on the memory enhancing effects of organization and structure at encoding (e.g., Craik & Tulving, 1975), researchers have also examined the use of structured notebooks to aid juror remembering. For example, Dann, Hans, and Kaye (2007) created a special juror notebook for trials involving DNA evidence. This notebook included a glossary of DNA terms as well as a DNA checklist. Although the notebook was not specifically structured to improve remembering of the evidence, it did result in jurors having a better comprehension of DNA evidence. This in turn might have ultimately led to better retention of the DNA evidence and its subsequent use in verdict deliberation. What this suggests is that when trials involve specialized evidence (including memory testimony), specialized notebooks might provide an excellent interpretive framework for jurors' understanding of that evidence. Thus, rather than simply providing jurors with blank paper, specifically designed notebooks that contain relevant information about specialized evidence in the trial might facilitate comprehension and memory for that critical evidence.

Others have created notebooks for jurors that are specifically directed at enhancing memory for all of the relevant evidence not just specialized information. For example, Hope et al. (2014) created what is called a trial ordered notebook.

Here, rather than a set of blank pages, the notebook contains headings that serve as organization cues to different parts of the trial: Opening Statements, First Witness, Second Witness, . . ., Closing Statements. Each of these main sections contained further subsections where specific notes could be made concerning what the prosecution said and what the defense said (e.g., Opening Statements: Prosecution, Defense). Hope et al. examined the effectiveness of their structured notebook compared with that of freestyle note taking when notes were available during retrieval. They found that the structured notebook contained more legally relevant details than the freestyle notes. Moreover, during the cued recall task, mock jurors who used the structured notebook had more complete recall of the trial information although it was no more accurate than those who penned freestyle notes. Of course, because the mock jurors had access to their notes during the cued recall, it is not clear whether the observed effects are due to enhanced encoding, enhanced retrieval, or both.

In order to disentangle the encoding and retrieval components of this advantage, Thorley, Baxter, and Lorek (2016) extended this line of research by comparing structured versus freestyle note taking in mock jurors who were either allowed to use their notes during recall or whose notes were confiscated. Five groups of participants watched a trial video with one-fifth not taking notes, two-fifths taking freestyle notes, and two-fifths taking trial structured notes. At recall, half of the freestyle and half of the structured note takers had access to their notes. The results revealed that note taking enhanced recall over non-note takers even without the notes being available during recall and there was no difference between the structured and freestyle note takers. What this demonstrates is that note taking enhances memory for evidence at the time of encoding. Interestingly, Thorley et al. also found enhanced recall due to note availability during retrieval. Specifically, recall was best for structured note takers whose notes were also available during test. Together, these findings suggest that the effects of note taking mainly benefit encoding but that additional beneficial effects occur at retrieval for those who took structured notes.

Thus, note taking is beneficial to jurors' memory and structured notebooks can aid the interpretation and comprehension of evidence. As the results of Thorley et al. (2016) suggest, although structured notes have a beneficial effect at encoding, they also aid at retrieval and such notes should be allowed when jurors are deliberating on the trial verdict. Of course the question remains as to whether these memory advantages are outweighed by jurors' inattention to the evidence during note taking itself. To date, the prevailing view is that note taking may actually make jurors pay closer attention to the evidence. Indeed, the Oklahoma Court of Criminal Appeals (*Cohee v. State*, 1997, p. 2) stated:

> We find jurors may benefit from notes in several ways: (1) jurors may follow the proceedings more closely and pay more attention as they take notes for later use; (2) jurors' memories may be more easily and reliably refreshed during deliberations; (3) jurors may make fewer requests to have portions of the

trial transcript read back during deliberations; and (4) the ability to use their notes may result in increased juror morale and satisfaction.

As a final consideration concerning the utility of note taking in the courtroom, recall the earlier discussion on stereotyping. Here stereotypes were said to bias jurors' perceptions of and memory for the evidence and that these effects occurred regardless of the court's admonishment not to allow these personal biases to influence a juror's interpretation of the evidence. Interestingly, there is some research to show that note taking coupled with subsequent review of those notes, can counter the effects of stereotypes. Specifically, Strub and McKimmie (2012) presented participants with a mock trial in which either a male or a female had been charged with a stereotypical masculine crime. There were three conditions: note taking with review, note taking with no review, and no note taking. Interestingly, for participants in the note taking with review condition, decisions as to guilt or innocence were less likely to reflect the influence of stereotyped processing.

Conclusion

In much of this book we have documented the role of memory in the context of those who testify in court (e.g., complainants, witnesses, defendants). In this chapter, we have looked at the importance of memory from the other side of the courtroom, namely, in those who hear the evidence and must retain it in memory in order to come up with a fair and just verdict. Of course, memory operates the same way in witnesses and jurors, so perhaps it is not too surprising that there are many similarities between the two when it comes to remembering. However, it is important to see how our reconstructive memory systems interact with the different task requirements (remembering events that have happened versus remembering evidence passively seen or heard in the courtroom).

This task for the juror is complicated by the fact that evidence is not always easy to understand. Often there are technical terms that need explanation and sometimes there are legal arguments that are difficult to comprehend. Faced with such a daunting task, it is no wonder jurors often employ techniques (e.g., stereotyping, schema construction) when trying to remember the evidence. Although note taking can have its advantages, there are still reservations associated with their use in all courtrooms.

As well, like the evidence itself, the person presenting the evidence may exhibit a variety of emotions, ones that can affect the jurors' mood and interpretation of the evidence (also see Chapter 6). Emotion not only affects what gets encoded and subsequently remembered, but it can also bias later decision making. We see just how these variables play out in the context of juror deliberations in the next chapter where we examine the effects of collaborative remembering and decision making.

10

COLLABORATIVE REMEMBERING IN EYEWITNESSES AND JURORS

I want you to bear in mind that the testimony at trial is the evidence, not the transcript. The transcript is not authoritative. If you remember something different from what appears in the transcript, your collective recollections is controlling. In other words, the transcripts may not serve as a substitute for the collective memories of the jury. . . .

(Jury instructions suggested by *U.S. v. Montgomery*,1998)

Remembering has mainly been studied in the context of the individual. Although for the most part this is appropriate if the goal is to discover the mechanisms underlying individual memory mechanisms, it is not always useful when trying to understand how people remember in groups. People are often likely to form and recall memories with others. That is, recalling information is a social event, something that happens in the context of other people. This is especially true in cases where there are multiple eyewitnesses to a crime or when jurors remember trial information when deliberating. Indeed, people often form (encode) and recall (retrieve) memories in the company of others. So the question is, does memory behave differently in a social context when encoding and retrieving events happens collaboratively in a group from when it happens individually?

The simple answer to this question is, yes. Most studies of collaborative remembering look only at the effects of retrieving information in groups, although there are some studies that have examined encoding in groups (see later in this chapter). What these studies have shown is that collaborative memory can be both good (increase the total amount remembered collectively) and bad (decrease the total amount remembered collectively). We begin by reviewing laboratory-based studies that have examined the costs and benefits of collaborative remembering. There has only been a minimal amount of research that has specifically examined the efforts of jury members to remember during deliberation or multiple eyewitnesses to recollect events. However, based on the laboratory studies and research that has been conducted thus far, we will consider the costs and benefits of collective remembering as it applies to eyewitness testimony and jury deliberation.

In this applied setting, it is important to consider three other important factors. First, the effects on remembering following the encoding of information in a group setting and, second, the role of emotion and its effect on collaborative memory. Finally, although research is limited, it is also important to consider any age differences in collaborative memory. Throughout this chapter, we will treat collaborative remembering as a unitary construct inasmuch as it affects eyewitnesses and jurors in a similar manner. However, where there are differences, we will note where they exist between collaboratively remembering eyewitnessed events and collaborative remembering of trial evidence during jury deliberations. What we shall see is that although the courts instruct jurors to rely on their collective memories over and above their note taking (if allowed) or even the re-reading of written transcripts, the laboratory-based evidence suggests that, in fact, the group dynamics and interpersonal interactions can act to both reduce remembering or, worse, alter what the jurors and eyewitnesses remember. Indeed, when it comes to jury deliberation, collective memories of jurors are not always the most reliable record of courtroom testimony. A similar consensus exists when it comes to the effects of collective remembering of eyewitnesses.

Reductions in memory when remembering collaboratively

We begin by outlining the collaborative remembering paradigm. Here, participants study materials (e.g., word lists, stories) individually. Next, there is a delay period ranging from a few minutes to a week or more. When the delay period is short, consisting of several minutes, participants engage in some sort of filler activity (e.g., playing Tetris). Following the delay, participants perform a memory test (e.g., free recall) in which they attempt to remember all of the studied information. Although this testing procedure can vary across studies (and these variations will be noted throughout this chapter), they all typically involve both individual remembering (remembering in isolation) and collaborative remembering (most often in groups of two or three).

The outcome from these studies has been viewed by some as counterintuitive. That is, individuals tend to remember less when recalling in collaborative groups than when they remember in isolation (for a review, see Rajaram & Pereira-Pasarin, 2010). Although the total amount remembered by the group is usually greater than that recalled by any one individual, the reduction in the total amount remembered becomes clear when one contrasts this group total with the cumulative memory of all individuals who recalled the information in isolation. This phenomenon, that there is less total information remembered in the group (also called *collaborative groups*) than in the cumulative memories from individuals who remembered in isolation (also called *nominal groups*), has been labeled *collaborative inhibition* (see Weldon & Bellinger, 1997). Interestingly, this memory deficit in group settings is reminiscent of similar deficits found in studies of brainstorming (Brown & Paulus, 2002) where fewer ideas are generated in collaborative groups than nominal ones.

So, why does remembering in a collaborative group reduce the total amount remembered compared with when individuals remember in isolation? One answer comes in the form of the *retrieval inhibition hypothesis* (Basden, Basden, Bryner, & Thomas, 1997). This theory posits that each collaborative group member has their own individual strategy for organizing information at study and an optimal retrieval strategy when asked to recall that information at test. When group members encounter different organizational and retrieval strategies during collaboration, their own individual strategies become disrupted resulting in all group members failing to recall to their maximum potential. As nominal group members are tested individually, they are not subjected to the same disruption.

This theory has received considerable support from studies that have examined factors that enhance or diminish collaborative inhibition. For example, Basden, Basden, and Henry (2000) manipulated category size of the to-be-studied word lists. Participants were asked to learn either six category lists made of fifteen items or fifteen category lists made up of six items. Although the number of items remained constant in both stimulus conditions, the category lists with more list items led to larger differences in group members' organizational strategies compared with the shorter category lists. As would be predicted by the retrieval disruption hypothesis, larger category lists led to increased collaborative inhibition.

Group dynamics can also influence collaborative inhibition. Group size is an important factor to consider from an ecological as well as theoretical standpoint. In a social context people often recall information in varying group sizes. Although the majority of research on collaborative memory focuses on triads (e.g., Basden et al., 1997; Weldon & Bellinger, 1997), there are studies that have directly compared group size. Consistent with the retrieval strategy hypothesis, as group size increases and group members encounter more diverse retrieval strategies (e.g., Thorley & Dewhurst, 2009), the effect of collaborative inhibition increases. Although this study only examined dyads, triads, and tetrads, this trend is particularly worrisome when it comes to twelve-person collaborative remembering during jury deliberation.

Retrieval disruption in many of these instances is a clear cost of collaboration on memory performance. There are other negative effects of collaboration that can occur in memory. Although most research refers to a disruption to recall that can later be recovered (Thorley & Dewhurst, 2009; Weldon & Bellinger, 1997), some studies have also shown that the blocking effect can cause long-term forgetting. For example, Henkel and Rajaram (2011) found evidence of permanent forgetting after an individual-collaborative-individual recall condition compared with repeated individual recall conditions, with more participants failing to recall items on the third recall task that they had successfully recalled during the first recall test with the intervening collaborative condition.

Of course, there is growing evidence that retrieval disruption might not be the only mechanism mediating collaborative inhibition (for a recent review, see Marion & Thorley, 2016). This evidence comes from two sources: the first is a failure to replicate some key findings that support the retrieval disruption hypothesis and the second is new evidence that *retrieval inhibition* may also play an important role in collaborative inhibition. We discuss each of these in turn next.

Concerning failures of replication, the retrieval disruption hypothesis predicts that collaborative inhibition should be reduced (or eliminated) when group members use similar rather than idiosyncratic encoding and retrieval strategies. Although some tests of this assumption have produced results that are consistent with this hypothesis (e.g., Barber, Rajaram, & Fox, 2012; Harris, Barnier, & Sutton, 2013), others have not (e.g., Barber & Rajaram, 2011; Dahlström, Danielsson, Emilsson, & Andersson, 2011). In addition, the retrieval disruption hypothesis predicts that collaborative inhibition should be reduced (or eliminated) when participants attempt to remember non-overlapping rather than overlapping information. That is, when participants are presented with lists containing overlapping items as well as non-overlapping information, and they attempt to remember information unique to their individualized lists, collaborative inhibition should be attenuated compared with when they are attempting to remember information shared across individuals. Again, although there are some studies whose results are consistent with this hypothesis (e.g., Basden et al., 1997, Experiment 3), others are not (e.g., Meade & Gigone, 2011, Experiment 1). In fact, in this latter study, collaborative inhibition was actually higher for the non-overlapping information than for the overlapping information.

Finally, concerning failures to replicate, the retrieval disruption hypothesis predicts that collaborative inhibition should be reduced (or eliminated) when the memory test does not rely on individual and idiosyncratic retrieval strategies. Specifically, when the tests themselves impose their own particular strategy, as when cued (rather than free) recall tests are administered or when recognition tests are employed, these tests are equally disruptive to individual strategies regardless of whether they are administered individually or in groups. Again, although some studies have confirmed this prediction (e.g., Barber, Rajaram, & Aron, 2010; Thorley & Dewhurst, 2009), others have not. In fact, reductions in collaborative inhibition have not been found in studies using cued recall (e.g., Kelley, Reysen, Ahlstrand, & Pentz, 2012; Meade & Roediger, 2009) or in studies using tests of recognition (e.g., Danielsson, Dahlström, & Andersson, 2011).

So, if retrieval disruption is not always the source of collaborative inhibition, what else could be the cause? Some have suggested that *retrieval inhibition* could also play a role in collaborative inhibition (e.g., Barber, Harris, & Rajaram, 2015). Retrieval inhibition is a form of suppression where cuing (either through others recalling information or cues presented as part of the memory task) selectively strengthens some items in memory while at the same time suppressing other, non-cued items making them unavailable for retrieval (also see Bäuml & Aslan, 2004). Retrieval inhibition is similar to the well-known *part-set cuing* effect where providing participants with retrieval cues not only can improve memory for those items that were cued but can also lower recall for the other list items for which no cues were provided (e.g., Nickerson, 1984; Slamecka, 1968). If retrieval inhibition also contributes to collaborative inhibition, then suppression of the non-cued items should persist and the participants who received part-set cuing should exhibit poorer memory compared with a free recall group. Moreover, if non-cued information has been rendered unavailable, this impairment should persist regardless of how those memory representations are subsequently probed (e.g., free recall or recognition) (see Aslan, Bäuml, & Grundgeiger, 2007; Bäuml & Aslan, 2006). In fact, Barber et al. (2015) found consistent support for the retrieval inhibition hypothesis across two experiments. So it would appear that there are at least two factors contributing to collaborative inhibition, retrieval disruption and retrieval inhibition.

Collaborative inhibition occurs for a variety of different memory representations not just word lists (related and unrelated) (e.g., Basden et al., 1997; Blumen & Rajaram, 2008; Weldon & Bellinger, 1997, Experiment 1) and stories (e.g., Takahashi & Saito, 2004; Weldon & Bellinger, 1997, Experiment 2). For example, collaborative inhibition has also been found when using pictures (Finlay, Hitch, & Meudell, 2000, Experiment 1), film clips (e.g., Andersson & Rönnberg, 1995), and emotionally laden events (e.g., Yaron-Antar & Nachson, 2006; see later discussion in this chapter). As well, collaborative inhibition tends to increase with group size (see Thorley & Dewhurst, 2009).

Improvements in memory when remembering collaboratively

Of course, collaborative remembering is not all bad. In fact, there are numerous studies showing that there are "downstream" benefits of collaborative recall (for a review, see Rajaram & Pereira-Pasarin, 2010). In particular, people who previously remembered in group settings have better subsequent memory than those who did not participate in collaborative remembering (e.g., Blumen & Rajaram, 2008; Weldon & Bellinger, 1997). There are several reasons for these benefits. The first reason concerns the fact that during group memory tests, participants are re-exposed to items they may have forgotten (or never successfully encoded in the first place) when other group members successfully remember them. What this means is that collaborative remembering provides all individuals with a relearning opportunity. Of course, participants may also be exposed to information that is falsely remembered by the other group members, something that could also increase subsequent false memories in later individual recall.

A second reason concerns the ability to rehearse the studied information through retrieval. That is, it is well known that a memory test can be more powerful than restudying the information on subsequent tests of memory (Karpicke & Roediger, 2008; Roediger & Karpicke, 2006). By retrieving the previously encoded information, participants can practice learning how to retrieve that information, something that when successfully accomplished, strengthens not just the memory representation itself but also the path(s) by which it is retrieved. Finally, collaborative remembering can improve an individual's memory by reducing subsequent errors in recall. Although information falsely recalled by other members of the group when not corrected by other group members might lead to subsequent false memories in individuals, errors in an individual's recall can be corrected by the group (e.g., Ross, Spencer, Blatz, & Restorick, 2008; Ross, Spencer, Lindardatos, Lam, & Perunovic, 2004).

False memories in collaborative remembering

As just noted, there is a possibility that collaborative remembering can lead to false memories. In fact, if fellow group members falsely remember something and are not corrected by other members in the group, such items can be falsely remembered in later recall by individuals who participated in collaborative remembering in that group. This is similar to what are known as *social contagion effects* where individuals' subsequent memory reports can become contaminated when others in a group merely suggest that certain events occurred that in fact did not happen (e.g., Roediger, Meade, & Bergman, 2001).

A small body of research has recently investigated the effect of collaborative remembering using the Deese/Roediger-McDermott (DRM) paradigm (Deese, 1959; Roediger & McDermott, 1995). Recall that in this paradigm, participants are presented with lists of semantically associated words (e.g., *bed, rest, awake, tried, dream*) that converge on a single, non-presented critical item, in this case, *sleep*. Previous research has shown that participants often falsely recall the critical lures, with levels of false memory equalling and sometimes exceeding that of correct memory.

Basden, Basden, Thomas, and Souphasith (1998) directly examined false recall in collaborative groups using DRM word lists. Trios studied DRM lists and later engaged in either turn-taking collaborative recall, where each group member contributes one item at a time in a sequential order, or nominal group recall. The collaborative and nominal trios falsely recalled an equivalent number of critical lures. Takahashi (2007) presented pairs with DRM lists but used free-for-all collaborative recall, where deliberation is allowed and participants respond freely. Again, both group types recalled an equivalent number of critical lures.

However, research has also shown (Thorley & Dewhurst, 2009) that turn-taking groups falsely recalled the most critical lures, with no difference between free-for-all and nominal groups. Furthermore, critical lure recall increased with group size (individuals, pairs, trios, and quartets) across all conditions. Thorley and Dewhurst (2009) argued that turn-taking recall places group members under pressure to contribute list words and the items the group members generate are often the strongly associated critical lures. This collaborative facilitation was not observed in the earlier Basden et al. (1998) study as the DRM lists they used had weaker associations to the critical lures. The members of their turn-taking trios were, therefore, less likely to think of the critical lures when under pressure to respond. Interestingly, Thorley and Dewhurst (2009) also found that participants who collaborated in the high-pressure turn-taking recall groups, later, falsely recalled more DRM critical lures than individuals who had previously worked alone. Furthermore, prior collaboration in a pair, trio, or quartet on a DRM recognition test enhanced true and false memory when given a subsequent individual recognition test. This suggests that collaboration causes long-term alteration of memory, for both true and, more worryingly, false events.

Importantly, there are also age effects for false memories in collaborative remembering (also see later discussion of age effects in this chapter). Although very little work has focused on children, one might predict that to the extent these errors are due to suggestibility and social contagion, younger children should be more susceptible to these errors than older children and adults (Howe, 2011; also see Chapter 8). However, to the extent that these errors are driven by internal, self-generated spontaneous false memories, young children might be less susceptible to such errors of remembering than older children and adults (e.g., Otgaar, Howe, Brackmann, & Smeets, 2016).

Concerning the effects of aging, Meade and Roediger (2009) found that older adults were more susceptible to false memories than younger adults as a result of collaborative remembering. Ross et al. (2008) reported similar findings for older adults. Specifically, they found that collaborative remembering resulted in more self-generated false memories for older than younger adults. However, both younger and older adults were able to successfully edit false memories produced by another person through subsequent discussion. This reduction in overall false recollection may have occurred because the collaborative recall groups in this study were comprised of spouses. It is well known that in such dyads, it is much easier to correct each other's recollection than it is in a group comprised of strangers.

This latter point is quite important. Although both collaborative inhibition and false memories are reduced in groups where people know one another, presumably because they feel more comfortable communicating with each another, higher rates of collaborative inhibition and false memories are normally seen in groups of strangers (e.g., Meade & Roediger, 2009; Peker & Tekcan, 2009). This is critical forensically because typically, eyewitnesses to a crime do not know each other very well and subsequent discussion of the incident witnessed could increase false memory rates among witnesses. Similarly, members of a jury are strangers and discussions of the facts heard or seen at trial during deliberation could result not only in higher rates of collaborative inhibition but also in uncorrected false memories for "facts" that were not in evidence.

Effects of collaborative encoding

Of course, the effects on memory of collaboration are not just restricted to retrieval, but can often be seen during encoding. For example, often there are multiple witnesses to an event and jurors are together when they hear the evidence in a case. However, unlike the research on collaborative remembering, the research on collaborative encoding is quite sparse. In one relatively recent study, Barber et al. (2010) had either individuals or dyads create meaningful sentences using unrelated word pairs. Later, participants were asked to recall the second word in the pair when given the first word (i.e., a paired-associate test). There were three conditions during retrieval: alone, intact dyad (same person as during encoding), and changed dyad (different person from encoding). As it turned out, collaborative encoding impaired memory in all of these three retrieval conditions including the intact dyad condition.

They attributed these deficits to two factors. The first was that individuals working alone during sentence construction produced better integrated, more cohesive sentences and this was related to subsequent recall. The second was that when sentences were constructed in dyads, despite its level of cohesiveness, if it was created by the other person in the dyad, recall was not improved. What this suggests is that self-generated information is better retained than other-generated information.

Age and collaborative memory

Studies of the development of collaborative memory in children are also quite scarce. Indeed, only a few studies have investigated collaborative recall in children. For example, Andersson (2001) compared performance on a spatial memory task in 7-year-old and 15-year-old pairs. Pairs were in one of three conditions – reciprocal friends, non-reciprocal friends, and non-friends. Andersson found not only that older children outperformed younger children, but also that only the reciprocal friends performed comparably with their nominal equivalents. Non-reciprocal friends and non-friends performed at a lower level than their nominal equivalents. Andersson argued that younger children had inferior cognitive abilities and poor strategic planning at encoding. The results also suggest that children of all ages may benefit from collaborating with friends due to a possible "common ground" or what is referred to in the literature as a transactive memory system.

In contrast, Leman and Oldham (2005) compared three collaborative groups (two 7-year-olds, two 9-year-olds, and a 7- and a 9-year-old) and their nominal group equivalents on a word list recall task (unrelated words). Pairs containing older children (9-year-olds) recalled more than those containing just younger children (two 7-year-olds). However, pairs containing the older children (two 9-year-olds, and a 7- and a 9-year-old) recalled less than their nominal group equivalents. Conversely, the younger children (two 7-year-olds) recalled as many words as their nominal group equivalents. Collaboration therefore, seems to be inhibited in pairs containing older children.

In the most recent study, Gummerum, Leman, and Hollins (2013) examined age differences in 7- and 9-year-old children when they recalled shared versus unshared information. Children studied one of three word lists consisting of ten words each. Across three of the lists, seven items were identical (shared information) and three were unique (unshared information). Later, some of the children recalled the lists in isolation and the others recalled the lists in groups composed of three children. The results showed more collaborative inhibition in 9-year-olds than 7-year-olds. That is, 9-year-olds recalled less information in groups than when cumulative recall was obtained from children recalling alone, whereas there was no difference for the 7-year-olds. Moreover, 7-year-olds showed little if any collaborative inhibition for either the shared or unshared information whereas 9-year-olds showed collaborative information for both types of information.

The attenuation (or absence) of collaborative inhibition in young children has been interpreted in terms of the development of children's understanding of coordinated social activity (i.e., remembering in a group). Because the effects of interruptions caused by partners is not disruptive to young children's remembering (e.g., they expect that groups engage in turn taking), this leaves them less vulnerable to collaborative inhibition (e.g., Leman & Oldham, 2005). Of course, these effects could also come about because younger children (e.g., 7-year-olds) use fewer and less sophisticated organization strategies during encoding and retrieval than older children (e.g., 9-year-olds) so that interruptions are not as detrimental to overall recall (e.g., Howe, 2011).

Considerably more research has examined collaborative remembering in older adults (for a review, see Blumen, Rajaram, & Henkel, 2013). Importantly, though, like the research with children, collaborative inhibition has routinely been found in older adults (e.g., Henkel & Rajaram, 2011; Meade & Roediger, 2009; Ross et al., 2004, 2008). For example, Henkel and Rajaram (2011) examined younger and older adults' collaborative remembering using categorized word lists. After studying the word lists, there were three memory tests. The first and last tests were always taken individually with the second test either being taken individually as well or in a group (triads). They found that although older adults recalled less overall than younger adults, regardless of age, collaborative remembering resulted in both costs and benefits. Specifically, during collaborative remembering both true and false recall rates were reduced, but there was also more reminiscence with some participants exhibiting improved memory scores on the post-collaborative memory test. Although these post-collaborative (downstream) benefits were initially lower for older than younger adults, other research has shown that they are similar following a one-week delay after collaboration (Blumen & Stern, 2011). Thus, although there are developmental differences in the amount remembered by older and younger adults, the magnitude of both positive and negative effects of collaborative remembering are developmentally invariant, at least in the long run.

Emotion and collaborative remembering

Although we have discussed the role of emotion in memory earlier (see Chapter 6), often collaborative remembering is uniquely affected by emotion. That is, eyewitnessed events are frequently emotional and arousing as is the testimony heard by many jurors. Despite the importance of emotion in memory, and the presence of emotional information in both eyewitness and juror memory, there are only a handful of studies that have examined how emotional information affects collaborative remembering. In the first of these, Yaron-Antar and Nachson (2006) examined memory for the assassination of Israel's Prime Minister Itzhak Rabin both in individuals as well as in groups. They found the usual collaborative inhibition effect. Specifically, on aggregate (nominal group), individuals produced more (accurate and inaccurate) details about the event than the pooled responses from members of the collaborative group. Others who have examined collaborative remembering of the death of someone famous who was in the public eye (in this case, "The Crocodile Hunter") found no effect of collaborative versus individual remembering on people's memory for episodic details of where and when they heard the news about his death (Harris, Barnier, Sutton, & Keil, 2010). However, they did find that collaborative remembering led to more distortions in people's memory for their experienced emotions, distortions that included an overall reduction in how they remembered the intensity of their feelings and how shocked they were at the news.

These findings are not just limited to deaths of public figures. Indeed, similar effects have been reported when the to-be-remembered material consisted of emotional films (Wessel, Zandstra, Hengeveld, & Moulds, 2015). Again, people who recalled in collaborative groups (triads) remembered fewer (correct and incorrect) details about the films than individuals working in isolation.

Although these results are of considerable interest, none of these studies included a neutral control event so that appropriate conclusions about the effect of emotion on collaborative remembering could be drawn. That is, in the absence of examining how these same people remember more mundane or neutral events, it is difficult to know how emotion impacted collaborative versus individual remembering. Moreover, the events examined in these studies were negatively valenced so it is not clear whether it is emotion (positive or negative) *per se* that influences collaborative versus individual remembering or whether these effects are specific to negative valence.

These issues are important because there is evidence that it may be arousal (high vs. low) that influences memory not simply valence (positive vs. negative) (e.g., Yonelinas & Ritchey, 2015; see Chapter 6 as well). If true, then perhaps the effects of collaborative remembering would be the same for both positive and negative memories given that their levels of arousal were similar. Alternatively, there is reason to suppose that valence is critical to memory even when arousal levels are controlled, particularly when it comes to remembering specific details and the reduction of incorrect memories (e.g., Kensinger, 2009; but see Howe et al., 2010; Porter, Taylor, & Ten Brinke, 2008).

These limitations (valence vs. arousal and emotional vs. non-emotional events) were examined in two recent experiments by Kensinger, Choi, Murray, and Rajaram (2016). The first experiment used the standard collaborative remembering paradigm and the second one used the social contagion paradigm. In both experiments, participants studied categorized lists consisting of photos that were either negatively valenced (e.g., a funeral which included a casket, hearse, and cemetery), positively valenced (e.g., a wedding which included a veil, flower girl, and bride), or neutral. All photos had been previously normed for valence and arousal. Items were selected so that they varied in valence but the negative and positive items were equated on arousal and were more arousing than the neutral photos.

Participants studied the lists individually and were required to make judgments as to how well a picture exemplar (e.g., a picture of Jupiter) fit with a category heading (e.g., astronomy) on a scale of one to five. Participants were also informed that there would be a later memory test for the specific exemplars. When participants returned 48 hours later, they were administered either an individual or group recognition test. Neither the images themselves nor the category labels were presented; instead they were presented with words that referred to the originally pictured items.

For the collaborative inhibition experiment, the results showed that emotion (both positive and negative) enhanced memory discriminability of the items (more hits and fewer false alarms) regardless of whether the memory test was administered individually or collaboratively (in triads). In the social contagion experiment, recall rather than recognition was used at test and participants were given the category label (e.g., funeral) and asked to remember items from the list (e.g., hearse, cemetery). Some participants recalled alone whereas others did so in a group (in pairs) where the second member of the pair was a confederate who intentionally gave incorrect answers. Finally, following the recall test and an additional 30-minute break (which included a Sudoku filler task), participants were tested individually on a recognition test. The results revealed that the misinformation supplied by the confederate had less impact on the subsequent recognition test for emotional information (both positive and negative) than for the neutral information.

Together, these findings indicate that emotion (positive and negative) enhances memory discrimination for both individual and collaborative remembering. Indeed, even in the face of misinformation being presented in a social contagion experiment, emotional information was less susceptible to subsequent distortion than neutral information. Of course, these experiments involved categorized lists of information that were unrelated across categories. Because of this, it is not clear that these findings generalize to the highly interrelated emotional information that is stored following the witnessing of a crime or hearing the emotional testimony of complainants in the courtroom.

Applications to collaborative eyewitness testimony

Although there has been extensive research on factors that affect eyewitness testimony, very little research has examined the effects of collaborative eyewitness discussion of events they witnessed as a group. However, consider the case review by Memon and Wright (1999) concerning the 1995 Oklahoma bombing. In April of that year, 186 people were killed and 600 injured after a bomb exploded in the Alfred P. Murrah Federal building in Oklahoma City. Timothy McVeigh was arrested and convicted of the bombings.

The main evidence for the conviction of McVeigh came from several witnesses who worked at Elliot's Body Shop where McVeigh rented the truck used in the bombing. Although CCTV footage was to show McVeigh arriving by taxi alone, one of the three eyewitnesses, when first questioned, stated that McVeigh was with a second man. This man wore a blue baseball cap with a zigzag pattern. At this first interview, the other two witnesses gave very sketchy descriptions of McVeigh and did not remember the second man. However, after the initial interviews, their memories transformed. They both became very confident that they could remember the second man, and one witness could even provide details of what he looked like – details that were very similar to those given by the first eyewitness (including a baseball cap with lightning stripes). Months later, the first witness confessed that he had recalled details of another customer who had rented a van the next day. Indeed, this was the case. Todd Bunting had arrived at 4pm the following day to pick up a rental truck. He wore a baseball cap with a blue and white zigzag pattern. But, how did the second witness come to recall the exact same error, and how did all three recall seeing a second man when McVeigh came alone? The answer may lie in the problem of cross-contamination. Later, the three witnesses admitted in testimony that they had discussed their memories prior to being questioned.

This case provides clear evidence for how a witness' memory report can influence that of another. The same effects have been demonstrated in laboratory-based research and similar findings have been demonstrated using more ecologically valid paradigms. For example, Gabbert et al. (2003; see also Gabbert, Memon, Allan, & Wright, 2004) found a "memory conformity" effect whereby post-event information provided by a co-witness was included in the eyewitness report of the second witness. Using a novel procedure, Gabbert et al. (2003) showed each member of a dyad a different video of the same event. Each video contained unique event items seen only by one witness. Dyads in the experimental group were encouraged to discuss the event. Finally, each witness performed an individual recall test. Performance was compared with that of a control group who did not discuss the event prior to recall. Seventy-one percent of witnesses (compared with 0% from the control condition) who had discussed the event went on to mistakenly recall items acquired during the discussion. Gabbert et al. (2003) refer to both cognitive factors, such as source confusion (e.g., Loftus & Hoffman, 1989), and to social factors, such as the individual's need for social approval (informational influence, Deutsch & Gerard, 1955) as the cause of these errors. Although such explanations will continue to be explored, it is clear from this research that the legal communities should take care when interviewing multiple witnesses and not give undue weight to the consistency of their independent statements when judging their accuracy (Gabbert et al., 2003).

Conclusion

Eyewitnesses must remember what they saw and frequently talk among themselves following the witnessed event. Similarly, jurors must remember the trial evidence if they are to reason using the facts of the case during their deliberations. In fact, at least 10% of what jurors talk about during deliberation is based on what they remember of the trial evidence (Warren & Kuhn, 2010). As noted in Chapter 9, many courts prefer to have jurors rely on their memories rather than on external aids such as note taking or trial transcripts. The (perhaps naïve) belief here is that even if an individual's memories are not always reliable, the collaborative recollections of all jurors should compensate for these individual errors. That is, twelve heads are better than one and that a fairly accurate representation of the trial evidence will emerge through the use of collaborative remembering.

Unfortunately, as with many naïve beliefs, collaborative remembering does not lead to better memory for eyewitnessed events or trial evidence. What the research reviewed in this chapter has shown is that collaborative remembering typically results in poorer overall memory across group members than the sum of the information recalled by those same people in isolation. This so-called collaborative inhibition arises due to retrieval disruption and retrieval inhibition, among other factors. However, following collaborative remembering there can be both costs and benefits in an individual's later recall. In terms of costs, collaborative remembering disrupts self-generated retrieval and can lead to extended retrieval inhibition or extended forgetting. It can also result in social contagion effects in memory; that is, individuals not only forget information (errors of omission) but can also come to falsely remember information "recalled" by other group members, information that was not present in the original event (errors of commission).

In terms of benefits, groups perform better than any single individual on memory tests. This can be helpful particularly when groups are attempting to relate as much about an event as possible (e.g., when there are multiple eyewitnesses to a crime) or are trying to remember trial evidence when deciding the guilt or innocence of a defendant. In addition, although there are social contagion effects that occur during collaborative remembering, there are also opportunities for group members to "prune" the memory errors of others as well as a chance for individuals to rehearse and possibly reinstate memories for elements of events that actually did occur.

Developmentally, these costs and benefits appear to be invariant. That is, with the exception of children who are among the youngest tested in collaborative remembering studies (7-year-olds), all children show both the costs (e.g., collaborative inhibition) and benefits (e.g., rehearsal and reminiscence effects) of collaborative remembering. Similarly, for both young and old adults, these effects tend to be of a similar magnitude regardless of age, especially following a one-week post-collaborative delay.

It is important to note here that most of the studies on collaborative remembering take place with strangers as participants and the stimuli being remembered are word lists or very occasionally other materials such as stories (Johansson, Andersson, & Rönnberg, 2005), pictures (e.g., Kensinger et al., 2016), or film clips (e.g., Wessel et al., 2015). Although the use of strangers is relevant to both eyewitness recollection (where often bystanders witnessing a crime are strangers) and juror memory during deliberation (again, where jurors typically do not know each other prior to jury duty), the heavy reliance on the use of word lists or simple stories may make these findings difficult to generalize to the highly interrelated and often emotional nature of events that eyewitnesses and jurors collaboratively remember.

This limitation has been addressed in some recent work in which people are asked to remember personally relevant information (e.g., Harris, Keil, Sutton, Barnier, & McIlwain, 2011). Much of this work involves older couples who have known each other for many years and who have developed compatible retrieval strategies (e.g., well-developed systems of communication and joint remembering). Under these conditions, collaborative facilitation often occurs, not collaborative inhibition. Although clearly an interesting reversal of the usual collaborative inhibition, it is not clear to what extent such collaborative facilitation is determined by personal relationships rather than the fact that people are remembering personally relevant information.

Of course, as we just saw, some very recent studies of the effects of emotion on collaborative remembering also address the limited generalizability of some of the collaborative inhibition findings to eyewitnesses and jurors. Here, emotion seems to increase the discriminability of information in memory, making it less subject to the effects of distortion. However, these studies are somewhat limited inasmuch as they either did not contrast emotional and non-emotional information when both arousal and valence were controlled or when they were contrasted, the study materials were categorized lists of pictures, not well-integrated emotional events that one might encounter when witnessing a crime or listening to trial testimony. As always, further research is needed to tease these factors apart and allow us to better understand the effects of emotion and information relatedness on collaborative remembering among eyewitnesses and jurors.

PART 3

Conclusions and recommendations

11

CONCLUSIONS AND RECOMMENDATIONS FOR MEMORY AND THE LAW

We have covered a wide variety of topics in this volume, providing an overview of the literature relevant to how reliance on memory as evidence in the courtroom can lead to miscarriages of justice. In this chapter, we distill this broad-brush review by extracting the main conclusions that can be drawn from this research about memory as evidence and making some specific recommendations concerning the use of memory evidence in the judicial system. In doing this, we hope to provide guidance for students of all ages who are interested in memory, legal professionals who work in the justice system, and laypeople who may be called upon to adjudicate decisions in the jury room when memory serves as evidence.

We begin by reminding readers of what we said at the outset of this volume, as well as throughout it, that because memory is (re)constructive, it is fallible and prone to (re)creations of images and recollections that although "feeling" real, may be partly or wholly false. This is not because memory is inherently unfit for purpose but because its purpose is not solely to (accurately) remember the past. Rather, memory is used to extract meaning, solve problems, anticipate the future, and ultimately shape who we are. Importantly, because memory is used to extract meaning (going beyond the individual memory events), aid creative problem solving, and imagine the future, it involves inferences, going beyond the mere memory "records" created by encoding and storing experiences. It is because of this broader, more flexible set of functions that memory performs, that it does not provide an accurate, videotape-like encryption of the past.

Because of extensive research examining memory we, as scientists, know this basic assumption about memory. Unfortunately, this scientific understanding of memory is not what has shaped the role of memory in the justice system. Instead, a more "intuitive" understanding of how memory works has formed opinion about the role of memory in our legal system. As we have seen in this volume, these intuitive beliefs about memory are far from the whole truth. The assumption that memory is an accurate representation of the past is a deeply embedded belief in everyday thinking and, more worryingly, the legal system. Instead, as we know, we construct a narrative of the past by pulling together pieces of detail, for example, who we were with, where we were, any smells or tastes, when we were there. All these parts are not stored together, but rather distributed across multiple representational systems in the brain. When we are constructing our memory narrative, we know that we flesh out the details and fill-in-the-gaps with information that was not part of the event but makes sense given similar experiences in the past. This way our narrative becomes a coherent, but not necessarily an altogether true, story. With this view of memory, it is important to remember that more detail does not necessarily mean greater accuracy. That is, rather vague details associated with a memory narrative can be completely accurate and a highly detailed narrative can be completely false.

Finally, before moving on to our conclusions and recommendations, one last point is worth emphasizing – a memory, once formed, is not a fixed entity. The naïve misconception that once a memory is formed it remains stable in storage, although it may fade somewhat over time, is simply wrong. As the research reviewed in this volume attests, memories are malleable and, when reactivated, are subject to alteration depending on myriad factors including who you are speaking to and what questions are being asked of you. This has its most important implications when a witness or victim is questioned multiple times by police, investigators, in the courtroom, and even more generally in conversations with friends and family. If nothing else has been gleaned from reading this book, it should be remembered that memory is both fallible and malleable.

In what follows, we draw specific conclusions from the various chapters in this book and present them seriatim. We begin with what might be the most controversial of our conclusions, namely, whether there is any legitimacy to claims that memories can be repressed. As we noted in Chapter 2, there is no substance to the idea that memories (of trauma) are repressed in the classic sense, and thus, the "recovered memory" debate is moot. We therefore conclude that:

1. There is no scientific evidence to support the existence of a repressed memory mechanism.

Specifically, the evidence from memory research suggests that although people can and do forget experiences, even traumatic ones, the terms "repressed" and "recovered" are used inappropriately. Instead, it is much more likely that apparent periods of forgetting are a result of normal memory mechanisms, including normal forgetting, failure to understand the traumatic nature of the event, failures of metamemory, intentional avoidance (or forgetting), and infantile and childhood amnesia, all of which have been adequately documented by ample scientific research.

Of course, in the courtroom, it is difficult to determine with a high degree of certainty whether a memory is about a real or an implanted event. As we noted in Chapter 2, many a "recovered" memory may contain both a kernel of "truth" as well as aspects that are illusory (Lindsay, 1998). We also pointed out that there exist some important factors that can assist triers-of-fact when they are assessing the plausibility of memory reports. These include how the "memory" was recovered (e.g., more confidence in a memory that was not recovered using imagination techniques or suggestive memory work), the likelihood of forgetting the event (happened early in life, happened a small number of times), and whether there is any corroborating evidence in support of the claim. Of course, recovered memories that appear relatively implausible (e.g., satanic ritual abuse) should always be treated with caution.

In cases where recovered memories do form the majority of the evidence, an expert memory witness should be called upon to inform the triers-of-fact about the science of such "memories." This is because, among other things, there exist a number of naïve beliefs about repressed memories, ones that run opposite to scientific fact and that are held not just by laypeople, but also by those in the legal arena (see Chapter 3). Indeed, a recommendation that falls out of Chapter 3, and one that is consistent with the recommendations of the National Research Council (2014), is that:

2. All law enforcement and legal professionals require training in the nature of memory.

With proper training concerning the reconstructive nature of memory (see Chapter 5 as well), along with some specific education concerning foibles that are characteristic of memory when it comes to remembering (traumatic) events, perhaps there will be fewer miscarriages of justice. As we saw in Chapter 2, there have been a number of well-documented cases in Europe and the USA where people alleging they recovered repressed memories of childhood sexual abuse have led to wrongful convictions of innocent people. Proper training in the malleability of memory and what constitutes "normal" recollection of events would go a long way toward avoiding wrongful convictions in the future.

Related to this issue, as well as that concerning repressed/recovered memories, is research on false and implanted memories. As we saw in Chapters 4 and 8, self-induced as well as suggestion-induced false memories arise more often than many laypeople would think. Here, we reviewed scientific evidence that memories for entire events that did not happen can be created. Indeed, sometimes it is easier to create negative false memories than positive or emotionally neutral ones.

In such cases, the person with an implanted memory will not have had a prior recollection of the event and thus, implanted memories may appear to be "recovered." Although for obvious reasons scientists do not create entire memories for sexual abuse in controlled laboratory conditions, there is considerable evidence showing the ease with which researchers can implant false memories of both mundane and more negative events through suggestion. Indeed, a recent mega-analysis showed that 30.4% of people in implanted memory studies came to believe that entire events happened to them when in fact, they never did (Scoboria et al., 2017). Further, when the memory implantation procedure included self-relevant information combined with instructions to imagine that the event happened to them, this figure jumped to 46.1% or almost half of the participants.

As we saw in Chapter 4, children not only encode experiences differently from adults, but early memories are extremely labile and often do not survive into later childhood and adulthood (i.e., infantile and childhood amnesia). Even if such memories do survive, they are fragmented, devoid of contextualized meaning, and generally lack emotional content and temporal markers. Moreover, because childhood memories are subject to reactivation and subsequent reconsolidation, processes that can lead to systematic distortion and modification of the original memory trace, such memories may not be particularly accurate. These processes occur automatically, outside of conscious awareness, and as such represent critical changes to memories for originally experienced events that transpire without the rememberer even knowing they have happened. For these reasons, and because considerable time has usually elapsed between the time of the childhood event(s) and the time the adult is now attempting to recall these events, we urge caution when the evidence consists primarily of an adult's alleged memories of those childhood event(s):

3. When adults present evidence that consists of reconstructed memories of childhood events, extreme caution needs to be exercised when adjudicating such evidence.

As we saw in Chapter 7, eyewitness accuracy of identifications can be improved but this will involve new law enforcement training protocols, standardized procedures for administering lineups, and improvements in the handling of eyewitness identification in court. As indicated in the National Research Council (2014) report, initial confidence in an eyewitness identification is important to record and jurors should be made aware of this evidence. Moreover, this report also recommends that judges use their discretion to allow either expert testimony in their courtrooms about eyewitness identification or use clear and concise jury instructions about eyewitness identification. We wholeheartedly agree with these recommendations and would go a step further and not restrict this just to identifications only but extend it to knowledge of eyewitness memory more generally:

4. The malleable nature of memory, perception, and confidence, the limitations in our ability to recognize faces and individuals, and the current law enforcement procedures for eyewitness identification can all result in mistaken identifications.

Although children are capable of remembering events reliably (depending on a number of specific factors outlined in Chapter 8), when children's narratives are elicited under conditions of high interviewer bias, suggestive questioning, and a number of other specific conditions that may alter the accuracy of what is being remembered, caution needs to be exercised when evaluating these narratives. Procedures such as the NICHD interview protocol must be routinely implemented if we are to extract an unbiased account of events for use in the courtroom. Although considerable research remains to be done to verify specific techniques that elicit as accurate an account of an event as possible, courts still need to understand the complexity of the situation surrounding the effects of suggestibility on memory reports. Indeed, like our other conclusions, we believe that judges should enlist the help of expert witnesses or have standardized jury instructions when it comes to understanding the influence interviewing techniques can have on eyewitness testimony, particularly the testimony of young children:

5.   Interviewers need to use non-biased interview techniques especially with young children.

Although much of the research on memory and the law has focused on how eyewitnesses remember events, we also examined the role of memory in those triers-of-fact who must retain the evidence in memory in order to come up with a fair and just verdict. Of course, memory operates no differently in jurors than in witnesses, so it was perhaps not too surprising to see many similarities. However, it was instructive to examine differences in how our reconstructive memory system operates as a function of whether one is remembering events that have happened or simply remembering evidence that has been passively seen or heard in the courtroom.

Because the task confronting the juror can be daunting, in part because the evidence is not always easy to understand (e.g., use of technical terms that need explanation, legal arguments that are difficult to comprehend), it might be useful for jurors to be able to take notes in much the same manner as a judge. As noted in Chapter 9, although note taking can have its disadvantages, there are perhaps more benefits associated with this form of "external" memory than previously thought. Because structured notebooks appear to be of particular benefit, especially when those notebooks can be used during jury deliberation, we can recommend that:

6.   Jurors be allowed to take (structured) notes during the trial and use them to refresh their memory during deliberations.

We would like to emphasize that until naïve beliefs about memory are replaced by evidence-based, scientifically derived knowledge, expert evidence should not only be viewed as being of assistance in the courtroom, but should be mandated in cases where memory serves as (the only) evidence. Moreover, standardized jury instructions about memory should be used not just as a replacement for expert testimony when none is available, but preferably, to augment expert testimony. These instructions need to provide clear and concise information about the use of memory evidence in the courtroom. Importantly, information on how to interpret memory evidence as given by an expert, contained in jury instructions, or both does not usurp the jury's function. Rather, such information, like expert testimony concerning how to interpret DNA evidence, gives the jury the necessary tools to understand and give appropriate weight to memory evidence when deliberating their verdict. Without such tools, jurors must rely on their own naïve beliefs, something that, as we have seen in this book, can lead inexorably to wrongful convictions:

> 7a.　Expert evidence should be mandated in cases where memory serves as (the only) evidence.

> 7b.　Standardized jury instructions should be provided to assist jurors in their interpretation of memory evidence.

Finally, in an ideal world, we would like to see expert reports and testimony being commissioned by the court rather than by either (or both) sides (defense and prosecution) in an adversarial justice system. In this way, jurors can receive unbiased information about the nature of memory and its role when used as evidence in the courtroom. By unbiased we mean that such information is not perceived to be favoring one side or the other but is seen as it should be, scientifically independent facts that aid the interpretation of memory evidence. In addition, procedures would need to be in place that ensure that standardized qualifications are used to guarantee the authenticity of who is (and who is not) a memory expert. Indeed, once safeguards are in place, ones that determine the qualifications for those who can act as memory experts, court-appointed experts who provide commissioned reports would do so in a manner that is independent of any potential conflicts of interest in the interpretation of scientific research:

> 8a.　Standardized criteria need to be established and enforced as to the qualifications of a memory expert.

> 8b.　Expert reports should be commissioned by the court in order to provide unbiased information for jurors to use when interpreting memory evidence.

Of course, as with any set of conclusions and recommendations, these are only as good as the science behind them. We believe that the science reviewed in this volume supports these conclusions and recommendations but we also realize that considerable work remains in our search for a formal understanding of memory and its role in legal proceedings. Although additional research is needed on each of the topics raised in the chapters of this book, research that might alter some of these conclusions and recommendations, we are confident that if implemented, fewer miscarriages of justice will occur when memory serves as (the only) evidence.

REFERENCES

Ackil, J. K., & Zaragoza, M. S. (1998). Memorial consequences of forced confabulations: Age differences in susceptibility to false memories. *Developmental Psychology, 34*, 1358–1372.

Addis, D.R., Barsense, M., & Duarte, A. (2015). *The Wiley handbook on the cognitive neuroscience of memory*. Chichester, UK: Wiley.

Akehurst, L., Milne, R., & Köhnken, G. (2003). The effects of children's age and delay on recall in a cognitive or structured interview. *Psychology, Crime & Law, 9*, 97–107.

Alexander, K. W., Quas, J. A., Goodman, G. S., Ghetti, S., Edelstein, R. S., Redlich, A. D., Cordon, I. M., Jones, D. P. (2005). Traumatic impact predicts long-term memory for documented child sexual abuse. *Psychological Science, 16*, 33–40.

Alison, L., Kebbell, M., & Lewis, P. (2006). Considerations for experts in assessing the credibility of recovered memories of child sexual abuse: The importance of maintaining a case-specific focus. *Psychology Public Policy and Law, 12*, 416–441.

American Medical Association (AMA; Council of Scientific Affairs, 1993).

American Psychiatric Association (Board of Trustees, 1993).

Anderson, N. D., & Craik, F. I. (2000). Memory in the aging brain. In E. Tulving & F. I. M. Craik (Eds.), *Oxford handbook of memory* (pp. 411–425). New York: Oxford University Press.

Andersson, J. (2001). Net effect of memory collaboration: How is collaboration affected by factors such as friendship, gender, and age? *Scandinavian Journal of Psychology, 42*, 367–375.

Andersson, J., & Rönnberg, J. (1995). Recall suffers from collaboration: Joint recall effects of friendship and task complexity. *Applied Cognitive Psychology, 9*, 199–211.

Andreasen, N. C., O'Leary, D. S., Cizadlo, T., Arndt, S., Rezai, K., Watkins, G. L., Boles Ponto, L. L., & Hichwa, R. D. (1995). Remembering the past: Two facets of episodic memory explored with positron emission tomography. *American Journal of Psychiatry, 152*, 1576–1585.

Andrews, S. J., & Lamb, M. E. (2014). The effects of age and delay on responses to repeated questions in forensic interviews with children alleging sexual abuse. *Law and Human Behavior, 38*, 171–180.

Anzures, G., Quinn, P. C., Pascalis, O., Slader, A. M., Tanaka, J. W., & Lee, K. (2013). Developmental origins of the other-race effect. *Current Directions in Psychological Science, 22*, 173–178.

Archdiocesan Commission (1990). *The report of the Archdiocesan Commission of the inquiry into the sexual abuse of children by members of the clergy* (St. John's Winter Report). Newfoundland, Canada: Archdiocesan of St. John's.

Arndt, J. (2012). False recollection: Empirical findings and their theoretical implications. *Psychology of Learning and Motivation, 56*, 81–124.

Arnold, M. M., & Lindsay, D. S. (2002). Remembering remembering. *Journal of Experimental Psychology: Learning, Memory, and Cognition, 28*, 521–529.

Arnold, M. M., & Lindsay, D. S. (2005). Remembrance of remembrance past. *Memory, 13*, 533–549.

Aslan, A., Bäuml, K.-H., & Grundgeiger, T. (2007). The role of inhibitory processes in part-list cuing. *Journal of Experimental Psychology: Learning, Memory, and Cognition, 33*, 335–341.

Aslan, A., Staudigl, T., Samenieh, A., & Bäuml, K.-H. (2010). Directed forgetting in young children: Evidence for a production deficiency. *Psychonomic Bulletin & Review, 17*, 704–709.

Atance, C. M., & Sommerville, J. A. (2014). Assessing the role of memory in preschoolers' performance on episodic foresight tasks. *Memory, 22*, 118–128.

Bahrick, L. E., Parker, J. F., Fivush, R., & Levitt, M. (1998). The effects of stress on young children's memory for a natural disaster. *Journal of Experimental Psychology: Applied, 4*, 308–331.

Barber, S. J., Harris, C. B., & Rajaram, S. (2015). Why two heads apart are better than two heads together: Multiple mechanisms underlie the collaborative inhibition effect in memory. *Journal of Experimental Psychology: Learning, Memory, and Cognition, 41*, 559–566.

Barber, S. J., & Rajaram, S. (2011). Exploring the relationship between retrieval disruption from collaboration and recall. *Memory, 19*, 462–469.

Barber, S. J., Rajaram, S., & Aron, A. (2010). When two is too many: Collaborative encoding impairs memory. *Memory & Cognition, 38*, 255–264.

Barber, S. J., Rajaram, S., & Fox, E. B. (2012). Learning and remembering with others: The key role of retrieval in shaping group recall and collective memory. *Social Cognition, 30*, 121–132.

Bartlett, F. C. (1932). *Remembering: A study in experimental and social psychology.* Cambridge: Cambridge University Press.

Bartlett, J. C. (2014). The older eyewitness. In T. J. Perfect & D. S. Lindsay (Eds.), *The SAGE handbook of applied memory* (pp. 654–674). London, UK: Sage.

Basden, B. H., Basden, D. R., Bryner, S., & Thomas III, R. L. (1997). A comparison of group and individual remembering: Does collaboration disrupt retrieval strategies? *Journal of Experimental Psychology: Learning, Memory, and Cognition, 23*, 1176–1189.

Basden, B. H., Basden, D. R., & Henry, S. (2000). Costs and benefits of collaborative remembering. *Applied Cognitive Psychology, 14*, 497–507.

Basden, B. H., Basden, D. R., Thomas, R. I., & Souphasith, S. (1998). Memory distortion in group recall. *Current Psychology: A Journal for Diverse Perspectives On Diverse Psychological Issues, 16*, 225–246.

Bass, E., & Davis, L. (2008). *The courage to heal: A guide for women survivors of child sexual abuse* (4th Ed). New York: Harper Collins.

Bauer, P. J. (2007). *Remembering the times of our lives: Memory in infancy and beyond.* Mahwah, NJ: Erlbaum.

Bauer, P. J. (2009). The cognitive neuroscience of the development of memory. In M. Courage and N. Cowan (Eds.), *The development of memory in infancy and childhood* (pp. 115–144). Hove, UK: Psychology Press.

Bauer, P. J. (2015). A complementary processes account of the development of childhood amnesia and a personal past. *Psychological Review, 122*, 204–231.

Bauer, P. J., van Abbema, D. L., Wiebe, S. A., Cary, M. S., Phill, C., & Burch, M. M. (2004). Props, not pictures, are worth a thousand words: Verbal accessibility of early memories under different conditions of contextual support. *Applied Cognitive Psychology*, *18*, 373–392.

Bauer, P. J., Burch, M. M., van Abbema, D. L., & Ackil, J. K. (2008). Talking about twisters: How mothers and children converse about a devastating tornado. In M. L. Howe, G. S. Goodman, & D. Cicchetti (Eds.), *Stress, trauma, and children's memory development: Neurobiological, cognitive, clinical, and legal perspectives* (pp. 204–235). New York: Oxford University Press.

Bauer, P. J., Burch, M. M., Scholin, S. E., & Güler, O. E. (2007). Using cue words to investigate the distribution of autobiographical memories in childhood. *Psychological Science*, *18*, 910–916.

Bauer, P. J., & Larkina, M. (2014). Childhood amnesia in the making: Different distributions of autobiographical memories in children and adults. *Journal of Experimental Psychology: General*, *143*, 597–611.

Bauer, P. J., & Larkina, M. (2016). Predicting remembering and forgetting of autobiographical memories in children and adults: A 4-year prospective study. *Memory*, *24*, 1345–1368.

Baugerud, G. A., Howe, M. L., Magnussen, S., & Melinder, A. (2016). Maltreated and non-maltreated children's true and false memories of neutral and emotional word lists in the Deese/Roediger-McDermott task. *Journal of Experimental Child Psychology*, *143*, 102–110.

Bäuml, K.-H., & Aslan, A. (2004). Part-list cuing as instructed retrieval inhibition. *Memory & Cognition*, *32*, 610–617.

Bäuml, K.-H., & Aslan, A. (2006). Part-list cuing can be transient and lasting: The role of encoding. *Journal of Experimental Psychology: Learning, Memory, and Cognition*, *32*, 33–43.

BBC News. (2016, June 16), Sir Cliff Richard's full statement. Retrieved from www.bbc.co.uk/news/entertainment-arts-36547213.

BBC News. (2015, February 24), Sir Cliff Richard's privacy "breached by raid details release". Retrieved from www.bbc.co.uk/news/uk-england-south-yorkshire-31609227.

Beaudry, J. L., & Lindsey, R. C. L. (2006). Current identification procedure practices: A survey of Ontario police officers. *The Canadian Journal of Police and Security Services*, *4*, 178–183.

Benton, T. R., Ross, D. F., Bradshaw, E., Thomas, W. N. & Bradshaw, G. S. (2006). Eyewitness memory is still not common sense: Comparing jurors, judges, and law enforcement to eyewitness experts. *Applied Cognitive Psychology*, *20*, 115–129.

Beresford, J., & Blades, M. (2006). Children's identification of faces from lineups: The effects of lineup presentation and instructions on accuracy. *Journal of Applied Psychology*, *91*, 1102–1113.

Bernstein, D. M., & Loftus, E. F. (2009). How to tell if a particular memory is true or false. *Perspectives on Psychological Science*, *4*, 370–374.

Bjorklund, D. F. (1987). How changes in knowledge base contribute to the development of children's memory. *Developmental Review*, *7*, 93–130.

Bland, C. E., Howe, M. L., & Knott, L. (2016). Discrete emotion-congruent false memories in the DRM paradigm. *Emotion*, *16*, 611–619.

Bloodsworth, K. (2016, December 5), Innocence Project Cases. Retrieved from www.innocenceproject.org/cases/kirk-bloodsworth/.

Blumen, H. M., & Rajaram, S. (2008). Influence of re-exposure and retrieval disruption during group collaboration on later individual recall. *Memory*, *16*, 231–244.

Blumen, H. M., Rajaram, S., & Henkel, L. (2013). The applied value of collaborative memory research in aging: Behavioral and neural considerations. *Journal of Applied Research in Memory and Cognition, 2*, 107–117.

Blumen, H. M., & Stern, Y. (2011). Short-term and long-term collaboration benefits on individual recall in younger and older adults. *Memory & Cognition, 39*, 147–154.

Bodenhausen, G. V. (1988). Stereotypic biases in social decision making and memory: Testing process models of stereotype use. *Journal of personality and Social Psychology, 55*, 726–737.

Bohannon, J. N. (1992). Arousal and memory: Quantity and consistency over the years. In E. Winograd & U. Neisser (Eds.), *Affect and accuracy in recall: The problem of "flashbulb" memories* (pp.65–91). New York: Cambridge University Press.

Borawick v. Shay 68 F.3d 597 (2d Cir. 1995).

Bornstein, B. H., Witt, C. J., Cherry, K. E., & Greene, E. (2000). The suggestibility of older witnesses. In M. B. Rothman, B. D. Dunlop, & P. Entzel (Eds.), *Elders, crime and the criminal justice system: Myth, perceptions, and reality in the 21st century* (pp. 149–161). New York: Springer.

Bottoms, B. L., Shaver, P. R., & Goodman, G. S. (1996). An analysis of ritualistic and religion-related child abuse allegations. *Law and Human Behavior, 20*, 1–34.

Bourgeois, M. J., Horowitz, I. A., FosterLee, L., & Grahe, J. (1995). Nominal and interactive groups: Effects of preinstruction and deliberations on decisions and evidence in complex trials. *Journal of Applied Psychology, 80*, 58–67.

Brady, M. S., Poole, D. A., Warren, A. R., & Jones, H. R. (1999). Young children's responses to yes–no questions: Patterns and problems. *Applied Developmental Science, 3*, 47–57.

Brainerd, C. J., Reyna, V. F., Howe, M. L., & Kingma, J. (1990). Development of forgetting and reminiscence. *Monographs of the Society for Research in Child Development, 55* (3–4, Serial No. 222).

Bremner, J. D., Krystal, J. H., Southwick, S. M., & Charney, D. S. (1995). Functional neuroanatomical correlates of the effects of stress on memory. *Journal of Traumatic Stress, 8*, 527–553.

Brenneis, C. B. (1994). Can early childhood trauma be reconstructed from dreams? On the relation of dreams to trauma. *Psychoanalytic Psychology, 11*, 429–447.

Brewer, N., & Wells, G. L. (2006). The confidence-accuracy relationship in eyewitness identification: Effects of lineup instructions, foil similarity, and target-absent base rates. *Journal of Experimental Psychology: Applied, 12*, 11–30.

Brewer, W. F. (1986). What is autobiographical memory? In D. C. Rubin, D. C. Rubin (Eds.), *Autobiographical memory* (pp. 25–49). New York: Cambridge University Press.

Briere, J., & Conte, J. (1993). Self-reported amnesia for abuse in adults molested as children. *Journal of Traumatic Stress, 6*, 21–31.

Brigham, J. C., Maass, A., Snyder, L. D., & Spaulding, K. (1982). Accuracy of eyewitness identification in a field setting. *Journal of Personality and Social Psychology, 42*, 673–681.

British Psychological Society [Research Board] (2008). *Guidelines on memory and the law. Recommendations from the scientific study of human memory.* Leicester, UK: The British Psychological Society.

Brown, D., Scheflin, A. W., & Hammond, D. C. (1998). *Memory, trauma treatment, and the law.* New York: Norton.

Brown, D. A., & Lamb, M. E. (2009). Forensic interviews with children: A two-way street: Supporting interviewers in adhering to best practice recommendations and enhancing children's capabilities in forensic interviews. In K. Kuehnle & M. Connell (Eds.), *The evaluation of child sexual abuse allegations: A comprehensive guide to assessment and testimony* (pp. 299–325). Hoboken, NJ: Wiley.

Brown, D. A., Lamb, M. E., Lewis, C., Pipe, M., Orbach, Y., & Wolfman, M. (2013). The NICHD Investigative Interview Protocol: An analogue study. *Journal of Experimental Psychology: Applied*, *19*, 367–382.

Brown, D. A., Lewis, C. N., Lamb, M. E., & Stephens, E. (2012). The influence of delay and severity of intellectual disability on event memory in children. *Journal of Consulting and Clinical Psychology*, *80*, 829–841.

Brown, D. A., & Pipe, M. E. (2003). Individual differences in children's event memory reports and the narrative elaboration technique. *Journal of Applied Psychology*, *88*, 195–206.

Brown, E., Deffenbacher, K., & Sturgill, W. (1977). Memory for faces and the circumstances of encounter. *Journal of Applied Psychology*, *62*, 311–318.

Brown, R., & Kulik, J. (1977). Flashbulb memories. *Cognition*, *5*, 73–99.

Brown, V. R., & Paulus, P. B. (2002). Making group brainstorming more effective: Recommendations from an associative memory perspective. *Current Directions in Psychological Science*, *11*, 208–212.

Bruce, D., Wilcox-O'Hearn, L. A., Robinson, J. A., Phillips-Grant, K., Francis, L., & Smith, M. C. (2005). Fragment memories mark the end of childhood amnesia. *Memory & Cognition*, *33*, 567–576.

Bruce, V. (2009). Remembering faces. In J. R. Brockmole (Ed.), *The visual world in memory* (pp. 66–88). New York: Psychology Press.

Bruce, V., Burton, A. M., & Hancock, P. J. H. (2007). Remembering faces. In R. C. L. Lindsay, D. F. Ross, J. D. Read, & M. P. Toglia (Eds.), *The handbook of eyewitness psychology: Volume 2. Memory for people* (pp. 87–100). Mahwah, NJ: Erlbaum.

Bruck, M., & Ceci, S.J. (1995). Amicus brief for the case of *state of New Jersey v. Michaels* presented by committee of concerned social scientists. *Psychology, Public Policy, and Law*, *1*, 272–322.

Bruck, M., & Ceci, S. J. (1999). The suggestibility of children's memory. *Annual Review of Psychology*, *50*, 419–439.

Bruck, M., Ceci, S. J., Francoeur, E., & Barr, R. (1995). 'I hardly cried when I got my shot': Influencing children's reports about a visit to their pediatrician. *Child Development*, *66*, 193–208.

Bruck, M., Ceci, S. J., & Hembrooke, H. (2002). The nature of children's true and false narratives. *Developmental Review*, *22*, 520–554.

Buckner, R. L., Andrews-Hanna, J. R., & Schacter, D. L. (2008). The brain's default network: Anatomy, function, and relevance to disease. *Annals of the New York Academy of Sciences*, *1124*, 1–38.

Cabeza, R., & St. Jacques, P. L. (2007). Functional neuroimaging of autobiographical memory. *Trends in Cognitive Sciences*, *11*, 219–227.

Cahill, L., & McGaugh, J. L. (1998). Mechanisms of emotional arousal and lasting declarative memory. *Trends in Neurosciences*, *21*, 294–299.

Carretta, T. R., & Moreland, R. L. (1983). The direct and indirect effects of inadmissible evidence. *Journal of Applied Social Psychology*, *13*, 291–309.

Castelli, P. & Ghetti, S. (2014). Resisting imagination and confabulation: Effects of metacognitive training. *Journal of Experimental Child Psychology*, *126*, 339–356.

Ceci, S. J., & Bruck, M. (1993). The suggestibility of the child witness: A historical review and synthesis. *Psychological Bulletin*, *113*, 403–439.

Ceci, S. J., & Bruck, M. (1995). *Jeopardy in the courtroom*. Washington, DC: American Psychological Association.

Ceci, S. J., Fitneva, S. A., & Williams, W. M. (2010). Representational constraints on the development of memory and metamemory. *Psychological Review*, *117*, 464–495.

Ceci, S. J., & Friedman, R. D. (2000). The suggestibility of children: Scientific research and legal implications. *Cornell Law Review, 86,* 33–108.

Ceci, S. J., & Loftus, E. F. (1994). "Memory work": A royal road to false memories? *Applied Cognitive Psychology, 8,* 351–364.

Ceci, S. J., Loftus, E. F., Leichtman, M., & Bruck, M. (1994). The role of source misattributions in the creation of false beliefs among preschoolers. *International Journal of Clinical and Experimental Hypnosis, 42,* 304–320.

Ceci, S. J., Papierno, P. B., & Kulkofsky, S. (2007). Representational constraints on children's suggestibility. *Psychological Science, 18,* 503–509.

Ceci, S. J., Ross, D. F., & Toglia, M. P. (1987). Suggestibility of children's memory: Psycholegal implications. *Journal of Experimental Psychology: General, 116,* 38–49.

Chae, Y., & Ceci, S. J. (2005). Individual differences in children's recall and suggestibility: The effect of intelligence, temperament, and self-perceptions. *Applied Cognitive Psychology, 19,* 383–407.

Chae, Y., Goodman, G. S., Eisen, M. L., & Qin, J. (2011). Event memory and suggestibility in abused and neglected children: Trauma-related psychopathology and cognitive functioning. *Journal Of Experimental Child Psychology, 110,* 520–538.

Chan, J. C., & LaPaglia, J. A. (2013). Impairing existing declarative memory in humans by disrupting reconsolidation. *Proceeding of the National Academy of Science USA, 110,* 9309–9313.

Christianson, S. Å. (1992). Emotional stress and eyewitness memory: A critical review. *Psychological Bulletin, 112,* 284–309.

Christianson, S. Å. (2007). *Offenders' memories of violent crimes.* Chichester: Wiley.

Christianson, S. Å., & Engelberg, E. (1999). Memory and emotional consistency: The MS Estonia ferry disaster. *Memory, 7,* 471–482.

Christianson, S. Å., & Nilsson, L. (1989). Hysterical amnesia: A case of aversively motivated isolation of memory. In T. Archer, L. Nilsson, T. Archer, & L. Nilsson (Eds.), *Aversion, avoidance, and anxiety: Perspectives on aversively motivated behavior* (pp. 289–310). Hillsdale, NJ: Erlbaum.

Cheatham, C. L., & Bauer, P. J. (2005). Construction of a more coherent story: Prior verbal recall predicts later verbal accessibility of early memories. *Memory, 13,* 516–532.

Clancy, S. A., & McNally, R. J. (2005/2006). Who needs repression? Normal memory processes can explain "forgetting" of childhood sexual abuse. *Scientific Review of Mental Health Practice, 4,* 66–73.

Clark, J. W., Cramer, R. J., Percosky, A., Rufino, K. A., Miller, R. S., & Johnson, S. M. (2013). Juror perceptions of African American- and Arabic-named victims. *Psychiatry, Psychology, and Law, 20,* 781–794.

Clark, S. E. (2012). Costs and benefits of eyewitness identification reform psychological science and public policy. *Perspectives on Psychological Science, 7,* 238–259.

Clark, S. E., & Godfrey, R. D. (2009). Eyewitness identification evidence and innocence risk. *Psychonomic Bulletin & Review, 16,* 22–42.

Clark, S. E., Moreland, M. B., & Gronlund, S. D. (2014). Evolution of the empirical and theoretical foundations of eyewitness identification reform. *Psychonomic Bulletin & Review, 21,* 251–267.

Clark, S. E., & Tunnicliff, J. L. (2001). Selecting lineup foils in eyewitness identification experiments: Experimental control and real-world simulation. *Law and Human Behavior, 25,* 199–216.

Clifford, B. R., & Scott, J. (1978). Individual and situational factors in eyewitness testimony. *Journal of Applied Psychology, 63,* 352–359.

Cohee v. State, 942 P.2d 211 (Okla. 1997).

Cohen, G., & Faulkner, D. (1989). Age differences in source forgetting: effects on reality monitoring and on eyewitness testimony. *Psychology and Aging, 4,* 10–17.

Colloff, M. F., Wade, K. A., & Strange, D. (2016). Unfair lineups don't just make witnesses more willing to choose the suspect, they also make them more likely to confuse innocent and guilty suspects. *Psychological Science, 27,* 1227–1239.

Conway, M. A. (1996). Autobiographical knowledge and autobiographical memories. In D. C. Rubin (Ed.), *Remembering our past: Studies in autobiographical memory* (pp. 67–93). New York: Cambridge University Press.

Conway, M. A. (2005). Memory and the self. *Journal of Memory and Language, 53,* 594–628.

Conway, M. A. (2009). Episodic memories. *Neuropsychologia, 47,* 2305–2313.

Conway, M. A. (2013). On being a memory expert witness: Three cases. *Memory, 21(5),* 566–575.

Conway, M. A., & Fthenaki, A. (2000). Disruption and loss of autobiographical memory. In L. S. Cermak (Ed.), *Handbook of neuropsychology, 2nd Edition: Memory and its disorders* (pp. 281–312). Amsterdam: Elsevier.

Conway, M. A., Howe, M. L., & Knott, L. M. (2017). Psychology of memory and cognition. In B. K. Puri and I. Treasaden (Eds.), *Textbook of Forensic Psychiatry* (pp. 63–69). Abingdon, UK: CRC Press, Taylor and Francis Group.

Conway, M. A., Justice, L., & Morrison, C. (2014). Beliefs about autobiographical memory. *The Psychologist, 27,* 502–505.

Conway, M. A., Loveday, C., & Cole, S. N. (2016). The remembering-imagining system. *Memory Studies, 9,* 256–265.

Conway, M. A., & Pleydell-Pearce, C. W. (2000) The construction of autobiographical memories in the self-memory system. *Psychological Review, 107,* 261–288.

Conway, M. A., Pleydell-Pearce, C. W., & Whitecross, S. (2001). The neuroanatomy of autobiographical memory: A slow cortical potential study (SCP) of autobiographical memory retrieval. *Journal of Memory and Language, 45,* 493–524.

Conway, M. A., Pleydell-Pearce, C. W., Whitecross, S., & Sharpe, H. (2002). Brain imaging autobiographical memory. *Psychology of Learning and Motivation, 41,* 229–264.

Conway, M. A., Pleydell-Pearce, C. W., Whitecross, S., & Sharpe, H. (2003). Neuro-physiological correlates of autobiographical memory for experienced and imagined events. *Neuropsychologia, 41,* 334–340.

Conway, M. A., Turk, J. D., Miller, S. L., Logan, J., Nebes, R. D., Meltzer, C. C., & Becker, J. T. (1999). The neuroanatomical basis of autobiographical memory. *Memory, 7,* 1–25.

Costabile, K. A. (2009). Biased memory, biased verdicts: Memory effects in juror judgments. In M. E. Oswald, S. Bieneck, & J. Hupfeld-Heinemann (Eds.), *Social Psychology of Punishment of Crime* (pp. 315–355). London: Wiley-Blackwell.

Costabile, K. A., & Klein, S. B. (2005). Finishing strong: Recency effects in juror judgments. *Basic and Applied Social Psychology, 27,* 47–58.

Craik, F. M., & Jennings, J. M. (1992). Human memory. In F. M. Craik & T. A. Salthouse (Eds.), *The handbook of aging and cognition* (pp. 51–110). Hillsdale, NJ: Erlbaum.

Craik, F. I. M., & Tulving, E. (1975). Depth of processing and the retention of words in episodic memory. *Journal of Experimental Psychology: General, 104,* 268–294.

Crookes, K., & McKone, E. (2009). Early maturity of face recognition: No childhood development of holistic processing, novel face encoding, or face-space. *Cognition, 111,* 219–247.

Cutler, B. L., Penrod, S. D., & Martens, T. K. (1987). The reliability of eyewitness identification: The role of system and estimator variables. *Law and Human Behavior, 11,* 233–258.

Cyr, M., & Lamb, M. E. (2009). Assessing the effectiveness of the NICHD investigative interview protocol when interviewing French-speaking alleged victims of child sexual abuse in Quebec. *Child Abuse & Neglect, 33*, 257–268.

Dahlström, Ö., Danielsson, H., Emilsson, M., & Andersson, J. (2011). Does retrieval strategy disruption cause general and specific collaborative inhibition? *Memory, 19*, 140–154.

Dammeyer, M. D., Nightingale, N. N., & McCoy, M. L. (1997) Repressed memory and other controversial origins of sexual abuse allegations: Beliefs among psychologists and clinical social workers. *Child Maltreatment, 2*, 252–263.

Danielsson, H., Dahlström, Ö., & Andersson, J. (2011). The more you remember the more you decide: Collaborative memory in adolescents with intellectual disability and their assistants. *Research in Developmental Disabilities, 32*, 470–476.

Dann, B. M., Hans, V. P., & Kaye, D. H. (2007). Can jury trial innovations improve jury understanding of DNA evidence? *Judicature, 90*, 152–156.

D'Argembeau, A., Stawarczyk, D., Majerus, S., et al. (2010). The neural basis of goal processing when envisioning future events. *Journal of Cognitive Neuroscience, 22*, 1701–1713.

Davies, G., Tarrant, A., & Flin, R. (1989). Close encounters of the witness kind: Children's memory for a simulated health inspection. *British Journal Of Psychology, 80*(4), 415–429.

Davies, G., Westcott, H., & Horan, N. (2000). The impact of questioning style on the content of investigative interviews with suspected child sexual abuse victims. *Psychology, Crime & Law, 6*, 681–697.

Davis, D., & Loftus, E. F. (2012). Inconsistencies between law and the limits of human cognition: The case of eyewitness identification. In L. Nadel & W. P. Sinnott-Armstrong (Eds.), *Memory and Law* (pp. 29–58). New York: Oxford University Press.

De Bellis, M. D., Hall, J., Boring, A. M., Frustaci, K., & Moritz, G. (2001). A pilot longitudinal study of hippocampal volumes in pediatric maltreatment-related posttraumatic stress disorder. *Biological Psychiatry, 50*, 305–309.

Deese, J. (1959). On the prediction of occurrence of particular verbal intrusions in immediate recall. *Journal of Experimental Psychology, 58*, 17–22.

Deffenbacher, K. A. (1983). The influence of arousal on reliability of testimony. In S. M. A. Lloyd-Bostock & B. R. Clifford (Eds.), *Evaluating witness evidence* (pp. 235–251). Chichester, UK: Wiley.

Deffenbacher, K. A., Bornstein, B. H., McGorty, E. K., & Penrod, S. D. (2008). Forgetting the once-seen face: Estimating the strength of an eyewitness' memory representation. *Journal of Experimental Psychology: Applied, 14*, 139–150.

Deffenbacher, K. A., Bornstein, B. H., Penrod, S. D., & McGorty, E. K. (2004). A meta-analytic review of the effects of high stress on eyewitness memory. *Law & Human Behavior, 28*, 687–706.

Deffenbacher, K. A., & Loftus, E. F. (1982). Do jurors share a common understanding concerning eyewitness behavior? *Law and Human Behavior, 6*, 15–30.

Delaney, P. F., Sahakyan, L., Kelley, C. M., & Zimmerman, C. A. (2010). Remembering to forget: The amnesic effect of daydreaming. *Psychological Science, 21*, 1036–1042.

Deutsch M., & Gerard, H. G. (1955). A study of normative and informational social influence upon individual judgment. *Journal of Abnormal and Social Psychology 59*, 204–209.

Devine, P. G., & Ostrom, T. M. (1985). Cognitive mediation of inconsistency discounting. *Journal of Personality and Social Psychology, 49*, 5–21.

Devlin, Lord P. (1976). *Report to the Secretary of State for the Home Department on the Departmental Committee on Evidence of Identification in Criminal Cases.* London: HMSO.

Diamond, R., & Carey, S. (1977). Developmental changes in the representation of faces. *Journal of Experimental Child Psychology, 23*, 1–22.

Dolan, R. J. (2002). Emotion, cognition, and behavior. *Science, 298,* 1191–1194.

Dolan, Y. (1991). *Resolving sexual abuse: Solution-focused therapy and Ericksonian hypnosis for adult survivors.* New York: W. W. Norton & Co.

Dysart, J., & Lindsay, R. C. L. (2007). The effects of delay on eyewitness identification accuracy: Should we be concerned? In R. C. L. Lindsay, D. F. Ross, J. D. Read, & M. P. Toglia (Eds.), *The handbook of eyewitness psychology: Volume 2. Memory for people* (pp. 137–153). Mahwah, NJ: Erlbaum.

Easterbrook, J. A. (1959). The effect of emotion on cue utilization and the organization of behavior. *Psychological Review, 66,* 183–201.

Edwards, K., & Bryan, T. S. (1997). Judgmental biases produced by instructions to disregard: The (paradoxical) case of emotional information. *Personality and Social Psychology Bulletin, 23,* 849–864.

Eigsti, I.-M., & Cicchetti, D. (2004). The impact of child maltreatment on expressive syntax at 60 months. *Developmental Science, 7,* 88–102.

Eisen, M. L., & Carlson, E. B. (1998). Individual differences in suggestibility: Examining the influence of dissociation, absorption, and a history of childhood abuse. *Applied Cognitive Psychology, 12,* S47–S61.

Eisen, M. L., Goodman, G. S., Qin, J., Davis, S., & Crayton, J. (2007). Maltreated children's memory: Accuracy, suggestibility, and psychopathology. *Developmental Psychology, 43,* 1275–1294.

Eisen, M., Goodman, G. S., Ghetti, S., & Qin, J. (1999, July). *An examination of abuse disclosures in maltreated children.* Paper presented at the annual meeting of the Society for Applied Research in Memory and Cognition, Boulder, Colorado.

Eisen, M. L., Qin, J., Goodman, G. S., & Davis, S. L. (2002). Memory and suggestibility in maltreated children: Age, stress, arousal, dissociation, and psychopathology. *Journal of Experimental Child Psychology, 83,* 167–212.

Endres, J., Poggenpohl, C., & Erben, C. (1999). Repetitions, warnings and video: Cognitive and motivational components in preschool children's suggestibility. *Legal and Criminological Psychology, 4*(Part 1), 129–146.

Faller, K. C. (1988). Criteria for judging the credibility of children's statements about their sexual abuse. *Child Welfare: Journal of Policy, Practice, and Program, 67,* 389–401.

Felstead, K., & Felstead, R. (2014). *Justice for Carol: The true story of Carol Felstead.* Marsden Gate, UK: Amazon.co.uk.

Ferguson, S. A., Hashtroudi, S., & Johnson, M. K. (1992). Age differences in using source-relevant cues. *Psychology and Aging, 7,* 443–452.

Finlay, F., Hitch, G. J., & Meudell, P. R. (2000). Mutual inhibition in collaborative recall: Evidence for a retrieval-based account. *Journal of Experimental Psychology: Learning, Memory, and Cognition, 26,* 1556–1567.

Fitzgerald, J. M. (2000). Younger and older jurors: The influence of environmental supports on memory performance and decision making in complex trials. *The Journals of Gerontology Series B: Psychological Sciences and Social Sciences, 55,* 323–331.

Fitzgerald, R. J., & Price, H. L. (2015). Eyewitness identification across the life span: A meta-analysis of age differences. *Psychological Bulletin, 141,* 1228–1265.

Fivush, R., Hazzard, A., Sales, J. M., Sarfati, D., & Brown, T. (2003). Creating coherence out of chaos? Children's narratives of emotionally positive and negative events. *Applied Cognitive Psychology, 17,* 1–19.

Fivush, R., Peterson, C, & Schwarzmueller, A. (2002). Questions and answers: The credibility of child testimony in the context of specific questions. In M. Eisen, G. S. Goodman, & J. Quas (Eds.), *Memory and suggestibility in the forensic interview* (pp. 331–354). Hillsdale, NJ: Erlbaum.

Fivush, R., Sales, J. M., Goldberg, A., Bahrick, L., & Parker, J. (2004). Weathering the storm: Children's long-term recall of Hurricane Andrew. *Memory, 12,* 104–118.

Flango, V. E. (1980). Would jurors do a better job if they could take notes? *Judicature, 63,* 436–443.

Flowe, H. D., & Humphries, J. E. (2011). An examination of criminal face bias in a random sample of police lineups. *Applied Cognitive Psychology, 25,* 265–273.

Foa, E. B., & Rothbaum, B. O. (1998). *Treating the trauma of rape: Cognitive-behavioral therapy for PTSD.* New York: Guilford Press.

ForsterLee, L., & Horowitz, I. A. (1997). Enhancing juror competence in a complex trial. *Applied Cognitive Psychology, 11,* 305–319.

ForsterLee, L., Horowitz, I. A., & Bourgeois, M. (1994). Effects of note taking on verdicts and evidence processing in a civil trial. *Law and Human Behavior, 18,* 567–578.

ForsterLee, L., Kent, L., & Horowitz, I. A. (2005). The cognitive effects of jury aids on decision-making in complex civil litigation. *Applied Cognitive Psychology, 19,* 867–884.

Franklin v. Stevenson, 987 P. 2d 22, 1999, Utah: Supreme Court.

Fredrickson, R. (1992). *Repressed memories: A journey to recovery from sexual abuse.* New York: Simon and Schuster.

Frenda, S. J., Nichols, R. M., & Loftus, E. F. (2011). Current issues and advances in misinformation research. *Current Directions in Psychological Science, 20,* 20–23.

Friedman, W. J. (2014). The development of memory for the times of past events. In P. J. Bauer & R. Fivush (Eds.), *The Wiley Handbook of the Development of Children's Memory: Volume I* (pp. 394–407). West Sussex, UK: Wiley.

Friedman, W. J., Reese, E., & Dai, J. (2011). Children's memory for the times of events from the past years. *Applied Cognitive Psychology, 25,* 156–165.

Gabbert, F., Memon, A., & Allan. K. (2003). Memory conformity: Can eyewitnesses influence each other's memories for an event? *Applied Cognitive Psychology, 17,* 533–543.

Gabbert, F., Memon, A., Allan, K., & Wright, D. (2004). Say it to my face: Examining the effects of socially encountered misinformation. *Legal and Criminological Psychology, 9,* 215–227.

Gander, K. (2015), Cliff Richard investigation "increased significantly and involves more than one allegation", says police chief. *The Independent.* Retrieved from www.independent.co.uk/news/people/news/police-investigation-into-cliff-richard-increased-significantly-10070342.html.

Gardiner, J. M., & Richardson-Klavehn, A. (2000). Remembering and knowing. In E. Tulving & F. I. M. Craik (Eds.), *Handbook of memory* (pp. 229–244). Oxford: Oxford University Press.

Garrett, B. L. (2011). *Convicting the innocent: Where criminal prosecutions go wrong.* Cambridge, MA: Harvard University Press.

Garry, M., Manning, C. G., Loftus, E. F., & Sherman, S. J. (1996). Imagination inflation: Imagining a childhood event inflates confidence that it occurred. *Psychonomic Bulletin & Review 1996, 3,* 208–214.

Garven, S., Wood, J. M., & Malpass, R. S. (2000). Allegations of wrongdoing: The effects of reinforcement on children's mundane and fantastic claims. *Journal of Applied Psychology, 85,* 38–49.

Gates, H. L., Jr. (1995, October 23). Thirteen ways of looking at a black man. *The New Yorker,* 56–65.

Geraerts, E., Lindsay, D. S., Merckelbach, H., Jelicic, M., Raymaekers, L., Arnold, M. M., & Schooler, J. W. (2009). Cognitive mechanisms underlying recovered-memory experiences of childhood sexual abuse. *Psychological Science, 20,* 92–98.

Ghetti, S., & Bauer, P. J. (Eds.) (2012). *Origins of development and recollection*. New York: Oxford University Press.

Gilboa, A. L., Wincour, G., Grady, C. L., Hevenor, S. J., & Moscovitch, M. (2004). Remembering our past: Functional neuroanatomy of recollection of recent and very remote personal events. *Cerebral Cortex, 14*, 1214–1225.

Golding, J. M., & Long, D. L. (1998). There's more to intentional forgetting than directed forgetting: An integrative review. In J. M. Golding & C. M. MacLeod (Eds.), *Intentional forgetting: Interdisciplinary approaches* (pp. 59–102). Mahwah, NJ: Erlbaum.

Goodman, G. S. (2006). Children's eyewitness memory: A modern history and contemporary commentary. *Journal of Social Issues, 62*, 811–832.

Goodman, G. S., Bottoms, B. L., Schwartz-Kenney, B. M., & Rudy, L. (1991). Children's testimony about a stressful event: Improving children's reports. *Journal of Narrative & Life History, 1*, 69–99.

Goodman, G. S., Ghetti, S., Quas, J. A., Edelstein, R. S., Alexander, K. W., Redlich, A. D., . . . Jones, D. P. H. (2003). A prospective study of memory for child sexual abuse: New findings relevant to the repressed-memory controversy. *Psychological Science, 14*, 113–118.

Goodman, G. S., Magnussen, S., Andersson, J., Endestad, T., Løkken, L., & Mostue, C. (2007). Memory illusions and false memories in real life. In S. Magnussen & T. Helstrup (Eds.), *Everyday memory* (pp. 157–182). Hove, UK: Psychology Press.

Goodman, G. S., Ogle, C. M., Block, S. D., Harris, L. S., & . . ., Urquiza, A. (2011). False memory for trauma-related Deese-Roediger-McDermott lists in adolescents and adults with histories of child sexual abuse. *Development and Psychopathology, 23*, 423–438.

Goodman G. S., Quas J. A., Batterman-Faunce J. M., Riddlesberger M. M., &, Kuhn J. (1997). Children's reactions to a stressful event: influences of age, anatomical dolls, knowledge, and parental attachment. *Applied Developmental Science, 1*, 54–75.

Gordon, B. L., Schroeder, C. S., & Adams, J. M. (1990a). Children's knowledge of sexuality: A comparison of sexually abused and nonabused children. *American Journal of Orthopsychiatry, 60*, 250–257.

Gordon, B. L., Schroeder, C. S., & Adams, J. M. (1990b). Age and social-class differences in children's knowledge of sexuality. *Journal of Clinical Child Psychology, 19*, 33–43.

Green, D. M., & Swets, J. A. (1966). *Signal detection theory and psychophysics*. New York: Wiley.

Gronlund, S. D., Carlson, C. A., Dailey, S. B., & Goodsell, C. A. (2009). Robustness of the sequential lineup advantage. *Journal of Experimental Psychology: Applied, 15*, 140–152.

Gronlund, S. D., Goodsell, C. A., & Andersen, S. M. (2012). Lineup procedures in eyewitness identification. In L. Nadel & W. P. Sinnott-Armstrong (Eds.), *Memory and law* (pp. 59–83). New York: Oxford University Press.

Gross, J., & Hayne, H. (1996). Eyewitness identification by 5-to 6-year-old children. *Law and Human Behavior, 20*, 359–373.

Gummerum, M., Leman, P. J., & Hollins, T. S. (2013). Children's collaborative recall of shared and unshared information. *British Journal of Developmental Psychology, 31*, 302–317.

Habermas, T., & Bluck, S. (2000). Getting a life: The emergence of the life story in adolescence. *Psychological Bulletin, 126*, 748–769.

Haegerich, T. M., Salerno, J. M., & Bottoms, B. L. (2013). Are the effects of juvenile offender stereotypes maximized or minimized by jury deliberation? *Psychology, Public Policy, and Law, 19*, 81–97.

Hans, V. P., & Reyna, V. F. (2011). To dollars from sense: Qualitative to quantitative translation in jury damage awards. *Journal of Empirical Legal Studies, 8*, 120–147.

Hardy, L., & Parfitt, G. (1991). A catastrophe model of anxiety and performance. *British Journal of Psychology, 82*, 163–178.

Harris, C. B., Barnier, A. J., & Sutton, J. (2013). Shared encoding and the costs and benefits of collaborative recall. *Journal of Experimental Psychology: Learning, Memory, and Cognition, 39*, 183–195.

Harris, C. B., Barnier, A. J., Sutton, J., & Keil, P. G. (2010). How did you feel when "The Crocodile Hunter" died? Voicing and silencing in conversation influences memory for an autobiographical event. *Memory, 18*, 185–197.

Harris, C. B., Keil, P. G., Sutton, J., Barnier, A., & McIlwain, D. (2011). We remember, we forget: Collaborative remembering in older couples. *Discourse Processes, 48*, 267–303.

Hashtroudi, S., Johnson, M. K., & Chrosniak, L. D. (1989). Aging and source monitoring. *Psychology and Aging, 4*, 106–112.

Hastie, R., Penrod, S. D., & Pennington, N. (1983). *Inside the jury*. Cambridge, MA: Harvard University Press.

Havard, C., Memon, A., Clifford, B., & Gabbert, F. (2010). Comparison of video and static photo lineups with child and adolescent witnesses. *Applied Cognitive Psychology, 24*, 1209–1221.

Haxby, J. V., Connolly, A. C., & Guntupalli, J. S. (2014). Decoding neural representational spaces using multivariate pattern analysis. *Annual Review of Neuroscience, (June)*, 435–456.

Hayne, H. (2004). Infant memory development: Implications for childhood amnesia. *Developmental Review, 24*, 33–73.

Heaps, C., & Nash, M. (1999). Individual differences in imagination inflation. *Psychonomic Bulletin & Review, 6*, 313–318.

Heaps, C.M., & Nash, M. (2001). Comparing recollective experience in true and false autobiographical memories. *Journal of Experimental Psychology: Learning, Memory, and Cognition, 4*, 920–930.

Henkel, L. A., & Rajaram, S. (2011). Collaborative remembering in older adults: Age-invariant outcomes in the context of episodic recall deficits. *Psychology and Aging, 26*, 532–545.

Henry, L. A., & Gudjonsson, G. H. (2003). Eyewitness memory, suggestibility, and repeated recall sessions in children with mild and moderate intellectual disabilities. *Law & Human Behavior, 27*, 481–505.

Hershkowitz, I., Horowitz, D., Lamb, M. E., Orbach, Y., & Sternberg, K. J. (2004). Interviewing youthful suspects in alleged sex crimes: A descriptive analysis. *Child Abuse & Neglect, 28*, 423– 438.

Hershkowitz, I., Lamb, M. E., Katz, C. (2014). Allegation rates in forensic child abuse investigations: Comparing the revised and standard NICHD protocols. *Psychology, Public Policy, and Law, 20*, 336–344.

Heuer, L., & Penrod, S. (1988). Increasing jurors' participation in trials: A field experiment with jury note taking and question asking. *Law and Human Behavior, 12*, 409–430.

Heuer, L., & Penrod, S. (1994). Juror note taking and question asking during trial: A national field experiment. *Law and Human Behavior, 18*, 121–150.

Hirst, W., Phelps, E. A., Buckner, R. L., Budson, A. E., Cuc, A., Gabrieli, J. E., & . . . Vaidya, C. J. (2009). Long-term memory for the terrorist attack of September 11: Flashbulb memories, event memories, and the factors that influence their retention. *Journal of Experimental Psychology: General, 138*, 161–176.

Home Office. Memorandum of good practice on video recorded interviews with child witnesses for criminal proceedings. London: Author with Department of Health; 1992.

Home Office. Achieving the best evidence in criminal proceedings: Guidance for vulnerable and intimidated witnesses, including children. London: Author, 2002.

Honess, T. M., Charman, E. A., & Levi, M. (2003). Factual and affective/evaluative recall of pretrial publicity: Their relative influence on juror reasoning and verdict in a simulated fraud trial. *Journal of Applied Social Psychology, 33*, 1404–1416.

Hope, L., Eales, N., & Mirashi, A. (2014). Assisting jurors: Promoting recall of trial information through the use of a trial-ordered notebook. *Legal and Criminological Psychology*, *19*, 316–331.

Horowitz, I. A., & Bordens, K. S. (2002). The effects of jury size, evidence complexity, and note taking on jury process and performance in a civil trial. *Journal of Applied Psychology*, *87*, 121–130.

Horowitz, I. A., & ForsterLee, L. (2001). The effects of note taking and trial transcript access on mock jury decisions in a complex civil trial. *Law and Human Behavior*, *25*, 373–391.

Horry, R., Palmer, M. A., & Brewer, N. (2012). Backloading in the sequential lineup prevents within-lineup criterion shifts that undermine eyewitness identification performance. *Journal of Experimental Psychology: Applied*, *18*, 346–360.

Houston, K. A., Hope, L., Memon, A., & Read, J. D. (2013). Expert testimony on eyewitness evidence: In search of common sense. *Behavioral Sciences and the Law*, *31*, 637–651.

Howe, M. L. (1997). Children's memory for traumatic experiences. *Learning and Individual Differences*, *9*, 153–174.

Howe, M. L. (1998). Language is never enough: Memories are more than words reveal. *Applied Cognitive Psychology*, *12*, 475–481.

Howe, M. L. (2000). *The fate of early memories: Developmental science and the retention of childhood experiences*. Washington, DC: American Psychological Association.

Howe, M. L. (2005). Children (but not adults) can inhibit false memories. *Psychological Science*, *16*, 927–931.

Howe, M. L. (2011). *The Nature of Early Memory: An Adaptive Theory of the Genesis and Development of Memory*. New York: Oxford University Press.

Howe, M. L. (2013a). Feats of early memory: Courtroom tales of what adults claim to remember about early childhood events. In R. E. Holliday and T. A. Marche (Eds.), *Child Forensic Psychology* (pp. 39–64). New York: Palgrave-Macmillan.

Howe, M. L. (2013b). Memory development: Implications for adults recalling childhood experiences in the courtroom. *Nature Reviews Neuroscience*, *14*, 869–876.

Howe, M. L. (2013c). Memory lessons from the courtroom: Reflections on being a memory expert on the witness stand. *Memory*, *21*, 576–583.

Howe, M. L. (2014). The co-emergence of the self and autobiographical memory: An adaptive view of early memory. In P. J. Bauer & R. Fivush (Eds.), *The Wiley Handbook of the Development of Children's Memory: Volume II* (pp. 545–567). West Sussex, UK: Wiley.

Howe, M. L. (2015). Memory development. In R. M. Lerner (Ed.), *Handbook of child psychology and developmental science (7th Edition)*, L. S. Liben and U. Müller (Volume Eds.), *Volume 2: Cognitive Processes* (pp. 203–249). Hoboken, NJ: Wiley.

Howe, M. L., Candel, I., Otgaar, H., Malone, C., & Wimmer, M. C. (2010). Valence and the development of immediate and long-term false memory illusions. *Memory*, *18*, 58–75.

Howe, M. L., Cicchetti, D., Toth, S. L., & Cerrito, B. M. (2004). True and false memories in maltreated children. *Child Development*, *75*, 1402–1417.

Howe, M. L., Courage, M. L., & Peterson, C. (1994). How can I remember when "I" wasn't there: Long-term retention of traumatic experiences and emergence of the cognitive self. *Consciousness and Cognition*, *3*, 327–355.

Howe, M. L., Courage, M. L., & Peterson, C. (1995). Intrusions in preschoolers' recall of traumatic childhood events. *Psychonomic Bulletin & Review*, *2*, 130–134.

Howe, M. L., Courage, M. L., Vernescu, R., & Hunt, M. (2000). Distinctiveness effects in children's long-term retention. *Developmental Psychology*, *36*, 778–792.

Howe, M. L., & Knott, L. M. (2015). The fallibility of memory in judicial processes: Lessons from the past and their modern consequences. *Memory*, *23*, 633–656.

Howe, M. L., & Malone, C. (2011). Mood-congruent true and false memory: Effects of depression. *Memory, 19*, 192–201.

Howe, M. L., Toth, S. L., & Cicchetti, D. (2011). Can maltreated children inhibit true and false memories for emotional information? *Child Development, 82*, 967–981.

Howie, P., Kurukulasuriya, N., Nash, L., & Marsh, A. (2009). Inconsistencies in children's recall of witnessed events: The role of age, questions format and perceived reason for question repetition. *Legal and Criminological Psychology, 14*, 311–329.

Howie, P., Nash, L., Kurukulasuriya, N., & Bowman, A. (2012). Children's event reports: Factors affecting responses to repeated questions in vignette scenarios and event recall interviews. *British Journal of Developmental Psychology, 30*, 550–568.

Hulse, L. M., & Memon, A. (2006). Fatal impact? The effects of emotional arousal and weapon presence on police officers' memories for a simulated crime. *Legal and Criminological Psychology, 11*, 313–325.

Huntley, J., & Costanzo, M. (2003). Sexual harassment stories: Testing a story-mediated model of juror decision-making in civil litigation. *Law and Human Behavior, 27*, 29–51.

Ihlebaek, C., Love, T., Eilertsen, D. E., & Magnussen, S. (2003). Memory for a staged criminal event witnessed live and on video. *Memory, 11*, 319–327.

Innocence Project (2003). Retrieved from www.innocenceproject.org/cases/calvin-willis/

Innocence Project (2009). Retrieved January 20, 2016, from www.innocenceproject.org/docs/Eyewitness_ID_Report.pdf.

Innocence Project (2010). *250 Exonerated, Too Many Wrongfully Convicted.* Retrieved from www.innocenceproject.org/docs/InnocenceProject_250.pdf.

Jack, F., & Hayne, H. (2010). Childhood amnesia: Empirical evidence for a two-stage phenomenon. *Memory, 18*, 831–844.

Jenkins, P., & Maier-Katkin, D. (1991). Occult survivors: The making of a myth. In J. T. Richardson, J. Best, & D. G. Bromley (Eds.), *The Satanism scare* (pp. 127–144). Hawthorne, NY: Aldine de Gruyter.

Johansson, N. O., Andersson, J., & Rönnberg, J. (2005). Compensating strategies in collaborative remembering in very old couples. *Scandinavian Journal of Psychology, 46*, 349–359.

Johnson, M. T. (1993). Memory phenomena in the law. *Applied Cognitive Psychology, 7*, 603–618.

Justice, L. V., Morrison, C. M., & Conway, M. A. (2013). True and intentionally fabricated memories. *Quarterly Journal of Experimental Psychology, 66*, 1196–1203.

Karpicke, J. D., & Roediger, H. L. (2008). The critical importance of retrieval for learning. *Science, 319*, 966–968.

Kassin, S. M., Ellsworth, P. C., & Smith, V. L. (1989). The "general acceptance" of psychological research on eyewitness testimony: A survey of the experts. *American Psychologist, 44*, 1089–1098.

Kassin, S. M., & Studebaker, C. A. (1998). Instructions to disregard and the jury: Curative and paradoxical effects. In J. M. Golding & C. M. MacLeod (Eds.), *Intentional forgetting: Interdisciplinary approaches* (pp. 413–434). Mahwah, NJ: Erlbaum.

Kassin, S. M., Tubb, V. A., Hosch, H. M., & Memon, A. (2001). On the "general acceptance" of eyewitness testimony research: A new survey of the experts. *American Psychologist, 56*, 405–416.

Kassin, S. M., & Wrightsman, L. S. (1979). On the requirements of proof: The timing of judicial instruction and mock juror verdicts. *Journal of Personality and Social Psychology, 37*, 1877–1887.

Kassin, S. M., & Wrightsman, L. S. (1988). *The American jury on trial: Psychological perspectives.* New York: Hemisphere.

Keane, A. (2010). The use at trial of scientific findings relating to human memory. *Criminal Law Review, 1*, 19–30.

Keast, A., Brewer, N., & Wells, G. L. (2007). Children's metacognitive judgments in an eyewitness identification task. *Journal of Experimental Child Psychology, 97*, 286–314.

Kelley, M. R., Reysen, M. B., Ahlstrand, K. M., & Pentz, C. J. (2012). Collaborative inhibition persists following social processing. *Journal of Cognitive Psychology, 24*, 727–734.

Kensinger, E. A. (2009). Remembering the details: Effects of emotion. *Emotion Review, 1*, 99–113.

Kensinger, E. A., Choi, H.-Y., Murray, B. D., & Rajaram, S. (2016). How social interactions affect emotional memory accuracy: Evident from collaborative retrieval and social contagion paradigms. *Memory & Cognition, 44*, 706–716.

Kensinger, E. A., Piguet, O., Krendl, A. C., & Corkin, S. (2005). Memory for contextual details: Effects of emotion and aging. *Psychology and Aging, 20*, 241–250.

Kihlstrom, J. F. (1998). Exhumed Memory. In S. J. Lynn, & K. M. McConkey (Eds.), *Truth in memory* (pp. 3–31). New York: Guilford Press.

Kihlstrom, J. F., & Barnhardt, T. M. (1993). The self-regulation of memory, for better, and for worse, with and without hypnosis. In D. M. Wegner & J. W. Pennebaker (Eds.), *Handbook of mental control* (pp. 88–125). Englewood Cliffs, NJ: Prentice Hall.

Kimball, D. R., & Bjork, R. A. (2002). Influences of intentional and unintentional forgetting of false memories. *Journal of Experimental Psychology: General, 131*, 116–130.

Knott, L. M., & Thorley, C. (2014). Mood-congruent false memories persist over time. *Cognition and Emotion, 28*, 903–912.

Kobayashi, K. (2005). What limits the encoding effect of note-taking? A meta-analytic examination. *Contemporary Educational Psychology, 83*, 240–245.

Kobayashi, K. (2006). Combined effects of note-taking/-reviewing on learning and the enhancement through interventions: A meta-analytic review. *Educational Psychology, 26*, 459–477.

Kolber, A. J. (2006). Therapeutic forgetting: The legal and ethical implications of memory dampening. *Vanderbilt Law Review, 59*, 1561–1626.

Kramer, G. P., Kerr, N. L., & Carroll, J. S. (1990). Pretrial publicity, judicial remedies, and jury bias. *Law and Human Behavior, 14*, 409–438.

Kroes, M. C. W., Tendolkar, I., van Wingen, G. A., van Waarde, J. A., Strange, B. A., & Fernandez, G. (2014). An electroconvulsive therapy procedure impairs reconsolidation of episodic memories in humans. *Nature Neuroscience, 17*, 204–208.

Krug, K. (2007). The relationship between confidence and accuracy: Current thoughts of the literature and a new area of research. *Applied Psychology in Criminal Justice, 3*, 7–41.

Kvavilashvili, L., Mirani, J., Schlagman, S., & Kornbrot, D. E. (2003). Comparing flashbulb memories of September 11 and the death of Princess Diana: Effects of time delays and nationality. *Applied Cognitive Psychology, 17*, 1017–1031.

LaBar, K. S., & Cabeza, R. (2006). Cognitive neuroscience of emotional memory. *Nature Reviews Neuroscience, 7*, 54–64.

La Fontaine, J. S. (1998). *Speak of the devil: Tales of satanic abuse in contemporary England*. Cambridge: Cambridge University Press.

Lacy, J. W., & Stark, C. E. L. (2013). The neuroscience of memory: Implications for the courtroom. *Nature Reviews Neuroscience, 14*, 649–658.

Lamb, M. E., Hershkowitz, I., Orbach, Y., & Esplin, P. W. (2008). *Tell me what happened: Structured investigative interviews of child victims and witnesses*. Hoboken, NJ: Wiley.

Lamb, M. E., Orbach, Y., Hershkowitz, I., Esplin, P. W., & Horowitz, D. (2007). Structured forensic interview protocols improve the quality and informativeness of investigative interviews with children: A review of research using the NICHD investigative interview protocol. *Child Abuse & Neglect, 31*, 1201–1231.

Lamb, M. E., Orbach, Y., Sternberg, K. J., Aldridge, J., Pearson, S., Stewart, H. L., . . ., & Bowler, L. (2009). Use of a structured investigative protocol enhances the quality of investigative interviews with alleged victims of child sexual abuse in Britain. *Applied Cognitive Psychology, 23*, 449–467.

Lamb, M. E., Sternberg, K. J., & Esplin, P. W. (1995). Making children into competent witnesses: Reactions to the amicus brief re Michaels. *Psychology, Public Policy, And Law, 1*, 438–449.

Lamb, M. E., Sternberg, K. J., Orbach, Y., Esplin, P. W., Stewart, H., & Mitchell, S. (2003). Age differences in young children's responses to open-ended invitations in the course of forensic interviews. *Journal of Consulting and Clinical Psychology, 71*, 926–934.

Lamb, M. E., Sternberg, K. J., Orbach, Y., Hershkowitz, I., & Horowitz, D. (2003). Differences between accounts provided by witnesses and alleged victims of child sexual abuse. *Child Abuse & Neglect, 27*, 1019–1031.

Lampinen, J. M., Judges, D. P., Odegard, T. N., & Hamilton, S. (2005). Reactions of mock jurors to the Department of Justice guidelines for the collection and preservation of eyewitness evidence. *Basic and Applied Social Psychology, 27*, 155–162.

Lane, J. D., & Wegner, D. M. (1995). The cognitive consequences of secrecy. *Journal of Personality and Social Psychology, 69*, 237–253.

Lanning, K. V. (1992). A law-enforcement perspective on allegations of ritual abuse. In D. K. Sakheim & S. E. Devine (Eds.), *Out of darkness: Exploring Satanism and ritual abuse* (pp. 109–146). New York: Lexington.

LaRooy, D., Brown, D. A., & Lamb, M. E. (2013). Suggestibility and witness interviewing using the Cognitive Interview and NICHD Protocol. In A. Ridley, F. Gabbert, & D. LaRooy (Eds.), *Investigative suggestibility: Wiley series in psychology of crime, policing and law* (pp. 197–216). Chichester, UK: Wiley.

Larsen, S. (1996). Taking and use of trial notes by jury. *American Law Reports, 36*, 1–254.

Larsson, A., Granhag, P. A., & Spjut, E. (2003). Children's recall and the Cognitive Interview: Do the positive effects hold over time? *Applied Cognitive Psychology, 17*, 203–214.

La Rue, A. (1992). *Aging and neuropsychological assessment.* New York: Plenum Press.

Leichtman, M. D., & Ceci, S. J. (1995). The effects of stereotype and suggestions on preschoolers' reports. *Developmental Psychology, 31*, 568–578.

Leippe, M. R., Wells, G. L., & Ostrom, T. M. (1978). Crime seriousness as a determinant of accuracy in eyewitness identification. *Journal of Applied Psychology, 63*, 345.

Leman, P. J., & Oldham, Z. (2005). Do children need to learn to collaborate? The effect of age and age differences on collaborative recall. *Cognitive Development, 20*, 33–48.

Lichtenstein, M., & Srull, T. K. (1987). Processing objectives as a determinant of the relationship between recall and judgment. *Journal of Experimental Social Psychology, 23*, 93–118.

Lindsay, S. (1998). Depolarizing views on recovered memory experiences. In S. J. Lynn & K. M. McConkey (Eds.), *Truth in Memory* (pp. 481–495). New York: Guilford Press.

Lindsey, R. C. L., & Wells, G. L. (1985). Improving eyewitness identification from lineups: simultaneous versus sequential lineup presentations. *Journal of Applied Psychology 70*, 556–564.

Loftus, E. F. (1979). *Eyewitness testimony.* London: Harvard University Press.

Loftus, E.F. (1993). The reality of repressed memories. *American Psychologist, 48*, 518–537.

Loftus, E. F. (1998). The price of bad memories. *Skeptical Inquirer, 22*, 23–24.

Loftus, E. F. (2005). Planting misinformation in the human mind: A 30-year investigation of the malleability of memory. *Learning & Memory, 12*, 361–366.

Loftus, E. F. (2013). Eyewitness testimony in the Lockerbie bombing case. *Memory, 21*, 584–590.

Loftus, E. F., & Burns, T. E. (1982). Mental shock can produce retrograde amnesia. *Memory & Cognition, 10*, 318–323.

Loftus, E. F., Garry, M., & Feldman, J. (1994). Forgetting sexual trauma: What does it mean when 38% forget? *Journal of Consulting and Clinical Psychology, 62*, 1177–1181.

Loftus E. F., & Hoffman, H. G. (1989). Misinformation and memory: The creation of new memories. *Journal of Experimental Psychology: General 118*, 100–104.

Loftus, E. F., & Ketcham, K. (1994). *The myth of repressed memory.* New York: St. Martin's Press.

Loftus, E. F., Levidow, B., & Duensing, S. (1992). Who remembers best? Individual differences in memory for events that occurred in a science museum. *Applied Cognitive Psychology, 6*, 93–107.

Loftus, E. F., Loftus, G. R., & Messo, J. (1987). Some facts about 'weapon focus.'. *Law and Human Behavior, 11*, 55–62.

Loftus, E. F., & Palmer, J. C. (1974). Reconstruction of automobile destruction: An example of the interaction between language and memory. *Journal of Verbal Learning & Verbal Behavior, 13*, 585–589.

Loftus, E. F., & Pickrell, J. E. (1995). The formation of false memories. *Psychiatric Annals, 25*, 720–725.

Loftus, E. F., Polonsky, S., & Fullilove, M. T. (1994). Memories of childhood abuse: Remembering and repressing. *Psychology of Women Quarterly, 18*, 67–84.

Loftus, E. F., & Rosenwald, L. A. (1993, November). Buried memories and shattered lives. *ABA Journal*, 71–73.

Loftus, G. R., & Mackworth, N. H. (1978). Cognitive determinants of fixation location during picture viewing. *Journal of Experimental Psychology: Human Perception and Performance, 4*, 565–572.

Lowenstein, J. A., Blank, H., & Sauer, J. D. (2010). Uniforms affect the accuracy of children's eyewitness identification decisions. *Journal of Investigative Psychology and Offender Profiling, 7*, 59–73.

Lynn, S. J., Evans, J., Laurence, J.-R., & Lilienfeld, S. O. (2015). What do people believe about memory? Implications for the science and pseudoscience of clinical practice. *Canadian Journal of Psychiatry, 60*, 541–547.

Lyon, T. D. (2002). Expert testimony on the suggestibility of children: Does it fit? In B. L. Bottoms, M. B. Kovera, & B. D. McCauliff (Eds.), *Children, social science, and the law* (pp. 378–411). Cambridge: Cambridge University Press.

MacLeod, C. M. (1998). Directed forgetting. In J. M. Golding & C. M. MacLeod (Eds.), *Intentional forgetting: Interdisciplinary approaches* (pp. 1–58). Mahwah, NJ: Erlbaum.

Macrae, C. N., Bodenhausen, G. V., Milne, A. B., & Jetten, J. (1994). Out of mind but back in sight: Stereotypes on the rebound. *Journal of Personality and Social Psychology, 67*, 808–817.

MacLean, P. D. (1900). *The triune brain. Role in paleocerebral functions.* New York: Plenum Press.

Magnussen, S., Andersson, J., Cornoldi, C., De Beni, R., Endestad, T., Goodman, G. S., et al. (2006). What people believe about memory. *Memory, 14*, 595–613.

Magnussen, S., & Melinder, A. (2012). What psychologists know and believe about memory: A survey of practitioners. *Applied Cognitive Psychology, 26*, 54–60.

Magnussen, S., Melinder, A., Stridbeck, U., & Raja, A. Q. (2010). Beliefs about factors affecting the reliability of eyewitness testimony: A comparison of judges, jurors and the general public. *Applied Cognitive Psychology, 24*, 122–133.

Magnussen, S., Wise, R. A., Raja, A. Q., Safer, M. A., Pawlenko, N., & Stridbeck, U. (2008). What judges know about eyewitness testimony: A comparison of Norwegian and US judges. *Psychology, Crime & Law, 14*, 177–188.

Maguire, E. A. (2001). Neuroimaging studies of autobiographical event memory. *Philosophical Transactions of the Royal Society of London, Series B: Biological Sciences, 356*, 1441–1451.

Mallard, D., & Perkins, D. (2005). Disentangling the evidence: Mock jurors, inadmissible testimony, and integrative encoding. *Psychiatry, Psychology, and Law, 12*, 289–297.

Malloy, L. C., Katz, C., Lamb, M. E., & Mugno, A. P. (2015). Children's requests for clarification in investigative interviews about suspected sexual abuse. *Applied Cognitive Psychology, 29*, 323–333.

Malpass, R. S., Tredoux, C. G., & McQuiston-Surrett, D. (2007). Lineup construction and lineup fairness. In R. C. L. Lindsay, D. F. Ross, J. D. Read, & M. P. Toglia (Eds.), *The handbook of eyewitness psychology: Volume 2. Memory for people* (pp. 155–178). Mahwah, NJ: Erlbaum.

Manshel, L. (1990). *Nap time. Nap time.* New York: Kensington Publishing.

Manson v. Braithwaite (432 U.S. 98, 1977).

Maran, M. (2010). *My lie: A true story of false memory.* San Francisco, CA: Wiley.

Marion, S. B., & Thorley, C. (2016). A meta-analytic review of collaborative inhibition and postcollaborative memory: Testing the predictions of the retrieval strategy disruption hypothesis. *Psychological Bulletin, 142*, 1141–1164.

Matthews, R., Hancock, L., & Briggs, D. (2004). *Jurors' perceptions, understanding, confidence, and satisfaction in the jury system: A study in six courts.* London: Home Office.

Mazzoni, G., & Memon, A. (2003). Imagination can create false autobiographical memories. *Psychological Science, 14*, 186–188.

McClelland, J. L., & Chappell, M. (1998). Familiarity breeds differentiation: A subjective-likelihood approach to the effects of experience in recognition memory. *Psychological Review, 105*, 724–760.

McClelland, V. C., Schacter, D. L., & Addis, D. R. (2015). Contributions of episodic memory to imagining the future. In D. R. Addis, M. Barsense, & A. Duarte (Eds.), *The Wiley handbook on the cognitive neuroscience of memory* (pp. 287–308). Chichester, UK: Wiley.

McElvaney, R. (2015). Disclosure of child sexual abuse: Delays, non-disclosure and partial disclosure. What the research tells us and implications for practice. *Child Abuse Review, 24*, 159–169.

McFadyen, R. G., & Kitson, W. H. (1996). Language comprehension and expression among adolescents who have experienced childhood physical abuse. *Child Psychology & Psychiatry & Allied Disciplines, 37*, 551–562.

McGough, L. S. (1993). *Child witnesses: Fragile voices in the American legal system.* New Haven, CT: Yale University Press.

McKimmie, B., Masters, J. M., Masser, B. M., Schuller, R. A., & Terry, D. J. (2013). Stereotypical and counterstereotypical defendants: Who is he and was the case against her? *Psychology, Public Policy, and Law, 19*, 343–354.

McNally, R. J. (2003). *Remembering trauma.* Cambridge, MA: Harvard University Press.

McNally, R. J., Clancy, S. A., Barrett, H. M., & Parker, H. A. (2005). Reality monitoring in adults reporting repressed, recovered, or continuous memories of childhood sexual abuse. *Journal of Abnormal Psychology, 114*, 147–152.

McNally, R. J., & Geraerts, E. (2009). A new solution to the recovered memory debate. *Perspectives on Psychological Science, 4*, 126–134.

McWilliams, K., Goodman, G. S., Lyons, K. E., Newton, J., & Avila-Mora, E. (2014). Memory for child sexual abuse information: Simulated memory error and individual differences. *Memory & Cognition, 42*, 151–163.

Meade, M. L., & Gigone, D. (2011). The effect of information distribution on collaborative inhibition. *Memory, 19*, 417–428.

Meade, M. L., & Roediger, H. L. (2009). Age differences in collaborative memory: The role of retrieval manipulations. *Memory & Cognition, 37*, 962–975.

Megrahi v. Her Majesty's Advocate [2002] ScotHC 30 (14 March 2002).

Meissner, C. A., & Brigham, J. C. (2001). Thirty years of investigating the own-race bias in memory for faces: A meta-analytic review. *Psychology, Public Policy, and Law, 7*, 3–35.

Melinder, A., & Magnussen, S. (2015). Psychologists and psychiatrists serving as expert witnesses in court: What do they know about eyewitness memory? *Psychology, Crime & Law, 21*, 53–61.

Melinder, A., Scullin, M., Gavvold, T., & Iversen, M. (2007). The stability and generalizability of young children's suggestibility over a 44-month interval. *Psychology, Crime & Law, 13*, 459–468.

Memon, A., & Gabbert, F. (2003). Improving the identification accuracy of senior witnesses: do prelineup questions and sequential testing help? *Journal of Applied Psychology, 88*, 341–347.

Memon, A., & Higham, P. A. (1999). A review of the cognitive interview. *Psychology, Crime & Law, 5*, 177–196.

Memon, A., Hope, L., Bartlett, J., & Bull, R. (2002). Eyewitness recognition errors: The effects of mugshot viewing and choosing in young and old adults. *Memory & Cognition, 30*, 1219–1227.

Memon A., & Wright, D. B. (1999). Eyewitness testimony and the Oklahoma bombing. *The Psychologist, 12*, 292–295.

Mendoza-Dinton, R., Ayduk, O. N., Shoda, Y., & Mischel, W. (1997). Cognitive-affective processing system analysis of reactions to the O. J. Simpson criminal trial verdict. *Journal of Social Issues, 53*, 563–581.

Merckelbach, H., Muris, P., Rassin, E., & Horselenberg, R. (2000). Dissociative experiences and interrogative suggestibility in college students. *Personality and Individual Differences, 29*, 1133–1140.

Merckelbach, H., Smeets, T., Geraerts, E., Jelicic, M., Bouwen, A., & Smeets, E. (2006). I haven't thought about this for years! Dating recent recalls of vivid memories. *Applied Cognitive Psychology, 20*, 33–42.

Milne, R., & Bull, R. (2003). Does the cognitive interview help children to resist the effects of suggestive questioning? *Legal and Criminological Psychology, 8*, 21–38.

Mitchell, K. J., Johnson, M. K., & Mather, M. (2003). Source monitoring and suggestibility to misinformation: adult age-related differences. *Applied Cognitive Psychology, 17*, 107–119.

Morgan, C. A., III, Hazlett, G., Doran, A., Garrett, S., Hoyt, G., Thomas, P., et al. (2004). Accuracy of eyewitness memory for persons encountered during exposure to highly intense stress. *International Journal of Law and Psychiatry, 27*, 265–279.

Morgan, C. A., III, & Southwick, S. (2014). Perspective: I believe what I remember, but it may not be true. *Neurobiology of Learning and Memory, 11*, 101–103.

Morgan, C. A., III, Southwick, S. M., Steffian, G., Hazlett, G. A., & Loftus, E. F. (2013). Misinformation can influence memory for recently experienced, highly stressful events. *International Journal of Law & Psychiatry, 36*, 11–17.

Morris, G., & Baker-Ward, L. (2007). Fragile but real: Children's capacity to use newly acquired words to convey preverbal memories. *Child Development, 78*, 448–458.

Morrison, C. M., & Conway, M. A. (2010). First words and first memories. *Cognition, 116*, 23–32.

Mueller-Johnson, K., & Ceci, S. J. (2004). Memory and suggestibility in older adults: Live event participation and repeated interview. *Applied Cognitive Psychology, 18*, 1109–1127.

Mullally, S. L., & Maguire, E. A. (2014). Learning to remember: The early ontogeny of episodic memory. *Developmental Cognitive Neuroscience, 9*, 12–29.

Munsterberg, H. (1908). *On the Witness Stand*. New York: McClure.

National Research Council (2014). *Identifying the culprit: Assessing eyewitness identification*. Washington, DC: The National Academies Press.

Neil v. Bigger Screen (409 U.S. 188, 1972).

Neisser, U., & Harsch, N. (1992). Phantom flashbulbs: False recollections of hearing the news about Challenger. In E. Winograd, & U. Neisser (Eds.), *Affect and accuracy in recall: Studies of 'flashbulb' memories* (pp. 9–31). New York: Cambridge University Press.

Nelson, K. & Fivush, R. (2004). The emergence of autobiographical memory: a social cultural developmental theory. *Psychological Review, 111*, 486–511.

New Jersey Courts. (2012, July 19), Supreme Court releases eyewitness identification criteria for criminal cases. Retrieved from www.judiciary.state.nj.us/pressrel/2012/pr120719a.htm.

Nickerson, R. S. (1984). Retrieval inhibition from part-set cuing: A persisting enigma in memory research. *Memory & Cognition, 12*, 531–552.

Nigg, J. T. (2000). On inhibition/disinhibition in developmental psychopathology: Views from cognitive and personality psychology and a working inhibition taxonomy. *Psychological Bulletin, 126*, 220–246.

Orbach, Y., Hershkowitz, I., Lamb, M. E., Sternberg, K. J., Esplin, P. W., & Horowitz, D. (2000). Assessing the value of structured protocols for forensic interviews of alleged abuse victims. *Child Abuse & Neglect, 24*, 733–752.

Oregon v. Lawson, (SC S059306, 2012).

Ornstein, P.A. (1995). Children's long-term retention of salient personal experiences. *Journal of Traumatic Stress, 8*, 581–606.

Ost, J., Easton, S., Hope, L., French, C. C., & Wright, D. B. (2017). Latent variables underlying memory beliefs of Chartered Clinical Psychologists, Hypnotherapists, and undergraduate students. *Memory, 25*, 57–68.

Ost, J., Foster, S., Costall, A., & Bull, R. (2005). False reports of childhood events in appropriate interviews. *Memory, 13*, 700–710.

Ost, J., Wright, D. B., Easton, S., Hope, L., & French, C. C. (2013). Recovered memories, satanic abuse, Dissociative Identity Disorder and false memories in the UK: A survey of clinical psychologists and hypnotherapists. *Psychology, Crime & Law, 19*, 1–19.

Otgaar, H., Candel, I., & Merckelbach, H. (2008). Children's false memories: Easier to elicit for a negative than a neutral event. *Acta Psychologica, 128*, 350–354.

Otgaar, H., Candel, I., Merckelbach, H., & Wade, K. A. (2009). Abducted by a UFO: Prevalence information affects young children's false memories for an implausible event. *Applied Cognitive Psychology, 23*, 115–125.

Otgaar, H., Howe, M. L., Brackmann, N., & Smeets, T. (2016). The malleability of developmental trends in neutral and negative memory illusions. *Journal of Experimental Psychology: General, 145*, 31–55.

Otgaar, H., Howe, M. L., Memon, A., & Wang, J. (2014). The development of differential mnemonic effects of false denials and forced confabulations. *Behavioral Sciences and the Law, 32*, 718–731.

Otgaar, H., Howe, M. L., Smeets, T., & Wang, J. (2016). Denial-induced forgetting: False denials undermine memory, but external denials undermine belief. *Journal of Applied Research in Memory and Cognition, 5*, 168–175.

O'Toole, A. J., Roark, D. A., & Abdi, H. (2002). Recognizing moving faces: A psychological and neural synthesis. *Trends in Cognitive Sciences, 6*, 261–266.

Parker, J. F., Bahrick, L., Lundy, B., Fivush, R., & Levitt, M. (1998). Effects of stress on children's memory for a natural disaster. In C. P. Thompson, D. J. Herrmann, J. D. Read, & D. Bruce (Eds.), *Eyewitness memory: Theoretical and applied perspectives* (pp. 31–54). Mahwah, NJ: Erlbaum.

Paterson, H. M., & Kemp, R. I. (2006). Comparing methods of encountering post-event information: The power of co-witness suggestion. *Applied Cognitive Psychology, 20*, 1083–1099.

Patihis, L., Ho, L. Y., Tingen, I. W., Lilienfeld, S. O., & Loftus, E. F. (2014). Are the "memory wars" over? A scientist-practitioner gap in beliefs about repressed memory. *Psychological Science, 25*, 519–530.

Paunovic, N., Lundh, L.-G., & Oest, L.-G. (2002). Attentional and memory bias for emotional information in crime victims with acute posttraumatic stress disorder. *Journal of Anxiety Disorders, 16*, 675–692.

Pawlenko, N. B., Safer, M. A., Wise, R. A., & Holfeld, B. (2013). A teaching aid for improving jurors' assessment of eyewitness accuracy. *Applied Cognitive Psychology, 27*, 190–197.

Peker, M., & Tekcan, A. (2009). The role of familiarity among group members in collaborative inhibition and social contagion. *Social Psychology, 40*, 111–118.

Pennington, N., & Hastie, R. (1988). Explanation-based decision making: Effects of memory structure on judgment. *Journal of Experimental Psychology: Learning, Memory, and Cognition, 14*, 521–533.

Pennington, N., & Hastie, R. (1990). Practical implications of psychological research on juror and jury decision making. *Personality and Social Psychology Bulletin, 16*, 90–105.

Pennington, N., & Hastie, R. (1992). Explaining the evidence: Tests of the story model for juror decision making. *Journal of Personality and Social Psychology, 62*, 189–206.

Pennington, N., & Hastie, R. (1993). The story model for juror decision making. In R. Hastie (Ed.), *Inside the juror: The psychology of juror decision making* (pp. 192–221). New York: Cambridge University Press.

Penrod, S., & Heuer, L. (1996). Increasing juror participation in trials through note taking and question asking. *Judicature, 79*, 2–8.

Penrod, S., & Heuer, L. (1997). Tweaking commonsense: Assessing aids to jury decision making. *Psychology, Public Policy, and Law, 3*, 259–284.

Peters, D. P. (1988). Eyewitness memory in a natural setting. In M. M. Gruneberg, P. E. Morris, & R. N. Sykes (Eds.), *Practical aspects of memory: Current research and issues: Vol. 1. Memory in everyday life* (pp. 89–94). Chichester, UK: Wiley.

Peterson, C. (1996). The preschool child witness: Errors in accounts of traumatic injury. *Canadian Journal of Behavioral Science, 28*, 36–42.

Peterson, C. (1999). Children's memory for medical emergencies: Two years later. *Developmental Psychology, 35*, 1493–1506.

Peterson, C. (2012). Children's autobiographical memories across the years: Forensic implications of childhood amnesia and eyewitness memory for stressful events. *Developmental Review, 32*, 287–306.

Peterson, C., & Bell, M. (1996). Children's memory for traumatic injury. *Child Development, 67*, 3045–3070.

Peterson, C., Moores, L., & White, G. (2001). Recounting the same events again and again: Children's consistency across multiple interviews. *Applied Cognitive Psychology, 15*, 353–371.

Peterson, C., Morris, G., Baker-Ward, L., & Flynn, S. (2014). Predicting which childhood memories persist: Contributions of memory characteristics. *Developmental Psychology, 50*, 439–448.

Peterson, C., Pardy, L., Tizzard-Drover, T., & Warren, K. (2005). When initial interviews are delayed a year: Effect on children's 2-year recall. *Law & Human Behavior, 29*, 527–541.

Peterson, C., & Parsons, B. (2005). Interviewing former 1- and 2-year-olds about medical emergencies five years later. *Law & Human Behavior, 29*, 743–754.

Peterson, C., Warren, K., & Hayes, A. H. (2013). Revisiting Narrative Elaboration Training with an ecologically relevant event. *Journal of Cognition and Development, 14*, 154–174.

Peterson, C., & Whalen, N. (2001). Five years later: Children's memory for medical emergencies. *Applied Cognitive Psychology, 15*, 7–24.

Phelps, E. A. (2004). Human emotion and memory: interactions of the amygdala and hippo-campal complex. *Current Opinion in Neurobiology, 14*, 198–202.

Phelps, E. A. (2012). Emotion's impact on memory. In L. Nadel & W. P. Sinnott-Armstrong (Eds.), *Memory and law* (pp. 7–26). New York: Oxford University Press.

Pickel, K. L. (1995). Inducing jurors to disregard inadmissible evidence: A legal explanation does not help. *Law and Human Behavior, 19*, 407–424.

Piper, A. J., Pope, H. J., & Borowiecki, J. I. (2000). Custer's last stand: Brown, Scheflin, and Whitfield's latest attempt to salvage 'dissociative amnesia.' *Journal of Psychiatry & Law, 28*, 149–213.

Police and Criminal Evidence Act Codes of Practice, Code D (2011). Retrieved from www.gov.uk/government/publications/pace-code-d-2011.

Poole, D. A., Lindsay, D. S., Memon, A., & Bull, R. (1995). Psychotherapy and the recovery of memories of childhood sexual abuse: U.S. and British practitioners' opinions, practices, and experiences. *Journal of Consulting and Clinical Psychology, 63*, 426–437.

Poole, D. A., & White, L. (1991). Effects of question repetition on the eyewitness testimony of children and adults. *Developmental Psychology, 27*, 975–986.

Pope, H. G., Jr., Oliva, P. S., & Hudson, J. I. (1999). Repressed memories: The scientific status. In D. L. Faigman, D. H. Kaye, M. J. Saks, & J. Sanders (Eds.), *Modern scientific evidence: The law and science of expert testimony* (Vol. 1, pp. 115–155). St. Paul, MN: West Publishing.

Porter, S., Taylor, K., & Ten Brinke, L. (2008). Memory for media: Investigation of false memories for negatively and positively charged public events. *Memory, 16*, 658–666.

Porter, S., Yuille, J. C., & Lehman, D. R. (1999). The nature of real, implanted, and fabricated memories for emotional childhood events: Implications for the recovered memory debate. *Law and Human Behavior, 23*, 517–537.

Pozzulo, J. D., & Lindsay, R. C. L. (1998). Identification accuracy of children versus adults: a meta-analysis. *Law and Human Behavior, 22*, 549–570.

Pritchard, M. E., & Keenan, J. M. (1999). Memory monitoring in mock jurors. *Journal of Experimental Psychology: Applied, 5*, 152–168.

Putnam, F. W. (1997). *Dissociation in children and adolescents*. New York: Guilford Press.

Qin, J., Goodman, G. S., Bottoms, B. L., & Shaver, P. R. (1998). Repressed memories of ritualistic and religion-related child abuse. In S. J. Lynn & K. M. McConkey (Eds.), *Truth in memory* (pp. 260–283). New York: Guilford Press.

Quas, J. A., Thompson, W. C., & Clarke-Stewart, K. A. (2005). Do jurors "know" what isn't so about child witnesses? *Law and Human Behavior, 29*, 425–456.

R. v. Turnball, (98 Cr. App. R. 313, 1977).

Rabinowitz, J. C. (1984). Aging and recognition failure. *Journal of Gerontology, 39*, 65–71.

Rajah, M. N., Maillet, D., & Grady, C. L. (2015). Episodic memory in healthy older adults. In D. R. Addis, M. Barsense, & A. Duarte (Eds.), *The Wiley handbook on the cognitive neuroscience of memory* (pp. 347–370). Chichester, UK: Wiley.

Rajaram, S. (1993). Remembering and knowing: Two means of access to the personal past. *Memory & Cognition, 21*, 89–102.

Rajaram, S., & Pereira-Pasarin, L. P. (2010). Collaborative memory: Cognitive research and theory. *Perspectives on Psychological Science, 5*, 649–663.

Ran, A., Shapiro, T., Fan, J., & Posner, M. (2002). Hypnotic suggestion and the modulation of Stroop interference. *Archives of General Psychiatry, 59*, 1155–1161.

Raskin, D. C., & Esplin, P. W. (1991). Assessment of children's statements of sexual abuse. In J. Doris (Ed.), *The suggestibility of children's recollections* (pp. 153–164). Washington, DC: American Psychological Association.

Rausch, R. (1996). Effects of surgery on cognitive functioning. In J. C. Sackellares & S. Berent (Eds.), *Psychological disturbances in epilepsy* (pp. 245–258). Boston, MA: Butterworth Heinemann.

Raymaekers, L. H. C. (2013). *Recovering memories of childhood sexual abuse: From cognitive mechanisms to classification.* Unpublished doctoral dissertation, Maastricht University, The Netherlands.

Raymaekers, L. H. C., Smeets, T., Peters, M. J. V., Otgaar, H., & Merckelbach, H. (2012). The classification of recovered memories: A cautionary note. *Consciousness and Cognition, 21*, 1640–1643.

Reyna, V. F., Hans, V. P., Corbin, J. C., Yeh, R., Lin, K., & Royer, C. (2015). The gist of juries: Testing a model of damage award decision making. *Psychology, Public Policy, and Law, 21*, 280–294.

Richardson, R., & Hayne, H. (2007). You can't take it with you: The translation of memory across development. *Current Directions in Psychological Science, 16*, 223–227.

Riggins, T., Blankenship, S. L., Mulligan, E., Rice, K., & Redcay, E. (2015). Developmental differences in relations between episodic memory and hippocampal subregion volume during early childhood. *Child Development, 86*, 1710–1718.

Rimmele, U., Davachi, L., Petrov, R., Dougal, S., & Phelps, E. A. (2011). Emotion enhances the subjective feeling of remembering, despite lower accuracy for contextual details. *Emotion, 11*, 553–562.

Robbennolt, J. K., Groscup, J. L., & Penrod, S. (2014). Evaluating and assisting jury competence in civil cases. In I. B. Weiner & R. K. Otto (Eds.), *The handbook of forensic psychology (4th Edition)* (pp. 469–512). Hoboken, NJ: Wiley.

Roebers, C. M., Bjorklund, D. F., Schneider, W., & Cassel, W. S. (2002). Differences and similarities in event recall and suggestibility between children and adults in Germany and the United States. *Experimental Psychology, 49*, 132–140.

Roediger, H. L., & Karpicke, J. D. (2006). The power of testing memory: Basic research and implications for educational practice. *Perspectives on Psychological Science, 1*, 181–210.

Roediger, H. L., Meade, M., & Bergman, E. (2001). Social contagion of memory. *Psychonomic Bulletin & Review, 8*, 365–371.

Roediger, H. L., & McDermott, K. B. (1995). Creating false memories: Remembering words not presented in lists. *Journal of Experimental Psychology: Learning, Memory, and Cognition, 21*, 803–814.

Rogers, M. L. (1992). Evaluating adult litigants who allege injuries from child sexual abuse: Clinical assessment methods of traumatic memories. *Issues in Child Abuse Accusations, 4*, 221–238.

Rogers, M. L (1994). Factors to consider in assessing adult litigants' complaints of childhood sexual abuse. *Behavioral Sciences and the Law, 12*, 279–298.

Roozendaal, B., & McGaugh, J. L. (2011). Memory modulation. *Behavioral Neuroscience, 125*, 797–824.

Rosenhan, D. L., Eisner, S. L., & Robinson, R. J. (1994). Note taking can aid juror recall. *Law and Human Behavior, 18*, 53–61.

Rosenthal, R. (1964). The effect of the experimenter on the results of psychological research. *Bulletin of the Maritime Psychological Association. 13*, 1–39.

Rosenthal, R., & Rubin, D. B. (1978). Interpersonal expectancy effects: The first 345 studies. *Behavioral and Brain Sciences, 1*, 377–415.

Ross, M., Spencer, S. J., Blatz, C. W., & Restorick, E. (2008). Collaboration reduces the frequency of false memories in older and younger adults. *Psychology and Aging, 23,* 85–92.

Ross, M., Spencer, S. J., Linardatos, L., Lam, K. C. H., & Perunovic, M. (2004). Going shopping and identifying landmarks: Does collaboration improve older people's memory? *Applied Cognitive Psychology, 18,* 683–696.

Rubin, D. C. (2000). The distribution of early childhood memories. *Memory, 8,* 265–269.

Rubin, D. C., & Bernstein, D. (2007). People believe it is plausible to have forgotten memories of childhood sexual abuse. *Psychonomic Bulletin & Review, 14,* 776–778.

Ruva, C. L., & Guenther, C. C. (2015). From the shadows into the light: How pretrial publicity and deliberation affect mock jurors' decisions, impressions, and memory. *Law and Human Behavior, 39,* 294–310.

Ruva, C. L., Guenther, C. C., & Yarborough, A. (2011). Positive and negative pretrial publicity: The roles of impression formation, emotion, and predecisional distortion. *Criminal Justice and Behavior, 38,* 511–534.

Ruva, C. L., & McEvoy, C. (2008). Negative and positive pretrial publicity affect juror memory and decision making. *Journal of Experimental Psychology: Applied, 14,* 226–235.

Ruva, C. L., McEvoy, C., & Bryant, J. D. (2007). Effects of pretrial publicity and jury deliberation on juror bias and source memory errors. *Applied Cognitive Psychology, 21,* 45–67.

Sales, J. M., Fivush, R., & Peterson, C. (2003). Parental reminiscing about positive and negative events. *Journal of Cognition and Development, 4,* 185–209.

Sand, L. B., & Reiss, S. A. (1985). A report on seven experiments conducted by district court judges in the Second Circuit. *New York University Law Review, 60,* 423–497.

Sandrini, M., Cohen, L. G., & Censor, N. (2015). Modulating reconsolidation: A link to causal systems-level dynamics of human memories. *Trends in Cognitive Sciences, 19,* 475–482.

Sauerland, M., Raymakers, L. H. C., Otgaar, H., Memon, A., Waltjen, T. T., Nivo, M., Slegers, C., Broers, N. J., &, Smeets., T. (2016). Stress, stress-induced cortisol responses, and eyewitness identification performance, *Behavioral Sciences and the Law, 34,* 580–594.

Saywitz, K. J., & Snyder, L. (1996). Narrative elaboration: Test of a new procedure for interviewing children. *Journal of Consulting and Clinical Psychology, 64,* 1347–1357.

Schacter, D. L. (2012). Adaptive construction processes and the future of memory. *American Psychologist, 67,* 603–613.

Schacter, D. L., & Addis, D. R. (2009). On the nature of medial temporal lobe contributions to the constructive simulation of future events. *Philosophical Transactions of the Royal Society of London, Series B.: Biological Sciences, 362,* 773–786.

Schacter, D. L., Chamberlain, J., Gaesser, B., & Gerlach, K. D. (2012). Neuroimaging of true, false, and imaginary memories: Findings and implications. In L. Nadel & W. P. Sinnott-Armstrong (Eds.), *Memory and law* (pp. 233–262) New York: Oxford University Press.

Schacter, D. L., Koutstaal, W., Gross, M. S., Johnson, M. K., & Angell, K. E. (1997). False recollection induced by photographs: a comparison of older and younger adults. *Psychology and Aging, 12,* 203–215.

Schooler, J. W., Bendiksen, M., & Ambadar, Z. (1997). Taking the middle line: Can we accommodate both fabricated and recovered memories of sexual abuse? In M. A. Conway (Ed.), *Recovered memories and false memories* (pp. 251–292). New York: Oxford University Press.

Schreiber, N., Bellah, L. D., Martinez, Y., McLaurin, K. A., Strok, R., Garven, S., & Wood, J. M. (2006). Suggestive interviewing in the McMartin Preschool and Kelly Michaels daycare abuse cases: A case study. *Social Influence, 1,* 16–47.

Schwabe, L., Joëls, M., Roozendaal, B., Wolf, O. T., & Oitzl, M. S. (2012). Stress effects on memory: An update and integration. *Neuroscience and Biobehavioral Reviews, 36,* 1740–1749.

Schwabe, L., Nader, K., & Pruessner, J. C. (2014). Reconsolidation of human memory: Brain mechanisms and clinical relevance. *Biological Psychiatry, 76,* 274–280.

Schwabe, L., & Wolf, O. T. (2009). New episodic learning interferes with the reconsolidation of autobiographical memories. *PLoS ONE, 4,* e7519.

Schwartz, B. L., Howe, M. L., Toglia, M. P., & Otgaar, H. (Eds.) (2014). *What is Adaptive about Adaptive Memory?* New York: Oxford University Press.

Scoboria, A., Wade, K. A., Lindsay, D. S., Azad, T., Strange, D., Ost, J., & Hyman, I. E. (2017). A mega-analysis of memory reports from eight peer-reviewed false memory implantation studies. *Memory, 25,* 146-163.

Scott, S. (2001). *The politics and experience of ritual abuse: Beyond disbelief.* Philadelphia, PA: Open University Press.

Semmler, C., & Brewer, N. (2002). Effects of mood and emotion on juror processing and judgments. *Behavioral Sciences and the Law, 20,* 423–436.

Sharot, T., Martorella, E. A., Delgado, M. R., & Phelps, E. A. (2007). How personal experience modulates the neural circuitry of memories of September 11. *Proceedings of the National Academy of Sciences of the United States of America, 104,* 389–394.

Shaw, J. I., Garven, S., & Wood, J. M. (1997). Co-witness information can have immediate effects on eyewitness memory reports. *Law and Human Behavior, 21,* 503–523.

Simcock, G., & Hayne, H. (2002). Breaking the barrier? Children fail to translate their preverbal memories into language. *Psychological Science, 13,* 225–231.

Simcock, G., & Hayne, H. (2003). Age-related changes in verbal and nonverbal recall during early childhood. *Developmental Psychology, 39,* 805–814.

Simons, D. J., & Chabris, C. F. (2011). What people believe about how memory works: A representative survey of the U.S. population. *PLoS ONE, 6,* e22757.

Skagerberg, E. M., & Wright, D. B. (2008). The prevalence of co-witnesses and co-witness discussions in real eyewitnesses. *Psychology, Crime & Law, 14,* 513–521.

Skelton, F., & Hay, D. (2008). Do children utilize motion when recognizing faces? *Visual Cognition, 16,* 419–429.

Slamecka, N. J. (1968). An examination of trace storage in free recall. *Journal of Experimental Psychology, 76,* 504–513.

Smith, S. E., (1993). Body memories: And other pseudo-scientific notions of "survivor psychology." *Issues in Child Abuse Accusations, 5(4).*

Spiegel, D., & Scheflin, A. W. (1994). Dissociated or fabricated? Psychiatric aspects of repressed memory in criminal and civil cases. *International Journal of Clinical and Experimental Hypnosis, 42,* 411–432.

Spiers, H. J., & Bendor, D. (2014). Enhance, delete, incept: Manipulating hippocampus-dependent memories. *Brain Research Bulletin, 105,* 2–7.

Sporer, S. L., & Martschuk, N. (2014). The reliability of eyewitness identifications by the elderly: An evidence-based review. In M. P. Toglia, D. F. Ross, J. Pozzulo, & E. Pica (Eds.), *The elderly eyewitness in court* (pp. 3–37). New York, NY: Psychology Press.

State of Washington v. Ingram, No. 88–100752–1, Superior Ct., Olympia, Washington (1989).

State v. Michaels, 264 N. J. Super. 579, 631–32, 625 A.2d 489 (App.Div.1993).

State v. Michaels, 136 N. J. 299, 642 A.2d 1372 (1994).

Steblay, N. K., Besirevic, J., Fulero, S. M., & Jiminez-Lorente, B. (1999). The effects of pretrial publicity on juror verdicts: A meta-analytic review. *Law and Human Behavior, 23,* 219–235.

Sternberg, K. J., Lamb, M. E., Orbach, Y., Esplin, P. W., & Mitchell, S. (2001). Use of a structured investigative protocol enhances young children's responses to free-recall prompts in the course of forensic interviews. *Journal of Applied Psychology, 86,* 997–1005.

Strange, D. & Hayne, H. (2013). The devil is in the detail: Children's recollection of details about their prior experiences. *Memory, 21,* 431–443.

Strub, T., & McKimmie, B. (2012). Note takers who review are less vulnerable to the influence of stereotypes than note takers who do not review. *Psychology, Crime & Law, 18,* 859–876.

Strub, T., & McKimmie, B. (2016). Sugar and spice and all things nice: The role of gender stereotypes in jurors' perceptions of criminal defendants. *Psychiatry, Psychology, and Law, 23,* 487–498.

Stuber, M. L., Nader, K., Yasuda, P., Pynoos, R. S., & Cohen, S. (1991). Stress responses after pediatric bone marrow transplantation: Preliminary results of a prospective longitudinal study. *Journal of the American Academy of Child & Adolescent Psychiatry, 30,* 952–957.

Sui, J., & Humphreys, G. W. (2015). The integrative self: How self-reference integrates perception and memory. *Trends in Cognitive Sciences, 19,* 719–728.

Superior Court of New Jersey, Appellate Division, from *State of New Jersey v. Margaret Kelly Michaels,* appendix, Vol.1, Docket No.199–88T4.

Svoboda, E., McKinnon, M. C., & Levine, B. (2006). The functional neuroanatomy of autobiographical memory: A meta-analysis. *Neuropsychologia, 44,* 2189–2208.

Takahashi, M. (2007). Does collaborative remembering reduce false memories? *British Journal of Psychology, 98,* 1–13.

Takahashi, M., & Saito, S. (2004). Does test delay eliminate collaborative inhibition? *Memory, 12,* 722–731.

Talarico, J. M., & Rubin, D. C. (2003). Confidence, not consistency, characterizes flashbulb memories. *Psychological Science, 14,* 455–461.

Taub, S. (1999). *Recovered memories of child sexual abuse: Psychological, social and legal perspectives on a contemporary mental health controversy.* Springfield, IL: Charles C. Thomas.

Technical Working Group for Eyewitness Evidence [TWGfEE]. (1999). Eyewitness evidence: A guide for law enforcement (Report No. NCJ 178240). Washington, DC: United States Department of Justice, Offices of Justice Programs. Available at www.ncjrs.gov/pdffiles1/nij/178240.pdf.

The Royal Society (2011). *Neuroscience and The Law: Brain Waves.* London: The Royal Society.

Thompson-Cannino, J., Cotton, R., & Torneo, E. (2009). *Picking Cotton: Our memoir of injustice and redemption.* New York: St. Martin's Press.

Thorley, C., Baxter, R. E., & Lorek, J. (2016). The impact of note taking style and note availability at retrieval on mock jurors' recall and recognition of trial information. *Memory, 24,* 560–574.

Thorley, C., & Dewhurst, S. A. (2009). False and veridical collaborative recognition. *Memory, 17,* 17–25.

Tizzard-Drover, T., & Peterson, C. (2004). The influence of an early interview on long-term recall: A comparative analysis. *Applied Cognitive Psychology, 18,* 727–745.

Tulving, E. (1972). Episodic and semantic memory. In E. Tulving & W. Donaldson (Eds.), *Organization of memory* (pp. 381–403). New York: Academic Press.

Tulving, E. (1985). Memory and consciousness. *Canadian Psychology, 26,* 1–12.

Tunnicliff, J. L., & Clark, S. E. (2000). Selecting foils for identification lineups: Matching suspects or descriptions. *Law and Human Behavior, 24,* 231–258.

Tustin, K., & Hayne, H. (2010). Defining the boundary: Age related changes in childhood amnesia. *Developmental Psychology, 46,* 1049–1061.

Underwager, R., & Wakefield, H. (1990). New directions for the psychologist in child sex abuse cases. In the conference manuscript on *Defending a Case of Child Sexual Abuse,* Raleigh, NC: The North Carolina Academy of Trial Lawyers. New York: Guilford Press.

Underwager, R., & Wakefield, H. (1998). Recovered memories in the courtroom. In S. J. Lynn, K. McConkey, & N. P. Spanos (Eds.), *Truth in Memories* (pp. 394–434). New York: Guildford Press.

U.S. v. Montgomery, 150 F.3d 983, 999–1000 (9th Cir. 1998).

Valentine, T., Darling, S., & Memon, A. (2006). How can psychological science enhance the effectiveness of identification procedures: An international comparison. *Pub. Int. L. Rep., 11,* 21.

Valentine, T., Darling, S., & Memon, A. (2007). Do strict rules and moving images increase the reliability of sequential identification procedures? *Applied Cognitive Psychology, 21,* 933–949.

Valentine, T., & Heaton, P. (1999). An evaluation of fairness of police lineups and video identifications. *Applied Cognitive Psychology, 13,* S59-S72.

Valentine, T., & Mesout, J. (2009) Eyewitness identification under stress in the London Dungeon. *Applied Cognitive Psychology, 23,* 151–161.

Valentine, T., Pickering, A., & Darling, S. (2003). Characteristics of eyewitness identification that predict the outcome of real lineups. *Applied Cognitive Psychology, 17,* 969–993.

Van de Ven, V., Otgaar, H., & Howe, M. L. (in press). A neurobiological account of false memories. In H. Otgaar & M. L. Howe (Eds.), *Can we know what the truth is in the courtroom? Problems with deception, lies, and false memories.* New York: Oxford University Press.

van den Hout, M., Merckelbach, H., & Pool, K. (1996). Dissociation, reality monitoring, trauma, and thought suppression. *Behavioral Cognitive Psychotherapy, 24,* 97–108.

Vieira, K. M., & Lane, S. M. (2013). How you lie affects what you remember. *Journal of Applied Research in Memory and Cognition, 2,* 173–178.

Wade, K. A., Garry. M., Read, J. D., & Lindsay, D. S. (2002). A picture is worth a thousand lies: Using false photographs to create false childhood memories. *Psychonomic Bulletin & Review, 9,* 597–603.

Warren, J., & Kuhn, D. (2010). How do jurors argue with one another? *Judgment and Decision Making, 5,* 64–71.

Wegner, D. M. (1989). *White bears and other unwanted thoughts: Suppression, obsession, and the psychology of mental control.* New York: Viking.

Weldon, M. S., & Bellinger, K. D. (1997). Collective memory: Collaborative and individual processes in remembering. *Journal of Experimental Psychology: Learning, Memory, and Cognition, 23,* 1160–1175.

Wells, C., Morrison, C. M., & Conway, M. A. (2014). Adult recollections of childhood memories: What details can be recalled? *Quarterly Journal of Experimental Psychology, 67,* 1249–1261.

Wells, G. L. (1978). Applied eyewitness-testimony research: System variables and estimator variables. *Journal of Personality and Social Psychology, 36,* 1546–1557.

Wells, G.L. (1984). The psychology of lineup identifications. *Journal of Applied Social Psychology. 14,* 89–103.

Wells, G. L. (1988). *Eyewitness identification: A system handbook.* Toronto, Canada: Carswell Legal Publications.

Wells, G. L., & Bradfield, A. L. (1998). "Good, you identified the suspect:" Feedback to eyewitnesses distorts their reports of the witnessing experience. *Journal of Applied Psychology, 83,* 360–376.

Wells, G. L., & Olson, E. A. (2003). Eyewitness testimony. *Annual Review of Psychology, 54,* 277–295.

Wells, G. L., Rydell S. M., & Seelau E. P. (1993). On the selection of distractors for eyewitness line-ups. *Journal of Applied Psychology, 78*, 835–844.

Wells, G. L., Seelau, E. P., Rydell, S. M., & Luus, C. E. (1994). Recommendations for properly conducted lineup identification tasks. In D. F. Ross, J. D. Read, & M. P. Toglia (Eds.), *Adult eyewitness testimony: Current trends and developments* (pp. 223–244). New York: Cambridge University Press.

Wells, G. L., Small, M., Penrod, S. J., Malpass, R. S., Fulero, S. M., & Brimacombe, C. A. E. (1998). Eyewitness identification procedures: Recommendations for lineups and photospreads. *Law and Human Behavior, 22*, 603–647.

Wells, G. L., Steblay, N. K., & Dysart, J. E. (2015). Double-blind photo lineups using actual eyewitnesses: An experimental test of a sequential versus simultaneous lineup procedure. *Law and Human Behavior, 39*, 1–14.

Wessel, I., Zandstra, A. R., Hengeveld, H. M., & Moulds, M. L. (2015). Collaborative recall of details of an emotional film. *Memory, 23*, 437–444.

White, T. L., Leichtman, M. D., & Ceci, S. J. (1997). The good, the bad, and the ugly: Accuracy, inaccuracy, and elaboration in preschoolers' reports about a past event. *Applied Cognitive Psychology, 11*, 37–54.

Widen, S. C., & Russell, J. A. (2013). Children's recognition of disgust in others. *Psychological Bulletin, 139*, 271–299.

Wilcock, R., & Bull, R. (2010). Novel lineup methods for improving the performance of older eyewitnesses. *Applied Cognitive Psychology, 24*, 718–736.

Williams, L. M. (1994). Recall of childhood trauma: A prospective study of women's memories of child sexual abuse. *Journal of Consulting and Clinical Psychology, 62*, 1167–1176.

Wise, R. A., Pawlenko, N. B., Safer, M. A., & Meyer, D. (2009). What U.S. prosecutors and defense attorneys know and believe about eyewitness testimony. *Applied Cognitive Psychology, 23*, 1266–1281.

Wise, R. A., & Safer, M. A. (2004). What U.S. judges know and believe about eyewitness testimony. *Applied Cognitive Psychology, 18*, 427–443.

Wise, R. A., Safer, M. A., & Maro, C. M. (2011). What U.S. law enforcement officers know and believe about eyewitness factors, eyewitness interviews, and identification procedures. *Applied Cognitive Psychology, 25*, 488–500.

Wixted, J. T., Mickes, L., Clark, S. E., Gronlund, S. D., & Roediger III, H. L. (2015). Initial eyewitness confidence reliably predicts eyewitness identification accuracy. *American Psychologist, 70*, 515–526.

Wixted, J. T., Mickes, L., Dunn, J. C., Clark, S. E., & Wells, W. (2016). Estimating the reliability of eyewitness identifications from police lineups. *Proceedings of the National Academy of Sciences, 113*, 304–309.

Wogalter, M. S., Malpass, R. S., & McQuiston, D. E. (2004). A national survey of police on preparation and conduct of identification procedures. *Psychology, Crime & Law, 10*, 69–82.

Wolf, O. T. (2009). Stress and memory in humans: Twelve years of progress? *Brain Research, 1293*, 142–154.

Wolf, S., & Montgomery, D. A. (1977). Effects of inadmissible evidence and level of judicial admonishment to disregard on the judgments of mock jurors. *Journal of Applied Social Psychology, 7*, 205–219.

Wolitzky, K., Fivush, R., Zimand, E., Hodges, L., & Rothbaum, B. O. (2005). Effectiveness of virtual reality distraction during a painful medical procedure in pediatric oncology patients. *Psychology & Health, 20*, 817–824.

Wyer, R. S., & Srull, T. K. (1986). Human cognition in its social context. *Psychological Review, 93*, 322–359.

Wypijewski, J. (2009, March 16). Crisis of faith: Carnal knowledge. *The Nation* (online edition).

Yaron-Antar, A., & Nachson, I. (2006). Collaborative remembering of emotional events: The case of Rabin's assassination. *Memory, 14*, 46–56.

Yonelinas, A. P., & Ritchey, M. (2015). The slow forgetting of emotional episodic memories: An emotional binding account. *Trends in Cognitive Sciences, 19*, 259–267.

Yuille, J. C., & Cutshall, J. (1986). Analysis of statements of victims, witnesses, and suspects. In J. C. Yuille (Ed.), *Credibility assessment: NATO Advanced Institutes Series[Series D: Behavioral and social sciences]* (Vol. 47, pp. 175–191). New York: Kluwer Academic/Plenum Press.

Yuille, J. C., Davies, G., Gibling, F., Marxsen, D., & Porter, S. (1994). Eyewitness memory of police trainees for realistic role plays. *Journal of Applied Psychology, 79*, 931–936.

Zezima, K., & Carey, B. (2009, September 10). Ex-priest challenges abuse conviction on repressed memories. *New York Times* p. A13 (New York Edition).

Zhang, W., Gross, J., & Hayne, H. (2017). The effect of mood on false memory for emotional DRM word lists. *Cognition and Emotion, 31*, 526–537.

INDEX